Steinbeis-Beratungszentrum
Transgenerationale Übertragungen
Saseler Mühlenweg 62
22395 Hamburg

Steinbeis-Edition

Marlene Gottwald graduated in Latin America Studies (M.A.) at the University of Cologne covering Political Science, Latin American History and Languages as well as International Law. Tracking both of her main fields of interest – the EU and Latin America – she has been working as a student assistant at the Jean Monnet Chair of Prof. Wessels, University of Cologne, and as an intern at the German Embassy in Brasília, Brazil. In her final thesis she focused on the strategic partnership between the European Union and Brazil in light of the concept of interregionalism. In 2010 Marlene was accepted to the Marie Curie Initial Training Network EXACT (EU External Action). As researcher, Marlene has worked at the Finnish Institute of International Affairs (FIIA) in Helsinki, the Trans European Policy Studies Association (TEPSA) in Brussels and the University of Edinburgh. In the framework of EXACT, Marlene wrote her PhD at the University of Edinburgh and the University of Cologne ('co-tutelle'). Her main research interests include the EU's Common Foreign and Security Policy, Humanitarian Interventions, the Responsibility to Protect (RtoP), Human Security, as well as the crises in Kosovo, Libya and Syria. In November 2014 Marlene joined the Steinbeis Foundation as project manager.

Marlene Gottwald

Europe's Responsibility to Protect

From Kosovo to Syria

Imprint

Marlene Gottwald
Europe's Responsibility to Protect. From Kosovo to Syria

1st edition, 2015 | Steinbeis-Edition, Stuttgart
ISBN 978-3-95663-025-5
Accepted at University of Cologne and University of Edinburgh, Dissertation 2014

Layout: Steinbeis-Edition
Cover picture: © Shutterstock / SC Designs
Production: WIRmachenDRUCK GmbH, Backnang

Steinbeis is an international service provider in entrepreneurial knowledge and technology transfer. The Steinbeis Transfer Network is made up of about 1,000 enterprises. Specialized in chosen areas, Steinbeis Enterprises' portfolio of services covers research and development; consulting and expert reports as well as training and employee development for every sector of technology and management. Steinbeis Enterprises are frequently based at research institutions, especially universities, which are constituting the Network's primary sources of expertise. The Steinbeis Network comprises around 6,000 experts committed to practical transfer between academia and industry. Founded in 1971, the Steinbeis Foundation is the umbrella organization of the Steinbeis Transfer Network. It is headquartered in Stuttgart, Germany.

176041-2015-02 | www.steinbeis-edition.de

Europe's Responsibility to Protect
From Kosovo to Syria

Inauguraldissertation

zur

Erlangung des Doktorgrades

der Wirtschafts- und Sozialwissenschaftlichen Fakultät der

Universität zu Köln

2014

vorgelegt

von

Marlene Gottwald

Dipl.-Reg.-Wiss.

aus

Leimen

Referent: Prof. Dr. Claire Duncanson

Korreferent: Prof. Dr. Wolfgang Wessels

Tag der Promotion: 09.09.2014

Inhalt

Tables

Boxes

Acknowledgements

I remember saying in late 2013 that "doing a PhD is like running around Arthur's Seat on a cold winter morning ... you get there eventually." (If you have ever been to Edinburgh you will know what I am talking about.) While there was no one to push me up or down the hill on that cold winter morning, there were many people – family, friends, colleagues, supervisors, and others – who supported me immensely throughout the PhD. I would therefore like to thank all the amazing people, who were with me from the beginning and those who I met during my PhD journey, which took me from Cologne to Helsinki to Brussels to Edinburgh and to many other great places.

Particularly, I would like to thank: my wonderful parents Carmen and Gerhard, for always believing in me; my awesome brother Julian for reminding me that life is not only about work (or the PhD); the lovely Irmgard for being the best grandmother ever; Chris for all his love and care, especially for never getting tired of listening and for dancing with me in the kitchen; Gwen, Jim, Joan and Rich for making me feel at home in Edinburgh; Eva, Katarina and Tini for being the most amazing friends and for visiting me at all the places I lived in during the past three years; Kaisa and Marikki for wonderful times in Helsinki and beyond; Andi for his encouragement; Nicole for her pragmatism and all the fun; Andrew for being the best Irish flatmate I have ever had; all my EXACT colleagues for making the PhD a truly unique experience; Wulf for all his efforts in running EXACT; Cera for sharing and caring; Iina for being my Ballet and Yoga buddy; Gaby for supporting my EXACT application; Funda for helping me to erase some of the doubts; Andy Hardie for helping me to reboot my confidence; Dr. Juha Jokela for his practical advice; Prof. John Peterson for his enthusiasm and dedication; Prof. Wolfgang Wessels for his valuable feedback and guidance; and finally Albert Einstein for this wisdom, which I wish someone would have told me when I started the PhD: "We cannot solve our problems with the same thinking we used when we created them."

Marlene Gottwald,
September, 2014

Preface

This study was conducted within the framework of the Marie Curie Initial Training Network EXACT (EU External Action) under the 7th Framework Programme of the European Commission from October 2010 to September 2013. The stated aim of the programme was to

> *critically examine EU External Action and its respective institutional architecture from a global perspective. This policy domain is one of the most challenging and significant fields of theory-led and empirically based research for scholars engaged in research focusing on foreign policy, international relations and European integration.* (EXACT website, www.exact-training.net, 11 January 2014)

The initial title of my Ph.D. project, when applying for the EXACT programme in January 2010, was "Human security on the EU foreign policy agenda, Strategic concepts of EU conflict prevention and crisis management in traditional and new fields of security policy". In my proposal, I had planned to analyse the utility of the human security concept in various areas of EU External Action (security and defence, trade, development and environmental policy). Soon I realised not only that my project was too broad and too ambitious, but also that operationalising the concept of human security bore more theoretical and analytical challenges than originally expected.

Since the start of the EXACT programme in October 2010, my research topic has changed substantially. Inspired by political debates and events surrounding the Arab Spring since December 2010 and my work at the FIIA in Helsinki and TEPSA in Brussels, the focus of my study shifted towards the relevance and the application of the Responsibility to Protect (RtoP) in European foreign policies as well as its link to human security. This change allowed me to look at a very topical debate while keeping my initial interest in conducting a PhD: the question of whether the academic debates on a changed conception of security and the shift from state to human security after the end of the Cold War had an actual impact on practice and policy-making. Without facing the challenge of operationalising the concept of human security I would still be able to assess its potential political impact in the form of the RtoP.

This study aimed to address EXACT research topic 3 on the European / Common Security and Defence Policy of the EU. Research topic 3 stipulated the engagement with the following:

> *Although the central domain of so called "high politics", defence cooperation has seen increasing activity at the European level. ... The policy domain however suffers both from deeply entrenched differences in opinion between the member states about appropriate fora for the formulation of defence policy as well as immense differences in military capabilities among the member states. ... EXACT... endeavours to apply a diverse set of theoretical approaches to the study of this area, including neo-institutionalist and constructivist approaches.* (Official EXACT website, www.exact-training.net / field of research, 10 March 2014)

In order to analyse the influence of the RtoP on European security and defence policies in response to mass atrocities this study has adopted a social constructivist approach. The focus is thus less on why the EU and its member states (re-)acted in a certain way but more on how European foreign policies are constructed. The extent to which member states are willing to cooperate within the EU framework in the area of military intervention plays thus a crucial role in the analysis. The question and approach chosen for this study therefore fit the purposes of the EXACT programme. Against this background, the following thesis seeks to make not only a theoretical contribution in studying EU external action from a social constructivist perspective but the empirical findings on European responses to crises in its neighbourhood are also of relevance to the 'real world'.

Participating in the EXACT programme has been a unique and much appreciated experience. I would therefore like to thank the coordinating institution of the programme, the Jean Monnet Chair of Prof. Dr. Wolfgang Wessels at the University of Cologne, Wulf Reiners and his team particularly, as well as the whole EXACT consortium.

Abbreviations

AMIS	African Union Mission in Sudan
AU	African Union
AWACS	Airborne Warning and Control System
CDU	Christian Democratic Union (Germany)
CFSP	Common Foreign and Security Policy
CHG	Civilian Headline Goal
Civ-Mil	Civilian-Military
CIVCOM	Civilian Aspects of Crisis Management
CMCP	Civil-Military Coordination
CON	British Conservative Party
CONOPS	Concept of Operations
CPCC	Civilian Planning and Conduct Capability
CSDP	Common Security and Defence Policy (former ESDP)
CSU	Christian Socialist Union (Germany)
CWC	Chemical Weapons Convention
DRC	Democratic Republic of Congo
EEAS	European External Action Service
ENP	European Neighbourhood Policy
EP	European Parliament
ESDP	European Security and Defence Policy
ESS	European Security Strategy
EU	European Union
EUFOR	EU Force
EUMM	EU Monitoring Mission
EUMS	EU Military Staff
FAC	Foreign Affairs Council
FDP	Federal Democratic Party (Germany)
FRY	Federal Republic of Yugoslavia

FSA	Free Syria Army
FYROM	Former Yugoslav Republic of Macedonia
HR	High Representative of the EU for Foreign Affairs and Security Policy
ICC	International Criminal Court
ICISS	International Commission on Intervention and State Sovereignty
ICJ	International Court of Justice
IDP	Internally Displaced Persons
IICK	Independent International Commission on Kosovo
ILC	International Law Commission
IRA	Irish Republican Army
JEM	Justice and Equality Movement
KFOR	Kosovo Force
KLA	Kosovo Liberation Army
KVM	Kosovo Verification Mission
LAS	League of Arab States
MDC	Mouvement de citoyens (France)
NATO	North Atlantic Treaty Organization
NGO	Non-Governmental Organisation
OAF	Operation Allied Force
OCHA	UN Office for the Coordination of Humanitarian Affairs
OIC	Organisation of Islamic Conference
OSCE	Organisation for Security and Cooperation in Europe
PDS	Party of Democratic Socialism (Germany)
PS	French Socialist Party
RtoP	Responsibility to Protect
RWP	Responsibility while Protecting

SDP	Social Democratic Party (UK)
SLM / A	Sudan Liberation Movement / Army
SPD	Social Democratic Party (Germany)
TEU	Treaty of the European Union
TNC	Transitional National Council
UK	United Kingdom
UMP	Union Popular Movement (France)
UN	United Nations
UNAMID	African Union / UN Hybrid Operation in Darfur
UNGA / GA	United Nations General Assembly
UNHCR	UN High Commissioner for Refugees
UNMIS	UN Mission in Sudan
UNSC / SC	United Nations Security Council
UNSG	United Nations Secretary General
UNSMIS	UN Supervision Mission in Syria
US	United States of America

Chapter 1: Introduction

The repeated horror of mass atrocities has been one of the most disconcerting developments in human history. It was not until after the cruelty of the Holocaust that the international community was compelled to make assurances aimed at ending suffering more seriously (Murray and Mckay, 2014: 12). Yet, the international community showed little commitment to the proclamation made after the Second World War of "Never Again" to genocide[1] in the decades that followed. By contrast, states stood by and watched tragedies such as the ethnic cleansing of Bosnians by the Serbs and the mass slaughter of the Tutsi population by the Hutus in Rwanda throughout the 1990s. Reaching the climax of the inability and / or failure of the international community to prevent or halt such events, it was during the 1999 crisis in Kosovo that the former UN Secretary-General Kofi Annan wrote a landmark article in which he essentially challenged the traditional view on state sovereignty and the non-intervention principle, claiming that the principle of sovereignty contained in the UN Charter should be re-interpreted as a responsibility to protect individuals (Bellamy, 2011).

Although arguably acting to stop mass atrocities, the Kosovo intervention by NATO revealed a mismatch between the aspirations of prevention, on one hand, and the number and capabilities of the troops that were actually employed, on the other. At the same time, post-Cold War security challenges and institutional shifts inside NATO, highlighted by the Kosovo crisis, initiated a fundamental rethinking of the role and the responsibility not only of the international community but also of the European Union (EU). Europe's inability to stop mass atrocities in its direct neighbourhood served as a wake-up call for the EU to meet the expectations and responsibilities set out in the Common Foreign and Security Policy (CFSP) not only on a rhetorical level but also in practice.[2] The subsequent construction of the Common

1 The proclamation of "Never Again" after the Second World War was codified in the Convention on the Prevention and Punishment of the Crime of Genocide, which was adopted by the United Nations General Assembly on 9 December 1948 as General Assembly Resolution 260.

2 Since the Maastricht Treaty, one of the main objectives of the EU is "to assert its identity on the international scene, in particular through the implementation of a common foreign and security policy including the eventual framing of a common defence policy, which might in time lead to a common defence" (Article B, TEU Maastricht).

Security and Defence Policy (CSDP)[3] and the EU's reasoning on its responsibility to act externally were to some extent affected by the predominant discourse on the Responsibility to Protect (RtoP), taking place at the United Nations (UN).

At the UN World Summit on 14 September 2005, UK Prime Minister Tony Blair (2005) stated on behalf of the EU:

> *The EU strongly welcomes the agreement on the responsibility to protect. We cannot stand by as genocide, war crimes, ethnic cleansing or other gross violations of international humanitarian law and human rights are committed. The primary responsibility for the protection of populations lies first and foremost with each individual state, as the Outcome Document recognises. However, where the state in question is unable or unwilling to do so, the international community can and should act through a comprehensive range of measures, including collective action through the Security Council, and in extreme cases, and out of necessity, by use of force, authorised by the Security Council. International recognition of this is an important step forward.*

Given EU member states' different historical backgrounds and capabilities, one might be sceptical that this rhetorical statement constituted a genuine pledge to follow through with the commitment of troops and resources that the implementation of the concept might demand. Significantly, more than a decade after its failures in the Balkans and the Kosovo crisis, the EU still appears unable to prevent or halt mass atrocities from occurring in its neighbourhood, as the crises in Libya and Syria have shown since 2011. Legitimately, the question that arises is whether the development of the RtoP and the establishment of the CSDP have changed anything. In this context, this thesis aims to investigate the influence of the RtoP as an emerging international norm on European policy responses to crises involving mass atrocities in its neighbourhood. Furthermore, it will analyse whether the RtoP in connection to the creation of the CSDP has had an impact on the EU's role as a security actor. In doing so, this study aims to make a small yet original contribution in four areas addressing a set of rather distinct literatures.

3 When created in 1999 this policy was labelled the European Security and Defence Policy (ESDP). With the entry into force of the Lisbon Treaty in 2009 it was renamed in Common Security Defence Policy (CSDP). The latter term is used consistently throughout this thesis even if referring to earlier stages in the European integration process.

The underlying research interest behind this thesis derives from the rise of debates since the end of the Cold War about the changing nature of security, the development of human security, and its actual effects on the foreign policy of states and other actors in the international system. A central argument to this study is that the RtoP's potential to make a difference in policy responses to mass atrocities derives from its roots in the concept of human security. Speaking to the human security, RtoP and humanitarian intervention literature, the analysis conducted here aims, first of all, to provide fresh insights into the policy impact of human security as well as on the relationship between human security and RtoP.

Second, this thesis seeks to enhance the understanding of the relevance of the RtoP for the development of the EU's CSDP and its practical application. On this note, the EU will be treated as potential norm entrepreneur for the RtoP on one hand and as potential security actor influenced by the RtoP as an emerging international norm on the other. Furthermore, the empirical analysis of European crisis responses also aims at providing an overview of single member states' interpretations of the RtoP and its impact on Europe more broadly.

Conceptualising the RtoP as an emerging international norm and analysing its influence on actual political behaviour speaks, thirdly, to the scholarly body on (international) norms. It is argued that independent of their label and status, also emerging international norms can have an impact if they are seen as a legitimate behavioural claim. On this basis, this thesis aspires to contribute not only to the discussion on the influence of norms but also on what constitutes a norm.

Finally, providing a detailed empirical analysis of European responses to the crisis in Libya and in Syria since 2011, the research results of this study can also be of practical value. Insights on how and in what circumstances the RtoP is used to legitimise a specific policy response can be relevant to future cases of mass atrocities. Furthermore, the extent to which member states are willing to cooperate within the EU framework on security and defence in response to a concrete crisis can provide evidence on the practical relevance of the EU as a security actor.

This introductory chapter will provide further details on the relevance of addressing the influence of the RtoP on European foreign policy as well as on the contributions this study intends to make. Against this background it will introduce the theoretical analytical framework applied throughout the empirical analysis. The following section begins by highlighting the development of the RtoP and its link to the concept of human security. The relevance of the RtoP for the development of a common European security and defence policy and the role of the EU as a security actor will be discussed in section 2. Section 2 also sets the theoretical groundwork of this study and discusses the concept of the RtoP as an emerging international norm as well as its scope. Against this background, section 3 defines the main research question, sets out the main line of argumentation and introduces the approach used to tackle the expressed research problem. The chapter concludes with a brief synopsis of the study's structure and the main themes addressed.

1.1 Human Security and the Responsibility to Protect

Tragedies such as the mass slaughter of the Tutsi population by the Hutus in Rwanda in 1994 and the ethnic cleansing of Bosnians by Serbs in 1995 challenged traditional security thinking. One result was the development of the human security concept. What was new in this context was the changing and deepening of perspective from an exclusively state-based conception of collective security to a people- and community-centred definition of human security (Werthes and Debiel, 2006: 7).

Since the inception of human security in the 1994 UNDP Human Development Report, an extensive body of literature has emerged to define and operationalise the concept.[4] However, almost two decades later there is still no agreement either amongst scholars or policy-makers on what human security genuinely means and what it implies (Alcalde and Bouchard, 2008; Bellamy and McDonald, 2002; Chandler, 2008). Nevertheless, the concept has been linked to a number of international policy initiatives such as the prohibition of anti-personnel landmines and child soldiers, the regulation of the international arms trade as well as the Responsibility to Protect.

The existing literature shows that human security has an influence on national and international discourses on these highly sensitive security issues (Alkire, 2003; Krause, 2007). The question, however, of whether the concept has a genuine impact on policy – as opposed to mere rhetoric – is still unexplored. While human security has rightly been criticized for its theoretical vagueness and incoherence (Chandler, 2008; Thomas and Tow, 2002), providing an analytical answer to the question of its policy relevance is not an easy task.

Keith Krause (2007: 4-5) has argued that it is only possible to link human security to specific policy areas when focusing on a narrow definition of the concept limiting it to its 'freedom of fear' component.[5] The 'freedom from fear' approach seeks to limit the practice of human security to protecting individuals from violent conflicts. With its focus on the protection of civilians, human security can be seen as the un-

4 For a detailed overview of the state of the art of human security, see Alkire, 2003.

5 According to the 1994 UNDP Report human security refers to both the 'freedom from fear' and 'the freedom from want'. While the former is defined as the freedom from violent threats to individuals' physical well-being, the latter includes threats such as hunger, disease and natural disasters.

derlying framework of the RtoP. In this context, human security can be understood as putting people's security concerns first, while at the same time aiming to prevent the use of power to threaten it.

The debate on the RtoP was launched under the aegis of United Nations Secretary General (UNSG) Kofi Annan (2000), in order to be able to respond to future cases akin to "Rwanda or Srebrenica – to gross and systematic human rights violations that affect every precept of our common humanity". Adopted during the UN World Summit in September 2005, the RtoP developed the older norm of humanitarian intervention[6] further in three ways (Thakur, 2006). First, RtoP placed more emphasis on the primary responsibility of the state to protect its citizens. Second, RtoP introduced a range of non-coercive means (e.g. diplomacy, humanitarian aid, sanctions and legal instruments) to be exhausted before considering the use of military force. Third, RtoP introduced the novel idea that the international community could and should use force (if necessary) to enforce the norm that states had a responsibility to protect their own citizens.

Humanitarian intervention was linked to the notion of states having a 'right to intervene' and therefore entailed the 'fear of domination' based on the dynamics of international power politics (idem). On the other hand, by taking into account the changing security concept from state to human security, RtoP promoted the notion of states having a 'responsibility to protect' people from mass atrocities (Evans, 2006: 708). The RtoP thus aimed to shift the perspective of intervention from the prospective interveners to those in need of support (Thakur, 2006).

Although the notion of humanitarian intervention is understood as reflecting state security and national interests more strongly, its humanitarian dimension is not dismissed altogether. While the lines between humanitarian intervention, human security and the RtoP can at times be unclear, this thesis builds on the argument that RtoP as a newly emerging international norm can potentially make a change in practice in comparison to its predecessor. This potential for change rests on the practical application of human security and the implementation of policies genuinely

6 Humanitarian intervention has been defined as "the use of force against a territorial state by another state or a collective group of states, with or without authorisation from the UNSC for the promotion or protection of basic human rights of individuals other than intervening states' own citizens, without the permission from the territorial state within whose border the use of force takes place" (Holzgrefe, 2003: 15).

designed to protect civilians possibly precluding and following up a military intervention with non-coercive means, such as preventive sanctions, diplomacy, humanitarian aid and legal instruments as well as reconstruction and transition support.

Against this background, the underlying aim of this thesis is to assess the policy impact of human security in the form of the emerging international norm of the RtoP. If the RtoP has an impact, a change in the design and the direction of policies taking into account the human security concept should be visible. However, if the new norm and the people-centred perspective are merely reflected in the discourse while policies focus almost exclusively on the use of military force, the impact of the RtoP remains superficial. Focussing on the actual policy impact of human security in the form of the RtoP aims at filling a gap in existing research.

Moreover, this thesis will provide fresh insights on the relationship between human security and the RtoP. After the Libyan intervention in 2011 the RtoP has become increasingly linked to the question of military intervention. Human security proponents such as Mary Kaldor (2012) and others have argued that a no-fly zone is not the right instrument to provide protection for civilians on the ground. Furthermore, it has been claimed that the military operation in Libya went beyond the UN mandate by extending air strikes to non-military areas in order to achieve a regime change. In the case of Syria, the RtoP only started to play a dominant role in European discourses once the US President Barack Obama threatened to use military force in Syria after the chemical weapon attacks in August 2013. The international as well as the European discourse crystallized around the need to punish the Syrian government for the alleged crimes rather than protecting the Syrian population. Throughout this study, we will be alert to the possibility that, perhaps ironically, the RtoP in practice has actually undermined the human security concept instead of respected it.

One way to combat the misuse of emerging international norms such as the RtoP and to increase its collective understanding can be via the activities of a norm entrepreneur. Within the existing literature on international norms, norm entrepreneurs play a crucial role in determining the extent to which an international norm is influential (Finnemore and Sikkink, 1998: 896). The goal of norm entrepreneurs is to make decision-makers perceive the proposed norm as legitimate and appropriate. With the aim of assessing the influence of the RtoP on European foreign policy-making, the EU will be considered as potential norm entrepreneur affecting the collective understanding of the RtoP within the European context. At the same time, it is assumed that the RtoP can in return have an impact on the EU's role as a security actor.

1.2 Europe's Responsibility to Protect

A basic commitment to a broad definition of human security can be seen in Article 21 of the Treaty on European Union, which spells out the general provisions of the EU's external action. It lists among other objectives the strengthening of international security, the consolidation and support of democracy, rule of law, and human rights and reinforcing the principles of international law. The European Security Strategy (2003) embraced the human security perspective in addition to a traditional state-centric view. It emphasised the notion of people-centred solutions combined with cooperative engagement. The Report on the Implementation of the ESS (2008), which aimed at reinforcing the previous strategy, reflected the human security concept more explicitly:

> *... the EU already contributes to a more secure world. We have worked to build human security, by reducing poverty and inequality, promoting good governance and human rights, assisting development, and addressing the root causes of conflict and insecurity* (Report on the ESS, 2008).

On the EU's role in crisis management the Report affirmed:

> *We need to continue mainstreaming human rights issues in all activities in this field, including ESDP missions, through a people-based approach coherent with the concept of human security* (idem).

Although the Implementation Report could be seen as a breakthrough in the institutionalisation of human security within the EU, little attention was actually given to defining it as a core narrative (Kaldor et al, 2007: 274). Within the EU foreign policy discourse and particularly in the area of security and defence, human security has rarely been adopted unambiguously. It has, however, been argued that the EU is actually 'doing' human security, yet, without explicitly using the term in its official language and documents (idem).

A joint EU position on the RtoP was adopted at the 2005 UN World Summit, with the UK Foreign Secretary, Jack Straw (2005), declaring on behalf of the EU that, "the EU welcomes the unprecedented recognition of the international community's responsibility to protect populations from genocide, war crimes, ethnic cleansing or crimes against humanity". The EU underlined that only if diplomatic and humanitarian measures do not show any immediate effect, it lies with the authority of the UNSC to permit enforcement measures as a last resort. On this note, the EU also emphasised the importance of the prevention of mass atrocities as part of the RtoP.

Since the endorsement of the RtoP during the 2005 UN World Summit, the EU had been an active promoter of the newly emerging international norm. The 2008 Implementation Report reaffirms:

> *Sovereign governments must take responsibility for the consequences of their actions and hold a shared responsibility to protect populations from genocide, war crimes, ethnic cleansing and crimes against humanity.*

The construction of the CSDP was not only influenced by the EU's failures in the Balkans throughout the 1990s and NATO's post-Cold War transformation, but was also informed by the development of the RtoP as emerging new international norm (Barnutz, 2010). The influence of the RtoP on the CSDP becomes evident in three respects. First, the EU developed the CSDP on the basis of a perceived responsibility to act externally in the area of security. Second, the type of intervention that has significantly shaped the role of the EU as a security actor is the use of force to prevent or halt mass atrocities. The crises around which the EU has designed its CSDP are mostly those with a humanitarian dimension (Lucarelli and Menotti, 2006: 148).

Third, the development of the RtoP on the UN level influenced the EU's reasoning on its international responsibility. The people-centred focus of external EU policies is influenced by the debate on the RtoP. According to Ian Manners (2006: 192), "the centrality of the concept of human rights and RtoP for EU policies is apparent in the EU's external action". According to Article 21 (TEU), the EU's external action shall be based on the principles of

> *democracy, the rule of law, the universality and indivisibility of human rights and fundamental freedoms, respect for human dignity, the principles of equality and solidarity, and respect for the principles of the United Nations Charter and international law.*

In this context the EU faces a two-fold dilemma between its aspirations to be a 'normative power' (Manners, 2000; 2002) and its commitment to multilateralism on one hand and its role as a security actor and its approach to the use of force and military interventions to prevent or halt mass atrocities on the other. As a normative power, the EU promotes the RtoP by invoking its international commitment and by the power of example. If successful as norm entrepreneur, the EU can influence what kind of crisis response is appropriate and legitimate. Yet, the EU seems to subscribe to an interpretation of the RtoP that emphasises the responsibility to prevent and conveys the understanding that force should be used only in rare and clearly defined circumstances. EU interventions, therefore, have more frequently taken the form of economic and political reconstruction and peacekeeping through presence on the ground. Furthermore, the geographical area of intervention has been limited to the EU's neighbourhood as evidenced by both actual performance and the European Security Strategy's prescription that interventions should only take place in a legal framework.

The EU's understanding of its international responsibility is, however, not only influenced by the development of the RtoP but also relates to the availability of security and defence capabilities. Despite the development of the CSDP and the establishment of civilian as well as military crisis management capabilities, the EU is still reliant on NATO or US assets and structures when it comes to military interventions. Member states remain the key actors within the CSDP and security and defence issues are therefore subject to intergovernmental decision-making. The extent to which the EU is able to react in response to mass atrocities with military means depends largely on the political will of the member states[7] to cooperate under the EU framework. The EU's understanding of the RtoP as well as its role as a normative power, acting with primarily civilian means, convey the image of a reluctant security actor that is dependent on the peculiar institutional structure of EU foreign policy dominated by intergovernmental decision-making.

Finally, the increasing link of the RtoP to the use of force in recent crises, such as in Libya and Syria since 2011, might have influenced the EU in the opposite direction. Understanding its responsibility more in terms of prevention and assistance, while

7 The "political will" of the member states should not be seen as an all-encompassing explanation for the impact of the CSDP in practice. Yet, as they remain the key actors within the CSDP, the question of whether member states are willing to act under the EU framework when applying the RtoP in practice can reveal crucial insights on the role of the EU as a security actor.

lacking the capabilities to undertake a military intervention on its own, the recent application of the RtoP might have made the EU an even more reluctant security actor. Consequently, the EU has become more averse to promoting the emerging international norm in response to mass atrocities in its neighbourhood. In contrast to the well-known 'capability-expectations gap'[8] (Smith, 1993) that is said to plague the EU's foreign policy, there might yet be a convergence between the EU's understanding of its responsibility and its capabilities.

Having outlined the EU's understanding of the RtoP as an emerging international norm, the question arises on what kind of theoretical basis it is possible to assess the influence of the RtoP on the EU's foreign policy on one hand and the EU's possible role as a norm entrepreneur for the RtoP on the other. The nature of EU foreign policy and the influence of international norms more general therein can be explained from different theoretical angles. The research interest behind this thesis is less to answer the question of why European actors respond (or not) to mass atrocities in their neighbourhood but rather to explain how these responses became politically possible and what role the RtoP played therein. On this note, it is argued that a social constructivist perspective is the most appropriate for exploring the influence of the RtoP on European foreign policies in response to mass atrocities.

The nature of EU foreign policy

A social constructivist perspective on EU foreign policy focuses on the nature of the EU's international action and the ways in which it acts as a normative exporter of values, beliefs and norms (Tonra and Christiansen, 2011). Instead of searching exclusively for causal explanations of choice and behaviour, a constructivist approach asks how such decisions are possible and what are the normative bases upon which such choices are made. Constructivists argue that international norms are not only important for understanding foreign policy behaviour in the neoliberal sense, but that in fact, they are crucial to explaining politics because they constitute identity and therefore interests (Katzenstein, 1996).

8 Analysing the international role of the EU, Christopher Hill (1993) identified a gap between what the EU promised to do on paper and what it was actually able to do in practice. In this context he conceptualized the "capability-expectations gap" as having three components: the ability to find a common agreement among the member states, the availability of resources and capacity, and the disposability of instruments at the EU level.

In contrast to the realist perspective, international norms matter as they shape national interests that are not exogenously given but constructed vial social interactions between agents and structure. Moreover, international norms do not only have an impact when they serve a certain purpose or fit a given material interest but also when they are perceived as legitimate and appropriate (see Kratochwil, 1989; Onuf, 1989). In getting behind the rationalist questions, the social constructivist perspective allows us to explore how a range of policy choices within the EU is defined and how these may be enabled or constrained by existing normative structures (see Onuf, 1998; Wendt; 1992).

The constructivist focus on EU foreign policy has opened new pathways to a discussion of the EU's international capacity, looking at the growth of a common European identity in foreign policy (Jørgensen, 1997), an analysis of the role of discourse and public opinion in the creation of such an identity (Larsen, 1997; H. Smith, 1995) and the implications of such a development in creating the EU as a normative actor – driven by its identity and norms rather than interests (Manners, 2000, 2002; Matlary, 2002). From the normative power perspective the construction of the EU on the basis of common values and shared norms as well as its specific constitution is what characterises it most as a foreign policy and security actor.

The EU as a normative (security) actor

From a constructivist perspective, understandings of the EU and its role in global politics are part of the intersubjective international structures (see Wendt, 1994). In this context, the EU contributes to the processes of constructing these international structures by using opportunities as well as through its "unique presence" (Bretherton and Vogler, 2006: 15). As a normative power the EU is able to shape the identities of others and change perceptions of what is 'normal'. The EU can thus be conceptualised as a changer of norms in the international system mostly by what it is and not what it does or says (Manners, 2002: 252).

Throughout this study the role of the EU as a normative power[9] will be approached from two angles. The first perspective looks at the EU as normative power and norm entrepreneur. It focuses on the ways in which the EU promotes the RtoP by

9 Throughout this thesis 'normative' refers to the use and the influence of norms in general and of the RtoP as emerging international norm specifically.

invoking international commitment and by the power of example (Forsberg, 2011: 1197–1198). From this perspective it will be analysed whether the EU acts as a successful norm entrepreneur for the RtoP and can therefore influence EU member states in their decisions on what kind of crisis response is appropriate and legitimate.

The second angle scrutinises whether the RtoP in return also has an influence on EU foreign policy and whether it enables or constrains the EU as a security actor. For the EU to be able to perform as an actor in the area of security and defence two factors are crucial: First, member states remain the key actors within the CSDP and therefore security and defence issues are subject to intergovernmental decision-making leaving little room for the EU to act independently. To what extent the EU is able to act depends, to a large extent, on the political will of the member states.[10] Furthermore, the EU's ability to act is influenced by the availability of security and defence resources. Chapter 2 will show that the EU has been active in developing civilian as well as military capabilities within the CSDP. Member states' commitment to contribute to the advancement of the EU's military capabilities, however, has not lived up to the expectations created on paper.

In this context, the concept of the EU as a security actor is defined as the willingness of the EU members to act collectively under the EU framework and the existence of capabilities adequate for the proposed crisis response. The influence of the RtoP on the EU as a security actor will be assessed by an empirical investigation of the EU's practice of the CSDP as well as the role member states envisage for the EU in response to mass atrocities. The focus is on the EU's conflict prevention and crisis management policies in response to mass atrocities in its neighbourhood and how much room for manoeuvre member states grant the EU as (security) actor. As an effective security actor the EU should be able to contribute significantly with its available crisis management instruments to putting an end to mass atrocities and finding a solution to the crisis.

From the analysis of the role of the EU in this thesis it will also be possible to draw conclusions back on the normative development of the RtoP and its influence in

10 The "political will" of the member states should not be seen as an all-encompassing explanation for the impact of the CSDP in practice. Yet, as they remain the key actors within the CSDP, the question of whether member states are willing to act under the EU framework when applying the RtoP in practice can reveal crucial insights on the role of the EU as a security actor.

general. If the EU is acting as a successful norm entrepreneur and security actor at the same time, the RtoP could be seen as an important trigger for action. The analysis of the link between the RtoP and the EU is therefore two-fold: First, it will be investigated to what extent the EU acts as a norm entrepreneur and is successful in convincing its member states of the legitimacy of the emerging international norm. Second, the EU's role as a security actor will be scrutinised by focusing on its contribution to the European crisis response and by analysing whether the RtoP can be seen as a trigger for decisive EU action. The two-way analysis of the influence of the RtoP on EU foreign policy from a constructivist perspective requires in a next step defining and conceptualising what (emerging) international norms are.

(Emerging) international norms

International norms differ in terms of status and level of institutionalisation. Martha Finnemore and Kathryn Sikkink (1998) made the argument that in order to reach the status of effective normative frameworks able to affect behaviour, international norms need to go through processes of emergence, evolution and institutionalisation or internalisation. They understand the evolution of international norms as a three-stage process, labelled the 'norm-life cycle' (Finnemore and Sikkink, 2001: 895). Therein, the first stage is the norm emergence, the second stage involves broad norm acceptance and the third stage is called 'norm cascade'. At the far end of the 'norm cascade' internalisation occurs. Norms thus reach a taken-for-granted quality or become institutionalised so that their matter is no longer subject of debate.

Emerging international norms, as in the case of the RtoP, are those that have not reached the status of clear and precise norms and have not found any institutionalisation into international treaties or customary law. Thomas Risse and Kathryn Sikkink (1999: 15) found in their research on human rights that "emergent international norms are often signalled by international declarations or programs of action from international conferences." The main difficulty at reaching the status of institutionalized and precise international norms can sometimes be explained by high levels of contestation and disagreement as well as by the consequent impossibility of finding approval by the majority of international actors (idem.). Thus, emerging international norms are those that have not reached the necessary *opinion iuris* among states to be regarded as customary law.

Contrary to common strands in the literature on international norms and their influence (see for example Björkdahl, 2002; Finnemore and Sikkink, 1998; Percy, 2007; Raymond, 1997), it is argued that the legal status of a norm cannot be equated with a norm's genuine influence.[11] In other words, proving the existence of a norm in legal terms is no substitute for analysing its effects on policy. By contrast, from an analytical perspective, the existence of a norm in legal terms and its prescriptive functions should be seen separately.

From a theoretical perspective this thesis aims to make a contribution as an original analytical assessment of the influence of (emerging) international norms on actual political behaviour. Yet, it also seeks to grapple with the question of what constitutes a norm. The distinction between a norm's constitutive and its prescriptive functions implies that emerging international norms, such as the RtoP, that have not (yet) evolved into legal norms, which are enshrined in a treaty or that are commonly viewed as customary legal norms, can also have an effect on actual political behaviour. In this context, this study aims to address a gap in the literature on international norms regarding the tangible influence of emerging international norms on foreign policy.

In their prescriptive functions (emerging) international norms specify standards of appropriate and legitimate behaviour (Katzenstein, 1996: 26). It is assumed that norms contribute to the formation of interests on the basis of which a certain political action is chosen as policy. From this perspective, an emerging international norm is defined as, at least partially, a collective understanding that creates expectations, as well as a standard that prescribes what legitimate and appropriate behaviour ought to be (adopted from Björkdahl, 2002: 21)[12].

Yet, from the influence of international norms on actual policy, it is possible to draw conclusions on the actual existence and the status of a norm. Consequently, the three stages of emergence, evolution and internalisation cannot be separated that clearly from one another but, in fact, influence each other. Although the focus of this study is on the 'strength' of norms in terms of their influence on actual po-

11 Martha Finnemore and Kathryn Sikkink (1998) argue that in order to be able to effectively affect behaviour international norms need to go through the process of emergence, evolution and internalization. The latter means that norms reach a taken-for-granted quality or become institutionalized in international law for example.

12 While norms also have a constitutive function as in determining interests and identities the emphasis here is on the regulative effect of norms as in their influence on actual policy (see Björkdahl, 2002).

litical behaviour (Finnemore and Sikkink, 1998: 892), the empirical findings can have important implications for the existence of norms in terms of their status and further development.

It is assumed that international norms have explanatory power, not independent of the structural environment or the situational context, but in the sense that they order the world, shape agendas and (re-)form interests. Instead of accepting or rejecting international norms as 'causal occurrences', a distinction is made between reasons and causes for action. Seeing international norms as reasons rather than causes it can be argued that absent the reasons the same 'causes' would not have the same causal capacity (Yee, 1996: 84). Norms may thus guide behaviour, provide mutual expectations about future action, or be ignored. However, they do not affect behaviour in the sense of 'A' causes 'B'.

Furthermore, the explanatory power of international norms is limited by two factors: First, international norms are not invalidated by a counterfactual incident. And second, the influence of norms cannot be assessed in dichotomous terms (Raymond, 1997: 218). As Kratochwil suggests, "although we may observe a certain regularity that might be caused by some underlying norm, we have no clear idea how this hunch can be translated into a causalmechanism so that we can establish the actual aetiology between norms and resulting behaviour" (Kratochwil, 2000: 63). Non-norm compliance can amount to violation, though does not necessarily lead to invalidation or ineffectiveness of the norm. But if one believed that norms are irrelevant, it would be difficult to understand why states almost always provide justification for non-compliance.[13]

It is acknowledged that the RtoP might be given as a reason for a specific action but that the emerging norm as such does not cause exclusively a certain political behaviour. Although this study is not explicitly designed to explain the causes of European crisis responses to mass atrocities, it should not be ignored that a certain foreign policy is always motivated by multiple factors and conditions. Since it is not that easy to clearly separate norms and interests from each other in political reality, it is

13 The question of norm compliance and non-compliance will however only be addressed implicitly. While the influence of (emerging) international norms cannot be measured in dichotomous terms and a case of non-compliance does not prove a norm as invalid, the criteria of compliance and non-compliance has not been included in the analytical framework as a distinct indicator.

vital to address some of the alternative explanations for European responses to crises in its neighbourhood before moving on to establishing the analytical framework designed to explore the influence of the RtoP as an emerging international norm. [14]

RtoP's scope

Commonly stated motivations for a specific crisis response alongside altruistic reasons such as the RtoP are self-interest or national interest. These can be of economic or geo-strategic nature or can be in the political interest of the decision-maker in charge (Krieg, 2013). Seen as exogenously given and not constructed, a deeper analysis of the following possible explanations would call for a more rational approach. At the same time any of the following explanations or 'causes' for a specific crisis response might still be legitimised by referring to the RtoP, which is precisely what this study will investigate.

In the case of Libya, economic interests can be related to the availability of natural resources such as oil and gas as well as the strategic importance for regional and global trade.[15] Both Libya and Syria are vital regions for counter-terrorism efforts and might pose a perceived threat to the national security of other states. Particularly the Gaddafi regime had been a problem for France and the UK before the 2011 civil war.

Gaddafi's intervention into the internal affairs of Chad in the 1980s led the French government to deploy military support to engage directly against the Libyan forces. Significantly, France lost an aircraft, Flight UTA 772, as a result of a Libyan bomb responsible for the death of all 171 persons on board. In case of the UK, the Gaddafi regime assumed responsibility for an attack on the government itself. It supplied the Irish Republican Army (IRA) with guns and explosives, which they used to bomb the Grand Hotel in Brighton in 1984 during the Conservative Party conference. Likewise, the UK and others (most notably the US) lost many citizens in the Libyan bombing of Pan Am Flight 103 over Lockerbie, Scotland, in 1988 (Fermor, 2012/12: 342–3).

14 The following section addresses causes and motivations for European responses to the crises in Libya and Syria since 2011 most commonly stated in the literature. Yet, the account of alternative explanations given here does not claim to be exclusive.

15 According to the 2006 BP statistical review of World Energy, Libya figure the top ten of world oil reserves with 39.1 billion barrels.

Moreover, the current state of political affairs, such as the popularity of the current government as well as upcoming elections can have an impact on a specific foreign policy agenda. The response to an external crisis can also be motivated by the need of diverting public attention away from domestic political questions. This might have been the case for France's response to the Libyan crisis under Nicolas Sarkozy, who was at the time of the Libyan crisis planning to impose highly unpopular austerity measures.

The lack of a more decisive response in the case of Syria could be explained by Russia's undisguised *Realpolitik*, the sectarian tensions on the ground, Iran's support to the Assad government as well as the military strength of the latter. Therefore internal dynamics matter as much as external factors. While in the case of Libya a military intervention was, from an operational point of view, not only feasible, there was also a greater amount of information on the conflict as well as a more united opposition than it was in the case of Syria for example. Externally, consensus among members of the international community and the UNSC can play an important role. The Libyan crisis has shown further that the support of regional partners and organisations can also be crucial.

The context on the ground in the crisis country is as influential as domestic politics. Furthermore, the decisions on how to respond to a specific crisis and whether to intervene with military means can be further influenced by strategic and economic interests. The response to a crisis outside a state's own territorial border can therefore never be explained by looking at one specific factor. An analysis of all possible reasons for European responses to the Libyan and Syrian crisis would go not only beyond the scope of this thesis but would also fail to satisfy the main research interest behind this study. The original focus of this analysis is to investigate the RtoP's scope of legitimising European crisis responses in general and specifically, the decision to authorise (or not) the use of force independent of all other causes for action mentioned in the previous paragraphs. The sole objective of assessing the RtoP's influence in terms of its legitimising effects provides operational clarity as well as fresh insights in how Europe understands and applies the emerging international norm.

1.3 Exploring the influence of international norms

Before introducing the analytical framework, it is essential to define the terms central to this study. Defining the RtoP, as it was developed by the UN, is initially straightforward. This thesis will show that, when it comes to the actual implementation of the RtoP in practice, understandings of what the emerging norm means and entails vary quite widely. Furthermore, while outlining the terms mass atrocities and the EU's neighbourhood is fairly straightforward, defining European foreign policy with its different dimensions requires some further elaboration.

Definitions

For the purposes of this study, the term European foreign policy is defined as encompassing two dimensions:

1. The foreign policy or external action of the EU institutions
2. The member states' or national foreign policies[16]

European foreign policy is defined as the sum of actions of the EU institutions and the member states. Therefore the term foreign policy is preferred over the term external action, which is particularly linked to 'communitarized' external policies of the EU. Given the particular nature of the EU, the conceptualisation of EU foreign policy is more complex than the definition of a state's foreign policy. The foreign policy of the EU is neither all-encompassing nor exclusive. All member states maintain their own national foreign policies, which may in part be defined with involvement from the EU.

EU foreign policy is defined as "EU actions that can be considered the output from the EU's multilevel system of governance in foreign policy" (Lucarelli, 2006: 9). When referring to member states foreign policies, the term national foreign policies will be used. The term European foreign policy refers to the sum of the EU's institutional and member states' individual foreign policies.

16 The term foreign policy refers to a range of measures relevant in the area of security and defence: diplomacy, sanctions, humanitarian assistance and military intervention.

The distinction between the EU's and member states' foreign policies is crucial in this framework as the aim is to not only to identify the influence of the RtoP on European foreign policy but also to explore the role of the EU as a security actor in its neighbourhood. It is assumed that the EU's role as security actor increases if EU actions form a significant part of European responses to mass atrocities. The nature of EU foreign policy and its role as a security actor are therefore closely linked.

The concept of the EU as a security actor is defined as the willingness of the EU member states to act collectively under the EU framework and the existence of capabilities that are adequate for the proposed response to mass atrocities in its neighbourhood (see chapter 4). The RtoP is defined as an emerging international norm. It has been included in several international declarations and agreements. Although none of these documents can be seen as binding sources of international law,[17] there is some evidence of an evolving legalisation of the norm (see chapter 2). Still, the RtoP cannot be seen as a consistent single norm but rather as a collection of existing expectations and new contested ones.

The RtoP exists in the guise of three pillars adopted in paragraphs 138 and 139 in the 2005 World Summit Outcome Document. Pillar one refers to the responsibility of each state to protect its population from genocide, war crimes, ethnic cleansing and crimes against humanity. For the purposes of this study, the term 'mass atrocities' includes one or more of these four RtoP crimes. Pillar two consists of the international community's responsibility to assist the state to fulfil its responsibility to protect, particularly by helping them to tackle the causes of mass atrocities, build the capacity to prevent these crimes, and address problems before they escalate.

Pillar three states that in situations where a state has manifestly failed to protect its population from the four crimes, it is the international community's responsibility to take timely and decisive action through peaceful diplomatic and humanitarian means and, if that proves inadequate, other more forceful means in a manner consistent with Chapters VI, VII and VIII of the UN Charter. While pillar one builds on existing sources of international treaty and customary law, pillars two and three are

17 As defined in Article 38 of the Statute of the International Court of Justice (ICJ) referring to "international conventions", "international custom, as evidence of a general practice accepted as law", and "general principles of law".

less determined and leave greater room for interpretation, which will be addressed throughout this thesis.

The European neighbourhood refers to all those countries that are included in the European Neighbourhood Policy (ENP).[18] The focus is on crises involving mass atrocities in the EU's neighbourhood because the expectations for the EU to respond to a conflict taking place on its doorstep are high not only from the inside but also from the outside. Since the financial crisis in 2008 and the outbreak of the Arab Spring in late 2010, the United States (US) under Barack Obama has demanded a greater security role for the EU outside its borders (see chapter 5; Biscop, 2011b). Moreover, the European Security Strategy (ESS, 2003) states that "neighbours who are engaged in violent conflict ... pose problems for Europe". It is thus also in the EU's own interest to provide security in its neighbourhood.

Research question and analytical approach

This thesis seeks to determine whether the development of the RtoP and the creation of the CSDP actually have made a difference in terms of 'whether' and 'how' the EU and its member states have responded to crises in its neighbourhood. Ascertaining the impact of a norm on actual policy can only be assessed through empirical investigation (see Kratochwil, 1989: 42). This study explores the influence of the RtoP as an emerging international on European foreign policy by means of an empirical analysis of pre- and post-RtoP cases of mass atrocities since the Kosovo crisis in 1999.

Research question
To what extent does the Responsibility to Protect have an influence on European responses to mass atrocities in its neighbourhood?

For the framework developed here, the most important characteristic of an international norm to be influential is that it is considered a legitimate behavioural claim (Florini, 1996: 365). International norms are not obeyed because they are enforced by a higher authority, but because they are seen as legitimate. The influence of in-

18 Includes Algeria, Armenia, Azerbaijan, Belarus, Egypt, Georgia, Israel, Jordan, Lebanon, Libya, Moldova, Morocco, Palestine, Syria and Ukraine (see http://eeas.europa.eu/enp/, 26 November 2013)

ternational norms can be assessed by showing that these norms are distinctively used in foreign policy decisions, in communicating the basis for those choices to a wider audience and by implementing the according actions.

The influence of the RtoP will be scrutinized by analysing to what extent the RtoP is seen as legitimating choices in European foreign policies made in response to crises involving mass atrocities. The legitimacy of the RtoP will be assessed by looking at whether the RtoP appears in European discourses on how to respond to these crises. Such an operationalisation of an international norm is independent of its formal status or label.

The legitimacy of the RtoP will be evaluated on the basis of two indicators: The first indicator is to analyse whether RtoP is used throughout the decision-making process. In this context, discourses will be examined with a focus on whether and how they refer to the RtoP. In other words, it will be investigated whether the language of the RtoP is used during the decision-making process. The second indicator looks at whether the foreign policy decisions are implemented accordingly. Building on the first indicator, the crucial question here is whether rhetorical statements are followed through in practice. This study investigates therefore not only language but also policy implementation. With the aim of assessing the policy impact of the changing security conception from state to human security, the analysis examines the extent to which rhetorical statements are followed through in practice.

Indicators to assess the legitimacy of the RtoP:

1. Foreign policy decision-making
2. Foreign policy implementation

Influence can range from thin to thick and will be measured on the basis of a four-value scale referring to high, moderate, low and no influence (see Cortell and Davis, 2002). Starting by the latter, RtoP has no influence if it is absent in the foreign policy decision-making process. The emerging norm has some influence if it appears in debates on how to best respond to mass atrocities such as in parliamentary debates or in bilateral or multilateral consultations between different actors. Moderate influence applies if the RtoP is not only used throughout the internal decision-making process but also as the basis for the foreign policy decision that is communicated to a wider audience. This usually happens in press statements or releases by the head of state or government or by the foreign minister. Finally, the RtoP has the highest influence if all three indicators apply and actors implement the policies according to their discourse. This means, that the previously communicated foreign policy decisions are implemented according to the stated aims and purposes. By contrast, if implemented policies reveal a different purpose than claimed in the discourse or change during the process of implementation the influence of the RtoP remains limited and the legitimacy as well as the legality of the actions can be questioned.

Influence	Indicator	Operationalization
No influence	No use	None
Low influence	Use in foreign policy decision-making process	Parliamentary debates, bilateral and multilateral consultations
Moderate influence	Use as basis for foreign policy decision communicated to wider audience	High-level press statements on policy response
High influence	According implementation of policies	No later change in policy; no hidden aim or agenda

Table 1: Scale to assess norm influence

The influence of the RtoP as an emerging international norm on European foreign policy is further affected by three factors, which should not be seen as distinct but rather as reinforcing and possibly conditioning each other.

1. RtoP's interpretation
2. Norm entrepreneurs
3. Crisis perception

The interpretation of the RtoP depends first of all on the determinacy of the norm, which refers to how precise it indicates the behaviour it expects in a given situation. Containing several dimensions, the RtoP cannot be seen as a single norm but rather as a collection of norms. Some components of the RtoP are based on existing norms of international treaty or customary law while other parts of the norm remain vague in prescription and reference. A joint interpretation of the RtoP can further be impaired by contestation due to the existence of conflicting and competing norms. As Antje Wiener (2007: 13) suggested, "norms are contested by default". In the case of the RtoP, long-standing traditions of sovereignty, territorial integrity and non-interference can be seen as the main conflicting or competing norms.

Second, the extent to which an international norm is influential, can be affected by the existence of norm entrepreneurs and organisational platforms, on which norm entrepreneurs may act to promote the norm (Finnemore and Sikkink, 1998: 896). Norm entrepreneurs can be critical if they call attention to an issue or even create issues using language that interprets and dramatises them. The construction of cognitive frames is an essential component of norm entrepreneurs' political strategies. In constructing their frames, norm entrepreneurs are confronted by firmly embedded existing norms and frames in their attempt to create alternative perceptions of both interest and appropriateness (idem: 898). Independent of the platform, norm entrepreneurs and organisations need to secure the support of other actors. They must try either to convince decision-makers that it is in their own interest to adopt the proposed norm or persuade them of the moral superiority of the norm (Nadelmann, 1990: 482). Successful norm entrepreneurs are able to frame normative ideas in such a way that they resonate with relevant audiences. The goal is to make decision-makers perceive the proposed norm as legitimate and appropriate.

The UN together with the International Commission on Intervention and State Sovereignty (ICISS) spearheaded by Canada have acted initially as the main norm entrepreneurs of the RtoP on the international level. Having promoted the RtoP since the 2005 World Summit, the EU can serve as additional norm entrepreneur, influencing particularly European responses to mass atrocities by using its normative power and fostering a collective understanding of the emerging norm. At the same time the RtoP can serve as a trigger for a decisive EU crisis responses increasing the EU's profile as a security actor.

Third, due to the – at least partial – indeterminacy of the RtoP, interpretation can vary not only among actors but might also differ from case to case. Depending on how the crisis in question is perceived by other actors, there might be a more or less shared understanding of what the RtoP means and entails in that specific case. Furthermore, agreement in one case can lead to greater disagreement with regard to another crisis. The influence of the RtoP as an emerging international norm is thus highly context-dependent. The 2005 World Summit agreed to limit the RtoP to be applied in the cases of four crimes: genocide, war crimes, crimes against humanity and ethnic cleansing. The limitation of the RtoP to the four crimes has been further affirmed in two cases of RtoP-misuse: the Cyclone Nargis in Burma and the Georgian-Russian War (see chapter 3). It is therefore assumed that the extent to which a crisis is perceived in one or more of these terms has an effect to the extent the RtoP influences foreign policy decision-making and implementation.

Factor	Operationalization	RtoP influence
Interpretation	Agreement on what the different RtoP components mean and entail; little contestation	Increases
	Diverging understandings of the RtoP's implications	Decreases
Norm entrepreneurs	Presence	Increases
	Absence	Decreases
Crisis perception	RtoP crimes: genocide, war crimes, crimes against humanity and ethnic cleansing	Increases
	Any other term	Decreases

Table 2: Factors affecting norm influence

Presumptions

On the basis of the link between the above-established factors affecting norm influence as well as against the background on the RtoP in theory and in practice provided in chapters 2 and 3, four presumptions on the RtoP's influence can be established. The four presumptions will be tested throughout the two in-depth case studies on the Libyan and the Syrian crisis in chapter 4 and 5. The aim is to reveal whether the RtoP actually makes a difference in whether and how Europe responds to mass atrocities in its neighbourhood.

The revision of four cases of RtoP implementation and non-implementation or abuse in chapter 3 will show that a shared understanding of the RtoP, its trigger and toolbox has not yet evolved among European countries. Moreover, in none of the four RtoP cases analysed in chapter 3 the EU or a member state has acted as successful entrepreneur for the RtoP and has therefore convinced other actors that the RtoP is the legitimate basis to act on.[19] Furthermore, the interpretation of the RtoP seems to vary from case to case. Against this background it will be tested throughout the empirical analysis (see chapters 5 and 6), whether the presence of a successful norm entrepreneur provides for a greater agreement on what the RtoP means and entails in a specific case and in general (see presumption I, box 1).

While the interpretation of the RtoP is highly-context specific and linked to the type of crisis that occurs, the way the crisis in question is perceived is another important factor for the RtoP's influence. If a crisis is perceived from the beginning in RtoP terms i.e. as involving the occurrence of mass atrocities the RtoP is very likely to be used in the foreign-policy decision-making process. At the same time, agreement on the general applicability of the RtoP does not imply that different actors correspond with each other on how the emerging norm will be implemented. Furthermore, even if there is agreement on the implementation of the RtoP, there might still be a mismatch between rhetoric and practice undermining the influence of the RtoP (see presumption II, box 1).

Having promoted the RtoP since its inception in the 2005 World Summit Outcome Document, the EU as a normative power can potentially act as a norm entrepreneur for the RtoP. If the EU succeeds in persuading national foreign policy decision-makers that the RtoP is legitimate and appropriate it increases the shared understanding as well as the influence of the emerging norm (see presumption III, box 1). Remaining the central actors within the area of security and defence, the EU's ability to act will depend further on the political will of the member states and the kind of role they envisage for the EU as a security actor. Acting as a norm entrepreneur for the RtoP can therefore potentially increase the EU's role as a security actor. Yet, the EU's role as a security actor in its neighbourhood is further linked to the de-

19 NB: In the case of the Cyclone Nargis in Burma, France tried to convinced its partners that the crisis in Myanmar was a RtoP case and that a military intervention was necessary, but failed due to the argument that the RtoP was limited to the four crimes (war crimes, crimes against humanity, genocide and ethnic cleansing) as determined in the 2005 Outcome Document and did therefore not apply to natural disasters (see chapter 3).

velopment and the impact of the CSDP. While the EU has developed military and civilian capabilities to manage crises in its neighbourhood (see chapter 2), it has to be examined in practice whether the available CSDP instruments are actually used in practice in relation to the RtoP (see chapters 3-5).

Finally, the case that the RtoP has no influence at all and / or is absent in European responses to mass atrocities in its neighbourhood will be considered (see presumption IV, box 1). The absence of the RtoP in the official discourse can imply that the RtoP is not perceived as a legitimate and appropriate norm to act upon in a specific case. On the other hand, this presumption could be challenged by the argument that the RtoP's absence in the European foreign policy discourse can signify influence. On this note, RtoP absence in the discourse of a specific actor can imply that this actor disproves the interpretation of the RtoP by other actors in the same case. Furthermore it might be the case that other considerations such as economic interests prevail over the protection of civilians or that the crisis in question does not matter for European security. Finally, the lack of reference to the RtoP can be linked to a general uncertainty on how to best respond to a crisis.

I. The existence of a norm entrepreneur can increase the collective understanding of the RtoP in a specific case but not in general.

II. The EU's role as norm entrepreneur can reinforce its role as security actor.

III. The perception of a crisis in RtoP terms (i.e. the four RtoP crimes) increases its influence but does not entail the implementation of the RtoP.

IV. RtoP has no influence at all and/or is absent in the crisis response.

Box 1: Presumptions

Research design

This thesis follows the structure of demand, supply and test. It is assumed that, amongst other events, the lessons learned from the Kosovo crisis and intervention in 1999 increased the demand for a new norm of protection for civilians from mass atrocities committed by their own governments, as well as for the development of joint European defence capabilities. On the supply side, the international community created the emerging norm of the RtoP and Europe started to build a Common Security and Defence Policy. While it is acknowledged that a number of factors and events since the end of the Cold War had an influence on the demand for a new norm on humanitarian intervention as well as on the creation of the CSDP, addressing the full spectrum of historical explanations would go beyond the scope of this thesis. Arguably reaching the climax of the humanitarian crises in the 1990s, the Kosovo crisis constituted a tipping point timely and discursively for the RtoP and the CSDP.

Furthermore, against the background of Rwanda and Srebrenica, the Kosovo experience essentially revived the debate on the need of a new international norm on how to respond to such grave human rights violations. At the same time, Kosovo exemplified once more the EU's inability to respond effectively to mass atrocities in its neighbourhood. Partly inspired by the same events, Kofi Annan promoted the development of the RtoP at the UN level, while Jacques Chirac and Tony Blair launched a key initiative to create the Common Security and Defence Policy. The 1999 Kosovo crisis and intervention will serve as a starting point for this analysis. Constituting a pre-RtoP crisis and intervention, the Kosovo crisis will provide the necessary background in order to be able to assess the influence of the RtoP in terms of whether it actually makes a difference in European responses to mass atrocities. Yet, the Kosovo crisis should not be understood as the sole trigger for the development of the RtoP and the CSDP but rather as an example illustrating the trends and dynamics of the 1990s.

Accordingly, the first part of this thesis focuses on European responses to the Kosovo crisis in 1999 and the development of the RtoP and the CSDP in theory and in practice. Against this background, the influence of the RtoP as an emerging international norm on European responses to mass atrocities will be 'tested' on the basis of an in-depth case study analysis. A common definition of a case study is: "the essence of a case study … is that it tries to illuminate a decision or set of decisions: why were they taken, how were they implemented, and with what result" (Schramm, 1971, cited in Yin, 2003: 22-23). Throughout this study a case is defined as a crisis involving the presumed or actual occurrence of mass atrocities in the EU's neighbourhood. The analytical focus is not on the conflicts as such but on the European response to them.

Case study selection

The Libyan and the Syrian crisis are chosen on the basis of their assumed variation in the influence of the RtoP as an emerging international norm on European responses to these conflicts. It is assumed that the two case studies display a different degree of RtoP influence, which is reflected in the different policies adopted in response to the crises. The choice of the two cases can also be explained by their relevance for the RtoP as an emerging international norm and the development of the CSDP.

The military intervention in Libya in 2011 constituted the first instance in which the UNSC authorised the use of military force for the protection of civilians against the will of a functioning *de jure* government on the basis of the RtoP (Williams and Bellamy, 2012). The Libyan civil war was also the first crisis on the EU's borders after the entry into force of the Lisbon Treaty in 2009. In light of the establishment of the *Common* Security and Defence Policy, the expectations on Europe to manage this crisis in its immediate neighbourhood were considerably high. The Libya crisis therefore revived not only the debate about the RtoP in general but also its relevance for the EU as security actor in its neighbourhood.

In the Libyan case, member states openly disagreed on how to respond adequately to the crisis. Germany decided to abstain in the voting on UNSC Resolution 1973 and therefore from any military engagement in Libya. France together with the UK and the US, by contrast, took the lead in establishing a no-fly zone over Libya. Although the CSDP had been fully operational since 2003, practical crisis management on the EU level remained limited to humanitarian assistance. The time frame for the analysis of the Libya crisis is from the outbreak of the violence in February 2011 until October 2011, flagged by former *de facto* Libyan leader Muammar Gaddafi's death and a de-escalation of the conflict.

The application of the RtoP in the case of the Libya crisis raised the stakes for the international responses to the crisis in Syria since March 2011.[20] While the UNSC condemned the violence against the Syrian civilians and sent UN observers to Syria, it has been unable to agree upon action aimed at halting the mass atrocities. Concerns that the NATO-led intervention in Libya went beyond the mandate issued in Resolution 1973 have left some UNSC members even more reluctant to place sole blame on the government for the crisis and to take robust action to stop the mass violence (ICRtoP, 2011). It was only after the "red line" set by the US, for the use of chemical weapons of mass destruction against the civilian population, was crossed on 21 August 2013, that the option of a military intervention was put back on the table. However, arguments in favour of intervention on the basis of the RtoP became blurred by claims about the necessity to punish the Syrian government. While the EU has been engaged in responding to the Syrian crisis with political and economic instruments, its profile as security actor remained even lower than in the Libyan crisis. The time frame for the analysis of the Syrian case study is set from March 2011 to September 2013 when the US, Russia and Syria agreed on the defection of the Syrian chemical weapons arsenal.

Units of analysis

The chosen units of analysis are the relevant UN and EU institutions as well as the three biggest EU member states France, Germany and the UK[21]. This choice is motivated by the necessity to analyse the impact of international norms that are powerful enough to decide whether to invoke or contest the legitimacy of norms. While member states have always been the central actors in the area of European security and defence, France, Germany and the UK, in particular, played a crucial role in the creation and constant further institutional development of the CSDP. Concentrating on the 'Big 3' when analysing the influence of the RtoP through a number of case studies, provides constancy since the French, German and British positions were equally vital from Kosovo to Syria. They can serve as an indicator for European unity and can pos-

20 At the time of writing the Syrian crisis was still ongoing, therefore an artificial but justifiable end point was set for the analysis of the case study.

21 The theoretical and analytical framework developed and applied in this thesis focuses on the construction of European foreign policies in response to crises in its neighbourhood and the influence of the RtoP therein. The aim is not to answer why certain policies have been adopted on the basis of for example different ideologies or interests incumbent to specific governments. The changes in national administrations in terms of personnel and party affiliation will therefore be noticed (see table 4 below) but will not play a role in the actual analysis.

sibly be trend setting within the EU. The focus on the 'Big 3' therefore aims at serving as a proxy when evaluating the impact of the RtoP on European foreign policy. Inside the member states, the analysis of foreign policy decision-making will be limited to the official discourse of the respective heads of state or government, the foreign ministers, the permanent representatives (Perm Rep) to the UNSC and parliamentary debates.

Actor	France[22]	Germany[23]	United Kingdom[24]
Head of State or Government	Nicolas Sarkozy (UMP[25])/ François Hollande[26] (PS[27])	Angela Merkel (CDU)	David Cameron (CON[28])
Foreign Minister	Alain Juppé (UMP)/ Laurent Fabius[29] (PS)	Guido Westerwelle (FDP)	William Hague (CON)
UN Perm Rep	Gérard Araud	Petter Wittig	Sir Mark Lyall Grant
Parliament[30]	Assemblée Nationale	Deutscher Bundestag	House of Commons

Table 3: Key actors in German, French and British foreign policy

22 Occasionally statements of further members of the French government will also be taken into account: Laurent Wauquiez (Secretary of State for European Affairs under Sarkozy); Michèle Alliot-Marie (Minister of the Interior under Sarkozy); François Fillon (Prime Minister under Sarkozy); Jean-Marc Ayrault (Prime Minister under Hollande); Jean-Yves le Drian (Defence Minister under Hollande).

23 In addition to the statements made by the main actors in German foreign policy, utterances made by Werner Hoyer (Minister of State at the Foreign Office under Westerwelle from 2009 to 2013) will occasionally also be referred to.

24 Additional statements that will be taken into account are by Alistair Burt (Parliamentary Under Secretary of State at the Foreign and Commonwealth Office from 2010 to 2013) and Jeremy Brown (Minister at the Foreign and Commonwealth Office since 2010 and Minister of State at the Home Office from 2012-2013).

25 Union for a Popular Movement.

26 As President of France Nicolas Sarkozy was in power from May 2006 until May 2012 when his successor François Hollande took over.

27 French Socialist Party.

28 British Conservative Party.

29 Alain Juppé served as Foreign Ministers under President Sarkozy from 2011 to 2012. After the elections in May 2012, Laurent Fabius was appointed Foreign Minister under President Hollande.

30 Members of the respective national parliaments will be cited with their first and last name throughout the empirical chapters of this study.

On the EU level the analysis focuses on the EU institutions that are most relevant for the foreign policy of the EU and who communicate their foreign policy decisions publicly[31] (listed in table 4).

Institution	Cast	Foreign policy function
The European Council (EC)	Heads of state or government	Key role in strategic direction, scope and main decisions of EU foreign policy.
The Foreign Affairs Council (FAC)	Foreign Minister of the member states + HR	Foreign policy decisions
The High Representative of the Union for Foreign Affairs and Security Policy (HR)	Lady Catherine Ashton	Conducts CFSP as mandated by the FAC; head of the European External Action Service (EEAS)
The Permanent President of the European Council	Herman Van Rompuy	External representation
European Commission (COM)	One member per member states + president	Humanitarian assistance and civilian protection
European Parliament (EP)	Directly elected 766 members	Opinion on foreign policy issues through reports, resolutions and parliamentary questions

Table 4: Key actors in EU foreign policy

Finally, the analysis takes into account the discourse of the UN institutions such as the UN Security Council and the UN General Assembly (UNGA). While the latter has been an important forum of debate for the application and further development of the RtoP as an emerging norm, the UNSC is the main authority responsible for its implementation. The positions of the permanent members of the UNSC (P5) – France, UK, the US, China and Russia – are crucial for the implementation of the RtoP as either of them can veto a UNSC resolution any time. Furthermore, the US is still a key actor in international security in terms of military capabilities and

31 There are further relevant institutions within the CSDP particularly the Political and Security Committee (PSC) as well as the military and civilian crisis management structures. However most of their documents and communications are confidential and not publicly available. While this study focuses on the official discourse on European response to mass atrocities, these bodies were widely excluded from the analysis.

resources. The military intervention in Libya in 2011 was another proof that Europe is still reliant on the military capacities and structures of its transatlantic partner.

Methods of analysis

Part two of this study traces the influence of the RtoP on European responses to the crises in Libya in 2011 and in Syria from 2011 to 2013. Instead of considering all the available information, the analysis of the two cases is structured according to a set of indicators, which derive from the previously developed theoretical and analytical framework.[32] In line with the chosen units of analysis, both case studies focus on the role of the UN, the EU, France, Germany and the UK. The analysis of the crisis response of each actor is divided in two parts: crisis perception and foreign policy response. The division between each actors' description of the crisis and its actual foreign policy response paves the way for assessing the influence of the RtoP according to the previously developed scale. On this basis, it will be possible to reveal whether rhetorical claims are followed through in practice. The case study analyses of the Libyan and the Syrian crisis will be structured as follows:

1. Role of the UN
    a) Crisis perception
    b) Crisis response
2. Role of the EU
    a) Crisis perception
    b) Crisis response
3. Crisis perception
    a) France
    b) Germany
    c) UK
4. Foreign policy response
    a) France
    b) Germany
    c) UK

32 See George and Bennett (2005: 67-72) for a detailed introduction of the method of structured focused comparison of case studies.

The case study analysis is further based on the methods of process-racing and discourse analysis. The former will be applied to trace the different stages in the European foreign policy decision-making process, on how to respond to the crises in Libya and in Syria. In line with the constructivist perspective adopted in this thesis, the method of process-tracing will be combined with a method of discourse analysis, which focuses on the examination of the official UN and EU discourses, as well as the discourses of the three biggest EU member states – France, Germany and the UK. The analytical focus of this study is on investigating the influence of the RtoP in terms of whether it is seen as a legitimate behavioural claim in front of a broad national and / or European audience. The analysis therefore concentrates on examining the official discourse available in publicly accessible documents issued by the French, German and British governments as well as by the EU and the UN. When tracing the legitimacy of the RtoP through a number of illuminating case studies from 1999 to 2011, centring on the official discourse appears to be a reliable and valid method. It is reliable due to the availability of comparable data across the different cases and valid as to the main aim of study of assessing the influence of the RtoP on European crisis responses in terms of its legitimacy.[33]

The method of process-tracing is used as a method that seeks to trace the intervening steps by which international norms influence political behaviour. The aim is to reveal the extent to which international norms influence actors' "receptivity to and assessment of incoming information about the situation, his definition of the situation, his identification and evaluation of options, as well as, finally his choice of a course of action" (George, 1979: 113). It therefore seems a plausible procedure for establishing an explanatory link between norms and policies. At the same time, detecting the intervening steps in the foreign policy decision-making process does not reveal whether or how norms cause action. The focus is on how a certain policy response became politically possible rather than why it happened.

The analysis of the Libyan and the Syrian crises (see chapters 4 and 5) traces the different stages in the European foreign policy decision-making process on how to respond to the conflict. Tracing this process aims at revealing how the outcome was

33 In line with the operationalization of influence of the RtoP as legitimacy in front of a broader national and / or European audience, the author predominantly refrained from conducting interviews with member states and / or EU officials.

influenced by the RtoP.[34] It involves exploring the discourse and the policies implemented by the actors chosen for the analysis (the UN, the EU, France, Germany and the UK). The start and end point for the process-tracing are the set time frames for the case study analysis. As the proposed and debated responses to the crises as well as the arguments used to justify a specific course of action constitute relevant evidence in this framework, the method of process-tracing will be combined with a method of discourse analysis.

Drawing on Martha Finnemore's study on humanitarian interventions (1996: 306) it is argued that the explanations actors give for why and how they respond to a specific crisis can constitute possible indicators of the influence of the RtoP. Accordingly, if actors claim that a certain foreign policy measure is adopted in order to protect the civilian population from mass atrocities then this can count as an instance of RtoP. This does not completely solve the problem of whether this action was carried out on the basis of another interest but it is analytically useful as it shows that the RtoP is seen as legitimate.

The method of discourse analysis allows the integration of different dimensions and perspectives of the subject studied by taking into account the intertextual and interdiscursive relations between different discourses as well as the institutional frames of a specific context of situation[35] (Wodak, 2008: 2). The core of the discourse analysis is "the systematic and explicit analysis of the various structures and strategies of different levels of text and talk" (Van Dijk, 2007, quoted in Wodak, 2008: 3). Discourse is defined as "linguistic action, be it written, visual or oral communication, verbal or non-verbal, undertaken by social actors in a specific setting determined by social rules, norms and conventions" (Wittgenstein, 1967 and Austin, 1962 quoted in Wodak, 2008: 5).

34 NB: According to George and Bennett (2008: 217), "the method of process-tracing needs to consider the possibility of alternative processes that lead to the outcome in question. It is important to examine the process-tracing evidence not only on the hypothesis of interest, but on alternative hypotheses that other scholars, policy experts and historians have proposed." Focusing on the hypothesis of interest can create a confirmation bias and lower the explanatory power of the chosen hypothesis. Therefore, the introduction tried to foreclose a range of alternative explanations in advance (see section on 'RtoP's scope' under 1.2).

35 Intertextuality refers to the fact that all texts are linked to other texts, both in the past and in the present. Interdiscursivity indicates that discourses are linked to each other by common topics or sub-topics (Wodak, 2008: 3).

In line with the constructivist theoretical framework adopted in this study, discourse is seen as social activity by which actors make meaning of a particular situation with the use of language. Analysing discourse means looking at patterns, commonalities and relationships that concern different texts and occasions. Discourse is therefore more abstract than text, which can be described as one specific and potentially unique realisation of a discourse (Wodak, 2008: 6). In this context, a text creates no sense in itself but only in connection with knowledge of the world and of the context.

The qualitative discourse analytical approach used throughout this thesis focuses on the analysis of political rhetoric (Reisigl, 2008). Political rhetoric analysis refers to the "analysis of the use of rhetorical means of persuasion by professional politicians" (Reisigl, 2008: 97). It distinguishes between three different dimensions of 'political': polity, politics and policy. The polity dimension constitutes the structural framework for political action. It manifests itself in basic political norms, principles, rules and values of a political system, as well as in the legal procedures and political institutions. Policy involves the content-related dimension of political action and refers thus to specific foreign policy instruments such as diplomacy, sanctions or military interventions. Politics refers to the articulation of political interests and positions. The main goals of political rhetoric are political justification and legitimation (idem.)

In accordance with the focus of this study the political rhetoric analyses examines the official discourses of the European foreign policy makers in response to the crises in Libya and Syria. The choice of categories for the political rhetoric analysis is connected to the indicators chosen for the case study analysis. Under the first denominator 'the role of the UN and the EU', the respective discourses and responses will be scrutinised in terms of their promotion of the RtoP. The focus here is also on how the UN and the EU perceive their own responsibility as well as the responsibility of others. Moreover, it will be analysed to what extent the RtoP is contested by referring to conflicting or competing norms such as sovereignty, territorial integrity and non-interference.

With regard to the 'crisis perception', the discourse analysis looks at how the crises in Libya and Syria are depicted. It focuses specifically on the terms with which the crises are described i.e. as armed conflicts or civil wars. Further it looks at how human rights violations are depicted and to what extent the crisis is linked to one or more of the four RtoP crimes. It further takes into account proposed and debated courses of actions and the ways they are legitimised. Specifically, the extent to which the choice of the respective foreign policy tool is based on the RtoP will be investigated. Finally, under the indicator 'foreign policy response', discourses on the implementation will be compared with previous discourses on how best to respond to the crisis in question. This category scrutinises the conformity of discourse and action and focuses on whether the previously stated aim of a proposed policy is actually implemented or whether the policy is amended *ex post.*

Step	Indicator for case study analysis	Categories for discourse analysis
1	Role of the UN and the EU[36]	Crisis reaction, understanding and implementation of the RtoP.
2	Crisis perception	Description of the crisis and proposed actions.
3	Foreign policy response	Conformity of discourse and action, achievement of previously stated aims, *ex post* legitimation.

Table 5: Steps and categories for discourse analysis

36 Influence as norm entrepreneurs depends further on the type of document: in case of the UN, a binding UNSC Resolution has greater influence as a press statement or a non-binding UNGA Resolution; in case of the EU the political weight of binding CFSP decisions and FAC conclusion is higher than of press statements or non-binding EP resolutions.

Data collection

The process-tracing and discourse analysis focuses on official documents (speeches, press releases, parliamentary debates) of the respective French, German and UK governments on their response to the Libyan and the Syrian crises in accordance to the above-established key actors in the respective national foreign policies (see table 3). Furthermore, documents issued by the relevant EU institutions (Council conclusion, statements, press release and fact sheets by the HR, the EEAS, the President of the European Council, the European Commission and the European Parliament) as well as reports, resolutions and statements of the UN institutions (UNSC and UNGA) have been collected. For each of the specific time frames of the crises in Libya and in Syria, approximately 250 official documents have been collected and analysed.

The primary sources have been complemented by scholarly literature on the RtoP, the CSDP, and French, German and British foreign policies. Finally, for the background on the Libyan and the Syrian crises also Think Tank policy analyses, media reports and newspaper articles have been taken into account. By the time of finishing this thesis the Libyan crisis dated back almost two years and has since then been covered extensively by scholars, think tankers and journalists. The Syrian crisis, by contrast, was at the time of writing still ongoing. Originally, the time frame for the Syrian crisis was set from March 2011 – the outbreak of the violence – to July 2012 – the third Russian and Chinese veto in the UN Security Council – and until summer 2013 it seemed very unlikely that the option of a military intervention would be seriously considered by members of the international community. As RtoP increasingly started to reflect in international and European discourses once US President Barack Obama threatened the Assad government with a military intervention, it seemed almost inevitable to extend the time frame for the Syrian case to September 2013. At the same time, the recency of the second case study implies a lower number of secondary sources and scholarly analyses of the Syrian crisis. Therefore, a slight imbalance between the data available on the Libyan and on the Syrian crisis has to be acknowledged.

1.4 Outline of the thesis

This thesis consists of two parts – background and case study analysis – each consisting of two chapters. Part I (chapter 2) starts by looking at the lessons learned from Kosovo and the development of the RtoP and the CSDP. It focuses on European responses to the Kosovo crisis and their positions on the military intervention that was conducted without authorization by the UN Security Council. The legality and the legitimacy of the humanitarian intervention will be highlighted. Furthermore, chapter 2 traces the development of the RtoP as deriving from the previously existing norm of humanitarian intervention. Finally, the chapter looks at the EU's role as evolving security actor. It examines specifically the development of the CSDP and the EU's understanding of responsibility in relation to the RtoP and the use of force.

Building on the historical narrative traced in chapter 2, chapter 3 elaborates on the practical application of the RtoP and the CSDP. It focuses on the question of whether a collective (European) understanding of what the RtoP means truly exists, and whether it emerged prior to the Libyan and Syrian crises in 2011. Chapter 3 reviews four cases of RtoP application and non-application in the period from 2005 to 2010: The Darfur crisis, the post-election violence in Kenya, Cyclone Nargis in Burma and the Russian-Georgian War.

Part II applies the theoretical and analytical framework developed here to explore the influence of the RtoP on European responses to the crisis in Libya from March to October 2011 (chapter 4) and the Syrian crisis from March 2011 to September 2013 (chapter 5). Based on the background established in part I, the in-depth case study analysis aims at revealing whether the RtoP as an emerging international norm actually makes a difference in whether and how Europe responds to mass atrocities in its neighbourhood since the Kosovo crisis in 1999.

Chapter 6 draws conclusions on the different degrees of RtoP influence, in terms of its rhetorical use and practical application, in both case studies. It also evaluates what has changed in comparison to the Kosovo crisis and the old norm of humanitarian intervention. It further validates or rejects the four presumptions introduced previously. Finally, Chapter 6 also discusses further existing scholarly arguments on the influence of the RtoP on international responses to both crises and predictions about the further development of the emerging norm.

The conclusion returns to the meta-question of this thesis: it assesses the policy impact of human security and its link to the RtoP, on the basis of the results from the case study analysis and comparison. The final chapter of the thesis also addresses the usefulness of the theoretical and analytical framework as well as its limitations. It moreover provides an outlook on further research in the area of human security, the RtoP, CSDP and beyond. Finally, it briefly illustrates the most recent developments on the security situations in Libya and Syria, just prior to the completion of this thesis by means of a short press review. A glance at the situations in Libya and Syria post-RtoP application or consideration can arguably provide further insights on the influence of the RtoP in the 'real world' and on the ground.

The RtoP has been on the international agenda for over a decade now and arguably, no single work can capture the significance of the emerging international norm for past and futures developments in international relations. Yet, this thesis seeks both breadth and depth in the analysis of the RtoP's influence on European foreign policy-making. With the aim of assessing whether the RtoP has made a difference since its creation in 2001, this study provides an overview of the RtoP's development and practical application from 2001 to 2011.

Furthermore, spurred by a revived debate on the RtoP in light of the Arab Spring since late 2010, this thesis offers an in-depth analysis of two case studies – the influence of the RtoP in the Libyan and the Syrian crisis since 2011. The introduction has set out the relevance of studying human security and the RtoP in academic and practical terms. Since both concepts derive from the policy world and are designed to be applied in international relations, assessing their significance empirically becomes imperative.

PART I

Chapter 2: Lessons learned from Kosovo? Developing the RtoP and the CSDP

The international responses to the wars of Yugoslavia's dissolution in the 1990s and to Bosnia in particular were in the eyes of many Europeans a collective failure (Rupnik, 2011: 17). The 'hour of Europe', the memorable phrase coined by Jacques Poos, the Foreign Affairs Minister of Luxembourg and President of the EU Council in July 1991 (quoted in idem), never arrived. The EU was unable to prevent genocide and ethnic cleansing in the Balkans. Yet, the Kosovo experience was also increasing the demand for Common European Security and Defence Policy (CSDP) (Peterson, 2003: 89). Arguably contributing to the ethos of the EU's development as a security actor but also to the debate on humanitarian interventions, this chapter departs from the lessons learned from the Kosovo intervention in 1999. Against this background, it traces the evolution of the Responsibility to Protect (RtoP) as an emerging international norm and the development of the EU's CSDP.[37]

In order to be able to assess whether the RtoP and the CSDP actually make a difference, this chapter establishes the historical background that is needed for this comparison. The emphasis of this chapter is therefore more on breadth than depth. It focuses on the extent to which the RtoP derives from the previous norm of humanitarian intervention and on whether the developments of the RtoP and the CSDP have had an impact on the role of the EU as a security actor. While this chapter is dedicated to the development of the RtoP and the CSDP from a historical perspective, the following chapter will scrutinize the RtoP's and CSDP's practical application as they evolved up until the time of the Libyan crisis in 2011.

The chapter starts by examining the norm of humanitarian intervention and its application to the Kosovo crisis in 1999. In line with the focus of this thesis, a

37 The 1999 Kosovo crisis and intervention should not be seen as the main cause for the creation of the CSDP or the RtoP. There were certainly many reasons for the further integration of security and defence policies within the EU, namely the end of the Cold War, a new security environment and the fear the US would turn its focus away from Europe as well as a debate about the 'raison d'être' of NATO (see Koenig, 2010). The Kosovo crisis is rather used as an example highlighting previously existing flaws and trends in EU foreign policy and the humanitarian intervention debate.

particular emphasis will be put on European responses (Germany, France and the UK) to the Kosovo crisis. Against this background, the chapter proceeds by tracing the development of the newly emerging international norm – the RtoP. In the third part, the creation and institutional evolution of the CSDP inspired by Europe's inability to react to the Kosovo crisis will be outlined. The fourth part will draw some preliminary conclusions on the theoretical developments in the transition from humanitarian intervention to the RtoP.

2.1 Humanitarian intervention and the 1999 Kosovo crisis

Introduction

Questions surrounding the existence of a legal right of humanitarian intervention, related to ethical considerations and the meaning of morality have been widely debated in the scholarly literature (see for example Chesterman, 2002; Pattison, 2008; Bellamy, 2011b). Looking at the practice of humanitarian intervention over the course of history reveals distinctive patterns that correspond, broadly, to interventions in the 19th century, the post UN Charter era and the more recent post-Cold War period. During the 18th and 19th century, philosophers of political liberalism such as John Stuart Mill related the concept of humanitarian intervention to the concept of human rights (Parekh, 1997: 142).[38] The lack of a general prohibition of the use of force within international relations, could be taken as an early justification for the existence of the practice of humanitarian intervention. The attempt to outlaw the use of military force between sovereign states after World War I led to a slight decline of the practice during the first half of the 19th century (idem).

The UN Charter laid down a new approach towards the concept of humanitarian intervention, turning the non-intervention principle into a universal norm of international law. Exceptions would allow the use of military force only in case of a threat to international peace and security or in compromise of states' right to self-defence if authorised by the UNSC under Chapter VII of the UN Charter. Since 1945, the

38 The concept of humanitarian intervention can be traced back even further to the 16th and 17th century and the discussion on 'just wars' particularly by Hugo Grotius (Welsh, 2012: 187).

UNSC has thus had the right to authorise the use of force and intervention in the domestic affairs of a state with the aim of ending gross human rights violations – but only under the condition that those constitute a threat to international peace and security (MacFarlane and Khong, 2006).

The end of the Cold War and the increasing number of internal armed conflicts and civil wars have led to a substantial change in approach to humanitarian intervention. It can be seen in the growing number of UNSC Resolutions under Chapter VII imposing economic sanctions or authorising the use of force (MacFarlane and Khong, 2006). In line with the evolving role of the UN, multilateralism became an additional condition for humanitarian intervention in the post-Cold War period (Seppä, 2011). Consensus concerning the question of when to intervene in a domestic crisis has not emerged among states or within international organisations, including the UN (MacFarlane and Khong, 2006). The UN practice was developed on a case-by-case basis and thereby initially refrained from developing criteria for humanitarian interventions. Nevertheless, the practice of intervention without authorisation by the UNSC has not disappeared, one of the most well-known example being NATO's intervention in Kosovo in 1999.

NATO's action in Kosovo is one of the most controversial interventions of the 1990s. Undertaken in 1999, it heated up the debate on authority, especially in the context of evolving state practice. Authorization of intervention in Kosovo seemed improbable because of the opposition of China and Russia. In fact, it was not even ever formally requested. NATO governments bypassed the UNSC and used 'humanitarian necessity' as their legitimate justification. The 1999 Kosovo intervention therefore involved a denial of traditional notions of national sovereignty. In the aftermath the intervention was widely referred to as 'illegal but legitimate' (see for example Badescu, 2011: 62).

Summary of the crisis

Ethnic Albanians, who comprised 80 per cent of Kosovo's population, actively opposed Serbian rule after the breakup of the former Yugoslavia[39] (Independent International Commission on Kosovo (IICK), 2000: 317). Slobodan Milosevic's government[40] in Belgrade vehemently discriminated against the Albanian population, depriving it of political and economic opportunities. In response to the discrimination, a non-violent resistance movement led by Ibrahim Rugova established parallel, unofficial and political structures for Albanians in Kosovo. Although it was fairly successful at providing services, the movement failed to advance the cause of Kosovar independence from Serbia. The failure became obvious in 1995 when the Dayton Agreement[41], which gave neighbouring Bosnia and Herzegovina its independence, excluded any nod to Kosovar's political aspirations. In response, the Kosovo Liberation Army (KLA) emerged and by 1997 it was openly advocating violence as the only route to independence. Aware that it lacked popular support and was weak compared to the Serbian authorities, the KLA deliberately provoked Serbian police and Interior Ministry attacks on Albanian civilians, with the aim of garnering support, specifically military intervention (Seybolt, 2008: 79). Violence escalated through most of 1998 (Posen, 2000).

Responding with diplomacy, European and US governments, initially sent mixed signals about their objectives (IICK, 2000: 131-61). In October 1998 Milosevic and the KLA agreed on a ceasefire, the withdrawal of some Serbian security forces and the deployment of international monitors under the authority of the Organization for Security and Cooperation in Europe (OSCE) (Weller, 1999: 274). The unarmed Kosovo Verification Mission (KVM) managed temporarily to constrain the KLA and Serb security forces while diplomats aimed for a political settlement. In the meantime, the KLA used the hiatus to strengthen its forces. In response the Federal Republic of Yugoslavia (FRY) stationed army units on the Kosovo border (Seybolt, 2008: 80).

39 Yugoslavia's dissolution was the result of a series of political upheavals and conflicts in the early 1990s after a political crisis in the 1980s. The breakup of Yugoslavia resulted in several inter-ethnic wars initially primarily affecting Bosnia and Croatia. After the end of World War II Yugoslavia was established as a Federation and divided into six Republics: Slovenia, Bosnia and Herzegovina, Serbia, Montenegro and Macedonia. The Kosovo Albanians starting to demand their autonomous province in the 1980s, resulting into ethnic tensions between Albanians and Serbs that lasted throughout the decade (for a detailed account of European reactions to the breakup of Yugoslavia see Almond, 1994 and Glenny, 1996).

40 President of the Federal Republic of Yugoslavia from 1997 to 2000.

41 The General Framework for Peace in Bosnia and Herzegovina, signed in Paris on 14 December 1995, aimed at ending the Bosnian War (1992-1995).

Violence increased again by December 1998 (IICK, 2000: 79). While the governmental and public debates about how to respond to the Kosovo crisis continued, the US government under Bill Clinton sought to confront the KLA and the FRY with an ultimatum during the negotiations in Rambouillet, France, in February 1999 (IICK, 2000, annex 3). The terms of the draft Rambouillet agreement, set out by the Contact Group[42], were more favourable to the Kosovar Albanians. Therefore Milosevic rejected them (idem: 153). The Rambouillet talks were followed by a number of military operations. In March 1999, NATO launched Operation Allied Force (OAF), a coercive bombing campaign over Kosovo and the rest of Serbia.

As soon as the NATO operation began, Serbian security forces started to strategically expel the Albanian population of Kosovo (Ball et al, 2002). As the KVM and all international aid personnel had withdrawn, there was no foreign presence to restrain the Serbian security forces' actions. Military, Interior Ministry and police forces systematically cleared villages and towns, driving hundreds of thousands of people towards the border with Albania and the Former Yugoslav Republic of Macedonia (FYROM). As part of the expulsion campaign, Serbian forces killed 10.000 – 12.000 Kosovar Albanians (Ball et al, 2002: 6). In addition some 863.000 people became refugees and 590.000 were internally displaced. Over 90 per cent of the Kosovar population were forced to leave their homes. It was the largest population displacement since the aftermath of the Second World War (IICK, 2000: 90, 201).

NATO then engaged in two humanitarian operations to address the need of hundreds of thousands of refugees: Operation Allied Harbour provided logistical assistance and direct aid in Albania, and Operation Joint Guardian did the same in the FYROM. When the war ended, the UNSC authorized NATO to send a ground force into Kosovo, known as the Kosovo Force (KFOR). The operation was designed to protect aid operations, protect the population and create a stable security environment for the international administration of the province.

The four NATO operations deployed to Kosovo involved different types of intervention ranging from logistics to coercion. Each of them met with different degrees

42 Including France, Germany, Italy, Russia, the UK and the US.

and failure (Seybolt, 2008: 81).[43] NATO initiated OAF on 14 March 1999 under the authority of the North Atlantic Council. Its two objectives were to coerce Milosevic to accept a political plan for Kosovo's autonomy and to prevent the Serbian government from killing and expelling Albanians, which would provoke a refugee flow that could destabilise neighbouring Albania and FYROM. The political objective was partially achieved, but the humanitarian impact of the operation was the opposite of what NATO political leaders intended (Hehir, 2009: 259).

The short-term humanitarian outcome was negative. NATO air strikes did not save any lives and caused between 600 and 5000 Serbian military deaths, 400 to 600 Serbian civilian deaths, and an unknown (but probably smaller) number of Kosovar Albanian civilian deaths (IICK, 2000: 306). OAF had an indirect role in thousands more civilian deaths because it provoked the Serbian security to attack. It must be clarified that NATO action did not cause the attack, which FRY officials had prepared in advance, however OAF strongly influenced the timing and the intensity of the attack that killed thousands and caused a sudden and massive refugee flow. However, the IICK (2000: 295) concluded that

> *Although the intervention produced temporary and severe worsening of the ordeal faced by the Kosovar Albanians, over time it adverted their worst fears of ethnic cleansing, and had the emancipatory effect for them of dismantling the oppressive Serb police and paramilitary structure.*

43 During OAF, five US guided bombs hit the Chinese Embassy in Belgrade, 'accidentally' according to then US President Bill Clinton. The bombs were intended to hit Yugoslav Federal Directorate for Supply and Procurement nearby the Chinese Embassy (see http://congressionalresearch.com/RS20547/document.php, retrieved 18 February 20).

European crisis responses

France

France was the first to recognize Yugoslavia diplomatically in 1996 and until the beginning of 1999 Paris had largely shown sympathy for Serbia's arguments concerning Kosovo. The French government under Jacques Chirac organised conferences in Rambouillet and in Paris in February 1999 and worked on a diplomatic solution (Stahl, 2008: 10). After the failure of the conferences and in view of unceasing reports of further atrocities in Kosovo, the US, the UK and Germany were increasingly willing to take severe actions against Milosevic. Additionally, Russia blocked the UNSC and the contact group – institutions favoured by France. Chirac and his government decided in favour of a military intervention under the guidance of the US, as in the case of the Second Gulf War and in Bosnia in 1995. France joined the NATO led military actions and actively participated in the air raids over Kosovo (Fortmann and Viau, 2000: 98).

The French government justified its participation in the intervention by relating the Kosovo crisis to its own security interests. France argued that a further escalation of violence in Kosovo would aggravate the refugee problem and would evoke the threat of a creation of a Greater Albania, which would destabilise the entire region:

> *... our military determination and our humanitarian commitment are part of a larger perspective – a true political and diplomatic vision. This is really about the preservation of balance on our continent.*[44] (Chirac, 12 April 1999)

The war opponents (*anti-frappes*) emphasised the omnipotence of the US and the powerlessness of Europe. The air raids were interpreted as if mainly the US had intended and initiated them while Europe and France had only acquiesced reluctantly (Stahl, 2010: 54). The *anti-frappes*' second objection focused on the legitimacy of the NATO attacks. For the first time after World War II, so they argued, there was a military operation against a sovereign state, which had neither started a war nor threatened one of NATO's member states. Furthermore, it was criticised that at-

44 "... Notre détermination militaire et notre engagement humanitaire s'inscrivent dans une perspective plus large, dans une véritable vision politique et diplomatique. Ce qui est en cause, c'est l'équilibre même de notre continent." (Author's own translation; applies to all quotes derived from French and German official documents or speeches.)

tacks defied the principle of sovereignty. It was moreover claimed that the operation violated international law as it contravened the UN Charter and was not covered by a UNSC Resolution. Hence, the attacks contradicted those values, which they pretended to stand for. Moreover, the missing international legitimisation was not compensated by national legitimisation. On the opposite side, French decision-makers decided on and initiated the attacks without prior consultation of the *Assemblée Nationale* (Stahl, 2008: 12)

However, the debate in parliament on 26 March 1999 clearly showed that all other parties – apart from the communist and the leftist republican *Mouvement de citoyens* (MDC) – as well as the '*nouveau philosophes*' and the vast majority of the political advisors in foreign affairs supported the intervention (idem.). Due to increasing criticism, the President entered the debate through televised speeches and the Prime Minister intervened through speeches in parliament and interviews. President Chirac said that what was going on in Kosovo was a "monstrous ethnic cleansing, planned and carried out with the greatest possible cynicism and greatest possible brutality by the Serbian regime."[45] (Chirac, 6 April 1999)

French representatives of government supported by popular intellectuals considered the current situation to be similar to past conflicts in the Balkans: the lessons from the war in Bosnia (France's representative at the UN, 24 March 1999), the stations of horror in Vukovar, Sarajevo and Srebrenica (Jospin, 26 March 1999) and the massacre of Raçak (Robert, 26 March 1999; Jospin, 26 March 1999). The intervention in Kosovo was described as "*guerre juste*" (Hervé de Charette, 27 April 1999). To shy away from an intervention would be no less for France "to lose her soul" (Chirac, 26 March 1999). Therefore, France's intervention was a "*combat de l'honneur*" (idem). The socialist prime minister agreed with Chirac that Kosovo was no longer an international conflict but a national matter that touched upon the foundations of the French nation (Jospin, 27 April 1999).

45 "... monstrueuse opération d'épuration ethnique planifiée et conduite avec le plus grande cynisme et la plus grande cruauté par le régime serbe."

Furthermore, the French President considered the actions against Serbia to be of a new quality that would raise the issue of intervention above traditional considerations:

> *... this war ... is exemplary. It is not grounded in economic or strategic aims, but in a moral conception of the nations.*[46] (Chirac, 3 May 1999)

The airstrikes were arguably not aimed at the people of Serbia, but against their oppressors. Thus, Chirac and Jospin succeeded in countering the *anti-frappes*' arguments. Their line of argumentation combined moral values and historical experiences (Stahl, 2010: 61). The French government emphasised the brutality and exceptionality of the Kosovo crisis and referred to the lessons that should be learned from past atrocities in Bosnia, in order to justify the international intervention in Kosovo. Questions of the legality and the legitimacy of the military operation were only raised by the opposition.[47]

46 "... le combat ... est exemplaire. Il n'est pas fondé dans les arrières pensées économique ou stratégique, mais sure une conception de la morale et de l'honneur des nations."

47 Early April 1999, close to 80 % of those interviewed were content with the government's policy on Kosovo (Cristophe et al., 1999).

Germany

The escalation of the Kosovo crisis hit Germany in a volatile situation on the domestic front (Stahl, 2008). The administration of Helmut Kohl (CDU[48]), which had already been voted out, was formerly still in office, and the newly elected red-green coalition had not yet been constituted. However, in both camps there was a consensus between the old and the new government that Germany would participate in the NATO-led air campaign on Yugoslavia without UNSC mandate.

One of the initial rather interest-based lines of argumentation of the proponents of military intervention was based on a debate established in the beginning of the 1990s – the so-called "out-of-area debate" which proposed an incremental expansion of German military involvement abroad (Stahl, 2008: 8). The outgoing Minister of Defence Volker Rühe as well as the head of the CDU / CSU[49] faction, Wolfgang Schäuble emphasised the importance of Germany's commitment to its allies (*Bündnisverpflichtung*). They cautioned further against a German special path (*Sonderweg*) that is Germany's refusal to show solidarity and act responsibly.

The lessons from the Bosnian conflict as well as Germany's history were substantial for outgoing Foreign Minister Klaus Kinkel's (FDP[50]) argumentation concerning the legitimisation of the German participation:

> *Those who do not stop the evil will take the blame for it; the lesson of Bosnia is also the lesson of our own German past. It also applies to Kosovo. We must not simply say that there should not be a second Bosnia, but we must ensure that there will not be a second Bosnia.*[51] (Kinkel, 16 October 1998)

The Kohl government verdict in the early 1990s, that no German soldier shall be deployed to regions where soldiers of the *Wehrmacht* fought during World War II, was rejected by Chancellor-elect Gerhard Schröder (SPD[52]):

48 Christian Democratic Union.
49 Christian Socialist Union (sister party to the CDU).
50 Liberal Democratic Party.
51 "'Wer das Böse nicht stoppt, wir Schuld am Bösen' [ist] die Lehre aus Bosnien, aber es ist auch die Lehre ... aus unserer eigenen deutschen Geschichte. Sie gilt auch für den Kosovo. Dort dürfen wir nicht nur sagen, dass es kein zweites Bosnien geben darf, sondern wir müssen dafür sorgen, dass es kein zweites Bosnien gibt."
52 Social Democratic Party.

> *I have a lot of respect for those who ask: Is it sensible for Germans to take part in view of World War II? The question whether Germans should participate can be asked; and it is not a cynical question. However, I believe that one can reverse the sentence: especially if there is historical guilt with respect to this region one can also redeem it by helping to prevent further killing.*[53] (Schröder, 24 February 1999)

In a speech at the party convention of the Greens in Bielefeld in May 1999, which had been specifically summoned, Foreign Minister Joschka Fischer got to the heart of the matter when he drew the lessons from his life and the German past. He recalled Srebrenica and Auschwitz, and arson attacks on a home for asylum-seekers in Solingen, Germany, to conclude his argumentation with the statement: "no more war, no more Auschwitz, no more genocide, no more fascism" (Fischer, 13 May 1999). However, many adherents of an absolute restraint of military force did not share his re-interpretation. Christian Ströbele (The Greens) avowed: "I am ashamed of my country, which is waging war in Kosovo again and which is throwing bombs on Belgrade again."[54] (Ströbele, 25 March 1999). The chairmen of the parliamentary group of the PDS Gregor Gysi added: "In this century, Germany no longer has any right at all to throw bombs on Belgrade"[55] (Gysi, 26 March 1999).

Similarly to France, only opponents to the intervention in Kosovo discussed questions of legality and legitimacy. The incumbent government justified its participation in the military operation mainly on the grounds of Germany's historic responsibility. The opposition used the same historical arguments against German involvement in the Kosovo intervention. The Kosovo intervention represented the first active participation of the German military after World War II.[56]

53 "Ich habe großen Respekt vor denjenigen, die fragen: ist es angesichts der Geschichte des Zweiten Weltkrieges vernünftig, dass die Deutschen dabei sind? Die Frage, ob die Deutschen dabei sein sollen, kann man stellen, und es ist keine zynische Frage. Aber für mich gilt, dass man diesen Satz auch umkehren kann: gerade wenn es eine historische Schuld in dieser Region gibt, kann man sich auch dadurch abtragen, dass man weiteres Morgen verhindern hilft."

54 "Ich schäme mich für mein Land, das jetzt wieder im Kosovo Krieg führt und das wieder Bomben auf Belgrad wirft."

55 "Deutschland hat in diesem Jahrhundert überhaupt kein Recht mehr, Bomben auf Belgrad zu werfen."

56 In April 1999, 63 per cent supported Germany's participation in the NATO campaign, whereas 34 per cent opposed it (Ramet and Lyon, 2001: 92).

The United Kingdom

British policy-makers almost enthusiastically supported military intervention in Kosovo in 1999. The British Prime Minister Tony Blair stated on 23 March 1999 at the House of Commons that "on the assumption [diplomatic efforts] produce no change in President Milosevic's position and the repression in Kosovo by Serb forces continues, Britain stands ready with our NATO allies to take military action". The main reasons for Britain's support was to avert "what would otherwise be a humanitarian disaster in Kosovo". Blair underlined his argument at first by describing the refugee situation. He explained that

> *10 per cent of the population are now homeless as a result of repression by Serb forces. 65.000 people have been forced from their homes in the last month, and no less than 25.000 in the four days since peace talks broke down. Only yesterday, 5.000 people in the Srbica area were forcibly evicted from their villages.* (Blair, 23 March 1999)

Furthermore, he referred to the number of deaths: "Since last summer 2000 people have died" (idem). Similar to France and Germany, the Prime Minster recalled the lessons learned from history:

> *We act also because we know from bitter experience throughout this century, most recently in Bosnia, that instability and civil war in one part of the Balkans inevitably spills over in the whole of it, and affects the rest of Europe too* (idem).

Due to the number of refugees of about 1 million, Blair concluded, that a solution to the conflict was in Europe's strategic interest.

On 14 April 1999, Foreign Secretary Robin Cook justified Britain's participation in the NATO intervention in Kosovo by referring to British security in relation to the role and the credibility of NATO:

> *Our national security depends on NATO. NATO now has a common border with Serbia as a result of the expansion to embrace Hungary and other countries of central Europe. Our borders cannot remain stable while such violence is conducted on the other side of the fence. NATO was the guaran-*

> *tor of the October agreement. What credibility would NATO be left with if we allowed that agreement to be trampled on comprehensively by President Milosevic and did not stir to stop him?* (Cook, 14 April 1999)

At the same time, Cook also made references to the experiences during the Second World War and emphasised Britain's historical responsibility as well as the consequences of inaction:

> *... in 1945 when together we surveyed what we found in Europe, we found death camps, we found indecent bureaucracy of the extermination programme, pathetic survivors and millions of victims and we said then: 'Never again'. That is the pledge that we must honour in Kosovo, because in the past two weeks we have again borne witness to forced movements by train, to thousands hungry and squalid in makeshift camps, to pathetic masses shorn of their homes and their papers for no reason other than ethnic identity. Had we done nothing in response, we would have been complicit in that evil. Had we done nothing, we would have betrayed the modern Europe we are trying to build* (Cook, 14 April 1999).

Tony Blair's Chicago speech on 22 April 1999 has been described as "a key 'moment' in the history of the liberal interventionist discourse" (Daddow, 2009: 549). In his address Blair highlighted the threats that both Saddam Hussein and Milosevic posed to the international order and called on NATO to maintain its credibility by standing firm over Kosovo, which "would ensure that others do not make the same mistake in the future" (Blair, 22 April 1999). He encouraged to rethink the notion of sovereignty in international relations and called for consideration to be given to identifying "the circumstances in which we should get actively involved in other people's conflicts". Blair raised five questions that would need to be answered prior to any intervention taking place:

> *Are we sure of our case? Have all diplomatic options been exhausted? Can military operations be sensibly and prudently undertaken? Are we prepared for the long term? And are there national interests involved? (idem).*

Against this background, Blair left no doubt that a military intervention in Kosovo would be justified. In line with Chirac, Blair explained that the intervention was "a just war based not on any territorial ambitions but on values. We cannot let the evil of ethnic cleansing stand" (idem.). Therefore, the principle of non-interference "must be qualified in important aspects. Acts of genocide can never be a purely internal matter" mainly because the atrocities might trigger "massive flows of refugees which unsettle neighbouring countries" (idem.). According to Blair, they can be identified as "threats to international peace and security" which are simultaneously threats to national security. He concluded that this new doctrine of humanitarian intervention was "the best way of defending [British] interests and the moral way of promoting our values" (idem.)

The opposition generally supported the approach taken by the government. However, William Hague reminded that NATO's credibility was at risk also because "decisive action" had not already taken place earlier (Hague, 23 March 1999). Criticism of the intervention was based on the lack of UNSC authorisation. Members of Parliament claimed that "the British government and other NATO governments are defying the charter, to which they are committed, and breaking international law" (Tony Benn, House of Commons, 23 March 1999). Finally, concerns were raised that there was no regional demand for the military operation and that peaceful means might not have been exhausted completely (Alice Mahon, House of Commons, 23 March 1999).[57]

The European Union

During the General Affairs Council from 21 to 22 February 1999, held in Luxembourg, the EU urged "the parties to the conflict to come to a comprehensive agreement including on the security aspects in the time remaining" (Council, 21-22 February 1999). The Council moreover "confirmed its preparedness to take the necessary action against any party responsible for a breakdown of the peace efforts at Rambouillet" (idem). Emphasising the need of a political solution to the crisis, the Council affirmed further that it "remained prepared to play an essential role in the implementation of an agreement, including in the civil implementation structures, not least through efforts of economic reconstruction and community building" (idem). Although an immediate end to the crisis did not seem tangible in mid-

57 By April 1999, 68 per cent of the British public supported the intervention in Kosovo (The Economist, 1999).

February 1999, the EU signalled its "readiness ... to devote significant resources to helping all the people of Kosovo to rebuild their lives in security" (idem).

As the Kosovo crisis escalated in March 1999, heads of EU member states and government agreed that

> *on the threshold of the 21st century, Europe cannot tolerate a humanitarian catastrophe in its midst. It cannot be permitted that, in the middle of Europe, the predominant population of Kosovo is collectively deprived of its rights and subjected to grave human rights abuses.* (European Council, 24-25 March 1999)

The Berlin European Council stressed further that

> *the countries of the European Union, are under a moral obligation to ensure that indiscriminate behaviour and violence, which became tangible in the massacre at Raçak in January 1999, are not repeated* (idem).

While no explicit statement on the question of military intervention was made, the EU felt responsible for dealing with the refugee problem as well as for providing "peace and cooperation in the region" as "the way to guarantee our fundamental European values, i.e. respect for human rights and the rights of minorities, international law, democratic institutions and the inviolability of borders." Without specifying with what means peace and security would be achieved, the EU displayed itself mainly as civilian and normative power[58] in response to the Kosovo crisis. However, taking place in the EU's immediate neighbourhood the Kosovo crisis was a particular security concern. Within the EU, the security concerns were related strongly to the fear that violence and civil war could spill over into other former Yugoslavian republics and other Balkan countries leading to large numbers of refugees and destabilisation of the whole region. Yet, the EU's institutional response to the Kosovo crisis in 1999 remained mainly rhetoric.

58 For a discussion on the EU's role as a civilian or normative power, see chapter 4.

Legality and legitimacy of the humanitarian intervention

The UNSC did not pass a resolution authorising military force in Kosovo in March 1999 leading to considerable controversy about the legality and the legitimacy of the intervention. An attempt by Russia, Belarus and India at introducing a draft resolution condemning the NATO intervention failed by twelve votes to three, Russia, China and Namibia voting in favour.[59] The NATO-led military intervention in Kosovo was thus neither sanctioned nor condemned by the UNSC but still sparked an extensive discussion on the lawfulness of the NATO campaign. Some commentators found the NATO intervention lawful, while others disagreed, judging it an illegal intervention that is breaching international law. Still others assessed the intervention as unlawful but legitimate constituting an action that would eventually be held as lawful.

David Chandler (2006: 17) advanced the view that the NATO operation breached two central provisions of the UN Charter:

- Article 2(4) stating that "all members shall refrain ... from the threat or the use of force against the integrity or political independence of any state"; and
- Article 2(7) prohibiting intervention in matters falling essentially within the domestic jurisdiction of any state subject to UNSC action under Chapter VII (principle of non-interference).

Furthermore, Chandler argued that the right of self-defence was not applicable, as no NATO member was threatened by the instability within Kosovo and the UNSC did not invoke Chapter VII. The 78-day bombing campaign against Kosovo was therefore an assertion by NATO countries of a right to intervene and to wage war without UNSC authorisation on the humanitarian ground of human rights protection (Chandler, 2006).

The initial discussion of the legality of the NATO intervention by the IICK ended inconclusively with an appreciation of the difficulty of reconciling what was done to protect the people of Kosovo with the core prohibition on recourse to non-defensive force that has not been authorized by the UN. At the same time, the Commission

59 The draft resolution stated that "such unilateral use of force constitutes a flagrant violation of the United Nations Charter, in particular Articles 2(4), 24 and 53" (UNSC, 26 March 1999).

took the view that the pattern of Serb oppression in Kosovo, the experience of ethnic cleansing a few years earlier in Bosnia, and the lack of an international response to the genocide in Rwanda in 1994 combined, create a strong moral and political duty on the part of the international community to act effectively in response to the gross human rights violations (IICK, 2000). While diplomacy failed to put an end to the conflict, the international community was left with the options of doing nothing or mounting a military intervention under NATO command.

The perspective adopted by the IICK supports the general assessment of the NATO campaign as illegal, yet legitimate. Such a conclusion relates to the controversial idea that a 'right' of humanitarian intervention is not consistent with the UN Charter if conceived as a legal text, but that it may, depending on the context, nevertheless, reflect the spirit of the Charter as it relates to the overall protection of people against gross abuse (idem). At the same time, humanitarian intervention may also be legitimately authorized by the UNSC but will still often be challenged legally from the perspective of the Charter obligations to respect the sovereignty of the member states.

In the aftermath of the controversial military campaign a debate ensued over whether the event marked a turning point in the law on humanitarian intervention and a departure from the strict conditions established in the UN Charter for the permissible use of force in international relations. One view was that even though the intervention could be justified on compelling moral and political grounds, Kosovo should not be considered a precedent for eroding the norms of international law on the prohibition of force and the principles laid down in the Charter (Simma, 1999). Others argued that although the non-authorised NATO intervention constituted a breach of the UN Charter, such breach could be seen as evidence of the emergence of a new doctrine of humanitarian intervention. This new norm would legitimize the use of force to impede a state from committing mass atrocities when the UNSC is incapable of responding to the crisis because of the veto (Cassese, 1999: 23).

A third view was that, in principle, the breach of existing rules of international law could lead to a transformation of the law. However, on factual and legal grounds, the NATO intervention lacked the basic requirement of an *opinio iuris*[60] for the

60 In international law, an opinio juris (an opinion of law) is the judgment of whether a state acted in a particular because it was legally obliged or not (Bederman, 2001: 15-16)

emergence of a new norm of international law (Francioni 2000; 2005). Martha Finnemore and Kathryn Sikkink (1998), in turn, suggested that the development of new norms depends crucially upon particular states acting as norm entrepreneurs who attempt to convince other states to adopt the norm concerned. In this context, Nicholas Wheeler (2000: 147) argued that NATO members, notably the Blair government, were advancing a new norm of humanitarian intervention without explicit UNSC authorisation. But, in the Kosovo case, NATO governments refused to acknowledge that they were challenging existing norms of the UN charter and thus never acted as full-blown norm entrepreneurs (idem). Finally the use of cluster bombs and the reliance by NATO on a high-altitude rule of engagement for its bombing sorties so as to minimize the risk of casualties to itself have been criticised and put the legitimacy of the NATO intervention into further question (Welsh, 2012).

Since the 1999 Kosovo intervention, members of the international community have begun advocating a right to undertake intervention to stop mass atrocities from occurring. In line with the debate surrounding the Kosovo intervention, their central concerns rested with whether the current regulations on the use of force in the UN Charter met the challenges of the post-Cold War world. In particular, they were concerned with the demands of addressing the rising numbers of humanitarian emergencies (Badescu, 2011). The post-Kosovo demand for a new norm on the protection of people from mass atrocities eventually resulted in the creation of the RtoP.

2.2 RtoP – a new international norm? Post-Kosovo: the development of the RtoP

Hitting the peak of the humanitarian intervention disasters throughout the 1990s, a revived debate ensued after the 1999 Kosovo crisis and intervention on how to ensure the protection of civilians from mass atrocities. Reacting to member state calls on a reform of existing principles on humanitarian intervention, former UN Secretary General (UNSG) Kofi Annan challenged the traditional view of state sovereignty and the non-intervention principle claiming that the principle of sovereignty contained in the UN Charter should be reinterpreted as responsibility to protect individuals[61]. In his *Millenium Report* to the UN General Assembly in 2000, Annan argued

> *If humanitarian is indeed an unacceptable assault on sovereignty, how should we respond to a Rwanda, to a Srebrenica, to gross and systematic violations of human rights that offend every precept of our common humanity?*

In 2001, the International Commission on Intervention and State Sovereignty (ICISS)[62] launched the debate about the responsibility to protect doctrine. In the correspondent report from December, the Commission captured that, based on the concept of state sovereignty and the principle of non-intervention, states have primarily the responsibility to protect their own citizens. But when states cannot or would not (anymore) protect their citizens in the face of serious crises, the responsibility shifts towards the international community. The responsibility of the international community therefore includes three elements: "To prevent, to react in the event that prevention failed and to rebuild societies where protection has failed" (MacFarlane and Khong, 2006: 178). In the report, RtoP was conceived as an attempt to reconcile the ambiguity surrounding cases of proposed military intervention as in the case of Kosovo by establishing thresholds based on traditional 'just war' principles.

61 The notion of sovereignty as responsibility, which can be seen as the precursor of the development of the RtoP, was originally coined by Francis Deng in 1996. According to Deng, sovereignty does not constitute an absolute right but should rather be seen as a conditional right. He argued further that when states do not conduct their internal affairs according to internationally recognized standards other states do not only have the right, but also the duty to intervene. He added that those governments that fail to protect their people shed their sovereignty. As a result, sovereignty was redefined as the responsibility to protect the people in a given country (Deng et al., 1996).

62 Members of ICISS: Gareth Evans (Australia), Mohamed Sahnoun (Algeria), Gisèle Côté-Harper (Canada), Lee Hamilton (United States), Michael Ignatieff (Canada), Vladimir Lukin (Russia), Klaus Naumann (Germany), Cyril Ramaphosa (South Africa), Fidel V. Ramos (Philippines), Cornelio Sommaruga (Switzerland,) Eduardo Stein Barillas (Guatemala), Ramesh Thakur (India).

Intervention was recommended when passing the threshold of a **'just cause'**, namely in the case of large-scale loss of life and / or large scale 'ethnic cleansing', "actual or apprehended" (ICISS, 2001: XII), caused by the state or facilitated by neglect or incapacity. In addition to this threshold, the Commission defined 'precautionary principles'. Hence, an intervention should be based on the **'right intention'**, meaning that the primary purpose of the intervention is the protection of human beings. The option of an intervention should be the **'last resort'** since other non-military options have to be exhausted beforehand. The means of the intervention should be **'proportional'** in scale, duration and intensity being the minimum necessary to secure human protection. And the intervention should have **'reasonable prospects'** referring to the existence of a reasonable chance of success. A particular thorny point was the question of 'right authority' and the legitimacy of interventions not authorised by the UNSC, on which the ICISS was unable to reach a clear agreement and thereby established a three-layered distribution of responsibility. If the state (primary level) and the domestic authorities in partnership, with outside agencies (secondary level) failed to avoid a humanitarian crisis and the responsibility consequently shifts to the international community (third level), the report holds the view that the primary legal authority lays with the UNSC.

The Report also established a mechanism to avoid a gridlock in the Security Council, by proposing a "code of conduct" for the use of veto concerning actions on the basis of the RtoP in the sense of a "constructive abstention" (ICISS, 2001: XIII). In cases where vital national interests were not claimed to be involved", a permanent member of the UNSC would not use its veto right to hinder the agreement on a resolution (idem.). Finally, the report emphasised the 'responsibility to rebuild' and that interveners should have a strategic plan about how they intend to 'rebuild' post-conflict societies.

In September 2003, the High Level Panel on *Threats, Challenges and Change* commissioned by Kofi Annan endorsed the emerging norm, including its criteria and precautionary principles, but abandoned the idea of including a "constructive abstention". The panel produced their report, *A More Secure World: Our Shared Responsibility*, in 2004, and it was the basis for preparing a UN reform package leading up to the 2005 World Summit. Over 170 heads of government participated in the discussion from 14-16 September 2005, leading to the World Summit Outcome Document, which was formally adopted by the General Assembly in Resolution 60 / 1 (2005). In paragraphs 138 and 139 of the Outcome Document, the UN member states agreed to the three major components of RtoP: (1) formal recognition of the responsibility of sovereigns to protect their own populations; (2) a commitment to develop the institutional capacities and behaviours necessary to prevent genocide and mass atrocities, assist states in the fulfilment of their responsibility, and improve the effectiveness of peaceful and consensual measure; (3) a reaffirmation of the idea that the Security Council has the authority to intervene if deemed adequate:

> *138. Each individual State has the responsibility to protect its populations from genocide, war crimes, ethnic cleansing and crimes against humanity. This responsibility entails the prevention of such crimes, including their incitement, through appropriate and necessary means. We accept that responsibility and will act in accordance with it. The international community should, as appropriate, encourage and help States to exercise this responsibility and support the United Nations in establishing an early warning capability.*
>
> *139. The international community, through the United Nations, also has the responsibility to use appropriate diplomatic, humanitarian and other peaceful means, in accordance with Chapters VI and VIII of the Charter, to help protect populations from genocide, war crimes, ethnic cleansing and crimes against humanity. In this context, we are prepared to take collective action, in a timely and decisive manner, through the Security Council, in accordance with the Charter, including Chapter VII, on a case-by-case basis and in cooperation with relevant regional organizations as appropriate, should peaceful means be inadequate and national authorities manifestly fail to protect their populations from genocide, war crimes, ethnic cleansing and crimes against humanity. We stress the need for the General Assembly to continue consideration of the responsibility to protect populations from genocide, war crimes, ethnic cleansing and crimes against humanity and its implications, bearing in mind the principles of the Charter and international law. We also intend to commit ourselves, as necessary and appropriate, to helping States build capacity to protect their populations from genocide, war crimes, ethnic cleansing and crimes against humanity and to assisting those which are under stress before crises and conflicts break out.*

The next important step in the RtoP's development was its inclusion in UNSC Resolution 1674 in April 2006. In operative paragraph 4 of that Resolution, on the protection of civilians in armed conflicts, the SC "reaffirms the provisions of paragraphs 138 and 139 of the 2005 World Summit Outcome Document regarding the Responsibility to Protect populations from genocide, war crimes, ethnic cleansing, and crimes against humanity." In 2009, the UN Secretary-General Ban Ki-moon released a report on "Implementing the responsibility to protect" proposing a comprehensive strategy for the implementation of what he then called the RtoP's three pillars:

- **Pillar one** refers to the responsibility of the state to protect its population from genocide, war crimes, ethnic cleansing and crimes against humanity and from their encouragement.
- **Pillar two** consists of the international community's responsibility to assist the state to fulfil its responsibility to protect, particularly by helping them to tackle the causes of genocide and mass atrocities, build the capacity to prevent these crimes, and address problems before they escalate.
- **Pillar three** states that in situations where a state has manifestly failed to protect its population from the four crimes, it is the international community's responsibility to take timely and decisive action through peaceful diplomatic and humanitarian means and, if that proves inadequate, other more forceful means in a manner consistent with Chapters VI, VII and VIII of the UN Charter.

The report was well received, as the ensuing debate in the General Assembly attests where a vast majority of the member states reaffirmed their commitment to the prevention and halting of mass atrocities. Over 50 states endorsed the proposed three-pillar strategy and there was unanimity on the importance of the first two pillars and the fundamental obligation to prevent mass atrocity crimes. The member states also agreed on restricting the scope of the RtoP to the four crimes of genocide, war crimes, ethnic cleansing and crimes against humanity. There was less agreement on the third pillar. Particularly non-Western governments argued that emphasis should be put on peaceful measures, under Chapter VI and VIII of the UN Charter, instead of coercive measures under Chapter VII (Bellamy, 2011b: 44).

The following debates in the GA in 2010 and 2011 concentrated on the aspects of early warning and the role of regional organizations in implementing RtoP. The importance of prevention in pillar two was stated in both occasions. During the latest debate a number of countries raised concerns and reservations about the manner in which NATO has used force to implement Resolution 1973 in Libya. These concerns point to the necessity of putting in place a more effective framework to protect populations in the midst of an armed conflict. Moreover it was stressed that pillar three, referring to timely and decisive action in the face of the four respective crimes, included peaceful, economic, diplomatic and humanitarian means. The use of force should be seen as a last resort (ICRtoP, 2011).

Criticism of the RtoP

Since the very beginning, the RtoP has been subject to criticism. Many, especially non-Western countries, see the RtoP as a dangerous and imperialist doctrine that undermines the sovereignty and political autonomy of the weaker states (Evans, 2007). They believe that the RtoP poses a threat to state sovereignty by misusing the concept of human rights protection, establishing a new form of colonialism (idem). RtoP is accused to be used by the powerful states (meaning those who have the means to intervene) as a "Trojan Horse" for hard interests in other weaker states. This is also related to the exclusive authority of the UNSC to mandate the use of force. Conversely to its proclaimed purpose, the new norm has been criticised for offering little actual protection to vulnerable population, reducing it to a rhetorical posturing (Bellamy, 2010).

The 2009 implementation proposal gave rise to more concerns. Ramesh Thakur, former member of the ICISS, criticised Annan's report with regard to three aspects (Thakur, 2009). First, Thakur argued that it was unrealistic to see the three pillars being of equal strength and weight and that the most important pillar should be the states' own responsibility. On the other hand, the most critical one was the international community's response to the outbreak of mass atrocities. On this note, Thomas Weiss (2001: 424) pointed out that the term 'international community' was rather vague. Therefore it remained unclear to whom exactly the responsibility to protect shifts and more specifically, who has the right to intervene. Second, Thakur contended – in line with Jennifer Welsh (2010: 55) – that since the Secretary

General favoured prevention over protection, states are likely to (already) shy away from preventive measures that interfere in their domestic affairs. And third, the report failed to clarify a number of key questions related to the implementation of the RtoP such as: When should RtoP be activated as an international responsibility? What are 'RtoP triggers'? Which principles guide the use of force? (Thakur, 2009)

In light of the development of the RtoP and its criticism, the question arises to what extent the RtoP can actually be seen as an international norm. In order to be able to assess the influence on the RtoP on actual policy-making it has to be defined further it terms of its status of a norm and its implications. The following section will therefore concentrate on the legal status and the determinacy of the RtoP as an emerging international norm.

RtoP as a norm

None of the documents in which the RtoP has been treated in depth can be seen as binding sources of international law, as defined in Article 38 of the Statute of the International Court of Justice (ICJ).[63] The extent to which the RtoP can be seen as a legal norm has consequently to be analysed on a more refined basis. Jennifer Welsh and Maria Banda (2010) scrutinized whether the inclusion of the RtoP in the 2005 World Summit Outcome Document represents a moment of legislation differentiating in negative and positive duties. As to the first category, Welsh and Banda (2010) suggested that a great deal of legalization has already occurred. Carsten Stahn (2007: 101), on the other hand, argued that the Outcome Document "leaves considerable doubt whether and to what extent states intended to create a legal norm". Stahn saw the inclusion of the RtoP in paragraphs 138 and 139 rather as a "curious mixture of political and legal considerations" that points towards a common lack of clarity about the meaning of the concept (idem: 108).

According to Alex Bellamy (2010), there is some evidence in the area of international law that a positive duty towards the RtoP exists. First, the International Court of Justice in *Bosnia vs. Serbia* found that states have a legal obligation to take all measures reasonably available to them to prevent genocide (ICJ, 2007). Second, the

63 Refers to "international conventions", "international custom, as evidence of a general practice accepted as law", and "general principles of law".

Common Article 1 of the Geneva Conventions (1949) requires that states "ensure respect" to international humanitarian law as well as obey it themselves. Third, the International Law Commission (ILC) proposed Draft Articles on the Responsibility of States for Internationally Wrongful Acts (ILC, 2001). Fourth, following an independent enquiry, the UNSG recognised the organisation's failure to prevent genocide in Rwanda as a failure of the whole system. And fifth, the UNSC included its first explicit reference to RtoP in Resolution 1674 on the protection of civilians in armed conflicts. The key significance of the latter stems from Article 25 of the UN Charter, which states that "the Members of the United Nations agree to accept and carry out the decision of the Security Council in accordance with the present Charter." Although Resolution 1674 falls short of a formal decision requiring that member states implement the RtoP, Bellamy (2010) argues that it can be seen as part of an ongoing process of legalisation.[64]

A consensus of the General Assembly – as it has been reached during the 2009 debate on Annan's implementation report – can be seen as a proxy for existence of an international *opinio iuris*. Accompanied by a consistent state practice, the GA's statements may reveal the existence or the emergence of new rules of customary international law. The analysis of the RtoP as a legal norm therefore has to look at its practical implementation. A consistent implementation of the RtoP, however, depends first of all on its determinacy. The more precisely a norm indicates the behaviour it expects in a given situation, the more likely it will be applied consistently (Finnemore and Sikkink, 1998).

The definition of the RtoP used throughout this study is the one stated in the Outcome Document, defining the three pillars of the RtoP. Containing several layers, RtoP cannot be seen as a single norm, but rather as a collection of shared expectation and values. While the first pillar can be seen as a reaffirmation of existing norms, it is much less clear what rights and duties pillars two and three place on the international community's responsibility of prevention and assistance. The indeterminacy of pillars two and three can be seen as the result of the member states' disagreement of what ought to be expected and an interest in preserving flexibility for the future (Bellamy, 2010).

64 For a detailed discussion on the legal status of UNSC Resolutions see (Kelsen, 1954).

Reviewing cases of RtoP implementation and non-implementation between 2005 and 2010, chapter 3 will show that a consistent state practice has not (yet) emerged. In fact, analysing the RtoP in practice reveals states' differing expectations and understanding of the rights and duties derived from the RtoP. RtoP is thus still widely seen as an emerging international norm with limited legal implications. Although not obtaining the legal label the RtoP can still have an influence on actual policies in response to mass atrocities, as this study aims to show.

One of the main concerns raised after the experience of the Kosovo intervention in 1999 was whether the current regulations on the use of force in the UN Charter still met the challenges of the post-Cold War world (Toope and Brunnée, 2010). As elaborated previously, the questions of military intervention presented a particularly thorny issue in the development of the RtoP. It has furthermore been suggested that the recent application of the RtoP in Libya and its consideration in Syria reveal that the emerging norm has become increasingly linked to the issue of military intervention. The role of the use of force within the RtoP will therefore be discussed separately throughout the next section.

RtoP and the use of force

The definition of the RtoP in the 2005 Outcome Document did not introduce any new right or 'responsibility' of military intervention for individual states. Rather, it keeps recourse to force firmly in the hands of the UNSC (Toope and Brunnée, 2010). The Document leaves open, however, whether collective action "in accordance with the Charter, including Chapter VII" presumes that a situation involving the listed four crimes must first be found to constitute a threat to international peace and security, whether all such situations would constitute threats to peace and security *per se*, or whether the UNSC can intervene whenever a state is "manifestly failing" to protect (idem.; quotes from paragraph 139 of the Outcome Document, 2005). It also remains unclear to what extent the UNSC has an obligation to intervene if necessary to protect populations form the listed crimes. The Document's reference to "case-by-case" decisions on the use of force would seem to suggest there is no such obligation.

In light of the weaknesses in the RtoP as articulated in the 2005 Outcome Document, the 2009 General Assembly debate raised concerns by many members, particularly about the use of force element in the emerging norm. The strong emphasis in the Secretary General's Implementation Report on the need for guidelines on the use of force underscores these concerns. The call for non-use of the veto in cases involving one of the four RtoP crimes can also be related to the use of force considerations. The veto power of the five permanent members of the UNSC undermines the generality of the protective force option and weakens the potential for consistent decision-making in the Council (Peters, 2012: 201). Although recognising RtoP's indeterminacy regarding the use of force in its different aspects, none of the above addressed concerns have resulted in a substantial change or amendment of the RtoP.

At the same time, Bellamy (2008) argued that the RtoP can make three contributions to the issue of military intervention. First, the RtoP aims at replacing the old norm of humanitarian intervention with a broad range of measures directed most importantly at preventing mass atrocities. Only if those measures fail, the use of military force will be considered. Second, by including political and diplomatic strategies, alongside legal, economic and military instruments, the RtoP advocates a comprehensive crisis response that can counter the temptation to envisage complex humanitarian emergencies in exclusively military terms. Third, by drawing attention to the protection of civilians from mass atrocities, RtoP can provide a new framework for the implementation of policies – "if translated 'from words into deeds'" (Bellamy, 2008: 630). Whether these contributions, that the RtoP can make, have an influence on the practice will be investigated throughout the next chapters of this thesis.

The previous sections have elaborated on the emergence of the RtoP as a new international norm in response to the experiences of the Kosovo intervention and claims about a reform of the existing normative framework for humanitarian interventions. The Kosovo war was, however, also a significant driver for the creation of the EU's Common Security and Defence Policy and the EU's role as a security actor in its neighbourhood. These developments will be examined in the following sections.

2.3 The EU as evolving security actor

The role of Kosovo and the RtoP

Lessons learned from the EU's failure in the Balkans, among them the need to establish autonomous military power, amplified in the wake of the Kosovo crisis. The EU's recurring inability to act served as a wake-up call for the EU to meet the expectations and responsibilities set out in the Common Foreign and Security Policy (CFSP), not only on a rhetorical level but also in practice. Since the Maastricht Treaty (1993), one of the main objectives of the EU was

> *to assert its identity on the international scene, in particular through the implementation of a common foreign and security policy including the eventual framing of a common defence policy which might in time lead to a common defence.* (Article B, TEU Maastricht)

As the Kosovo crisis escalated through 1998, British and French concerns over the EU's continued lack of hard power, primarily military capabilities, intensified to such an extent that in December they launched the key initiative that would transform the EU's international role (Shepherd, 2009: 517). At the Franco-British summit in St Malo, Chirac and Blair declared that the EU "must have the capacity for autonomous action, backed by credible military forces, the means to decide to use them, and the readiness to do so, in order to respond to international crisis" (Franco-British Summit, 1998). The Kosovo experience contributed to the ethos of the subsequent construction of a joint European security and defence policy. Some of lessons learned from the Kosovo crisis are reflected in the early institutional and instrumental set-up of the CSDP. Yet, the establishment of the CSDP was also influenced by NATO's transformation and move towards a more global role as well as internal EU dynamics between the member states. Furthermore, the following sections will show that the development of European security and defence capabilities was also informed by the parallel advance of the RtoP.

The development of the CSDP

At the Cologne summit in June 1999, the 15 EU member states officially launched the 'common European policy on security and defence' linking its core purpose to the Petersberg tasks. Agreed upon in 1992 by the Western European Union Council of Ministers, the Petersburg tasks defined the type of military action that the EU could undertake in the area of conflict management: humanitarian and rescue tasks, peacekeeping tasks and tasks of combat forces in crisis management, including peace-making. The CSDP was supposed to permit the EU the ability "to take decisions on the full range of conflict prevention and crisis management tasks" through the development of "a capacity for autonomous action, backed up by credible military forces" (European Council, 4 June 1999). This capacity would not be detrimental to NATO, it would be in accordance with the principles of the UN Charter and would entail the EU playing "its full role on the international stage".

The following December Council established the Helsinki Headline Goal (HHG) which envisaged an army corps of 50,000–60,000 troops, 100 ships and 400 aircraft deployable at 60 days' notice and sustainable for a year. This ambition was explicitly modelled on NATO's crisis management operations in the Balkans (Shepherd, 2009: 517). The aim was that, by 2004, the EU would be able to manage two conflicts simultaneously: one 'hard' mission of separating belligerent forces, and one 'light' mission such as a humanitarian operation.

Since the Franco-British summit at Le Touquet in February 2003 the focus has turned to a somewhat neglected component of the HHG, the aim "to provide smaller rapid response elements available and deployable at very high readiness" (European Council, 11 December 1999). The UK and France called for European improvements in "planning and deploying forces at short notice, including initial deployment of land, sea and air forces within 5–10 days" (Franco-British summit, 4 February 2003). In February 2004, the UK, France and Germany, translated this into the 'battlegroup' concept, a key element of the EU's 2010 Headline Goal.[65] As national or multinational configurations, the battlegroups were designed as a "mini-

65 The battlegroups are on paper battalion-sized units 1,500 strong, deployable within 5–10 days and sustainable for 30 days with the possibility of extending that to 120 days; in any six month period there are two battlegroups on standby at very high readiness for almost simultaneous deployment to undertake the full range of Petersberg tasks.

mum militarily effective, credible, rapidly deployable, coherent force package capable of stand alone operations, or for the initial phase of larger operations" (European Council, 2 November 2006). Alistair Shepherd (2008: 518) argued that the illustrative scenarios for the battlegroups matched the Kosovo requirements and the EU's subsequent efforts to rectify the shortcomings exposed during that crisis: separation of parties by force, conflict prevention, stabilization, reconstruction and military advice to third countries, evacuation operations in non-permissive environments and assistance to humanitarian operations (EU Council Secretariat, November 2006).

Another lesson from the Balkans and Kosovo specifically was the necessity of non-military crisis management.[66] The European Council emphasised the need for "the enhancement and better coordination of ... non-military crisis response tools", arguing that "developments inter alia in Kosovo have for their part underlined the importance of this task" (European Council, 11 December 1999). The 2000 Feira European Council outlined four priority areas for civilian management capabilities: police, rule of law, civilian administration and civil protection; and a set of 5000 police officers, 1000 deployable in 20 days by 2003. The EU's Helsinki statement on 'non-military crisis management' stressed the need to strengthen the synergy and responsiveness of national, collective and NGO resources, to enhance EU links with other organisations, and to promote EU autonomous action and inter-pillar coherence. The June 2004 European Council set out the Civilian Headline Goal (CHG). The quantitative component was met at the November 2004 commitment conference, where 5761 police, 631 rule of law experts, 562 administration experts and 4988 civil protection personnel were pledged.

The 2008 CHG also highlighted the growing civil-military focus of the ESDP, emphasising first a need to be able to "deploy civilian means simultaneously with military means at the outset of an operation" and second that "close cooperation and coordination with ... military efforts have to be ensured throughout all phases of [operation]. When necessary, civilian crisis management mission must be able to draw on military enabling capabilities." (Council of the EU, 17 December 2004) Furthermore, the 2003 European Security Strategy (ESS) stated that

66 The importance of civilian instruments in responding to the changing security environment after the end of Cold War was also emphasised by NATO in its strategic concepts of 1991 and 1999 (see Koenig, 2010: 7).

> *none of the new threats is purely military; nor can any be tackled by purely military means ... in failed states, military instruments may be needed to restore order ... Regional conflicts need political solutions but military assets and effective policing may be needed in the post conflict phases ... the European Union is particularly well equipped to respond to such multifaceted situations.* (ESS, 2003)

Yet, the specific nature of defence policy and military operations also led to the creation of a separate infrastructure designed to enable the EU to benefit from, in the words of the Saint Malo Declaration, "the appropriate structures and a capacity for situation analysis, sources of intelligence and capability for relevant strategic planning" (Grevi, 2007). Initial steps towards the construction of this infrastructure were taken with the creation of the Political and Security Committee, the EU Military Staff and the EU Military Committee (Howorth, 2007). This was subsequently expanded to the civilian dimension with the creation of the Committee for Civilian Aspects of Crisis Management (CIVCOM) during the Feira European Council in 2000 (Cross, 2010). The CIVCOM was supplemented in 2006 with the establishment of a Civil-Military Cell within the EUMS and, a year later, by the creation of a Civilian Planning and Conduct Capability (CPCC) located in the Council Secretariat. The concept of Civil-Military Coordination (CMCO) was reinforced by the establishment of the European External Action Service (EEAS) in the Lisbon Treaty in 2009, with the aim to enhance coordination between civilian and military actors at all stages of crisis management, particularly at the strategic planning phase.[67]

As an integral part of the CFSP, the institutional system of the CSDP overlaps to some extent with that of the CFSP. Member state sensitivity about the need to preserve autonomy when it comes to defence-related decisions has led to the emergence of a complex decision-making process that requires consensus between the member states. From the outset, the CSDP has been subject to inter-governmental decision-making, characterised by complex interactions between the Council Secretariat (headed by the Secretary General / High Representative for CFSP), the Brussels-based PSC and decision-makers in the national capitals (Grevi, 2009). In many respects, the recent Treaty revision confirmed existing practices on CFSP / CSDP and affirmed the standing of

67 The concept of CMCO can be seen as the key component of what is mostly called a European comprehensive approach to crisis management. As a new structure within the EEAS, the CMCO has been incorporated by the Crisis Management Planning Directorate (CMPD).

existing institutions (see Articles 38 on the PSC and 42 on the European Defence Agency). Apart from the EEAS, its major institutional innovation is that of the position of the High Representative of the Union for Foreign Affairs and Security Policy. Sceptics argue that the real problem of the CSDP lay not with the Treaty provisions or the institutions but with Europe's weak and underfunded militaries. Military spending in most EU states declined sharply after the Cold War, leaving the US to extent its lead in the application of new technologies and hardware (Howorth, 2000: 38).

Since its first mission in the Balkans in 2003, the EU's operations have varied widely in terms of its size, ranging from the modest (ten EU experts in rule-of-law missions in Georgia and 30 in Iraq) to Operation Althea in Bosnia Herzegovina, which involved up to 7,000 soldiers. The EU has launched military missions both autonomously (Artemis in DRC, EUFOR Chad) and with the support of NATO under the so-called 'Berlin Plus' arrangements, governing operational collaboration between the two institutions (Concordia in FYROM, Althea). Missions have also varied widely in nature, ranging from the military to police missions in the Balkans, DRC, Palestine and Afghanistan to rule-of-law missions (Georgia, Iraq), monitoring missions (Aceh, Georgia), security sector reform missions (DRC, Guinea Bissau) and border missions (Georgia, Palestine, Ukraine-Moldova).

Although the emphasis was on the military dimension when creating the CSDP, the first operation was a civilian one and since 2003 military missions have made up only a minority of deployments. While many CSDP missions, in fact, exhibit both military and civilian characteristics, what is significant is the increasing emphasis on the latter. In most cases, missions have occurred in places where a robust NATO presence (as in Kosovo, Bosnia and Macedonia) or a UN role (as in Congo and Kosovo) already paved the way for deployment. From the outset of the creation of common European security and defence policies in the aftermath of Kosovo, the expectations were stirred to develop the EU into a fully-fledged security actor including sufficient military capabilities. In practice, however, the EU's civilian crisis management record outweighs its military engagement by far. When looking at the development of the CSDP since 1999 until 2009, the 'capability-expectations gap' (Smith, 1993) seems to be a persistent feature of the EU's foreign policy. To what extent there is also a gap between the EU's understanding of its responsibility and its available crisis management resources and structures will be addressed in the following section.

The EU's responsibility (to protect)

The EU's understanding of its security role is inherently linked to its sense of responsibility. Panos Koutrakos (2013) has defined the EU's sense of responsibility as "a soft, almost moral, understanding of responsibility and it emerges from, and is deeply embedded in the EU's experience in legal and policy integration" (p. 89). The Laeken Declaration (2001), which kick-started the process of constitutional reform and led, ultimately, to the adoption of the Lisbon Treaty, states: "Now that the Cold War is over and we are living in a globalised, yet also highly fragmented world, Europe need to shoulder its responsibilities in the governance of globalisation."

The European Security Strategy points out further, that "Europe should be ready to share its responsibility for global security and in building a better world". And, once it has set out the security challenges facing the EU and the added value of its contribution, it states that a "European Union which takes greater responsibility and which is more active will be one which carries greater political weight". Five years later this sentence opens the 2008 Implementation Report: "[f]ive years on from [sic] adoption of the European Security Strategy, the European Union carries greater responsibilities than at any time in its history."

The EU's understanding of its international responsibility has been informed further by the RtoP as an emerging international norm. The EU started to engage with the RtoP shortly after it had been designed by the ICISS in 2001. However, in official EU documents the RtoP began to appear only after its inclusion in the 2005 Outcome Document. In a statement by the EU Presidency in April 2005, it acknowledged that if a state is unable or unwilling to protect its own citizens in a situation of genocide, war crimes, crimes against humanity or gross human rights violations, the international community has the responsibility to help protect these citizens. The EU emphasised that only if diplomatic and humanitarian measures do not show any immediate effect, it lies within the authority of the UN Security to permit enforcement measures as a last resort. At the same time, it stressed the importance of the prevention component of the RtoP (Dembinski and Reinold, 2011).

A further reference to the RtoP appears in the Consensus on Development from November 2005:

> *The EU also strongly supports the responsibility to protect. We cannot stand by, as genocide, war crimes, ethnic cleansing or other gross violations of international humanitarian law and human rights are committed. The EU will support a strengthened role for the regional and sub-regional organisations in the process of enhancing international peace and security, including their capacity to coordinate donor support in the area of conflict prevention.*

The 2008 Report on the Implementation of the ESS made the EU's support for the emerging norm even more explicit by stating that

> *Sovereign governments must take responsibility for the consequences of their actions and hold a shared responsibility to protect populations from genocide, war crimes, ethnic cleansing and crimes against humanity.* (p. 3)

At the same time the Report emphasises that the EU "must be clear that respect for sovereignty, independence and territorial integrity of states and the peaceful settlement of disputes are not negotiable" (p 2).

The picture that emerges from these rare statements shows, as Matthias Dembinski and Theresa Reinold (2011: 13) have argued, that the EU has developed a particular understanding of the RtoP norm that emphasises the responsibility to prevent and evidently conveys the understanding that force should be used in rare and clearly defined circumstances only. Furthermore, EU documents clearly indicate that local actors bear the prime responsibility to protect. If states prove then unable or unwilling to protect their population, their responsibility would pass over either to the UN or to the geographically responsible regional security organisation. Outside of Europe, the EU sees itself primarily in an auxiliary role. It will empower local actors or, if absolutely necessary, step in temporarily to fill the gap before local actors or the UN do (Gänzle and Grimm, 2010; Brosig, 2011).

While scholars have long been criticising the EU's 'capability-expectations gap' (Smith, 1993), the EU's understanding of its responsibility (to protect) seems to fit its capabilities much better. As predominantly civilian or normative actor, the EU's sees its responsibility mainly in the area of non-coercive crisis management. However, since the member states remain the key actors within the CSDP, their understanding of the responsibility (to protect) and of the EU's role matters at least as much as the EU's definition of responsibility (see chapter 3).

The EU and the use of force

Since the end of the Cold War, European governments have become more willing to deploy military capabilities for voluntary operations in the name of multilateral frameworks (Deighton, 2011: 315). EU governments claim that actions that involve the use of force "for voluntary operations are an essential and legitimate way of upholding international norms of behaviour for peaceful, just and well-functioning international systems" (idem). In developing its Common Security and Defence policy the EU has shifted its ground from civilian politics to becoming an actor with tools that extend to the military spectrum (idem: 317).

At first, the use of force seems to openly contradict the EU's aspiration to act as normative power and a force for good in its external action. Yet, intervention in support of shared norms could be regarded as a necessary requirement for the EU's role as a security actor. The ESS does not make any explicit reference to the use of force but rather refers to "military activities" and "robust intervention". The document confirms that the role of the EU as security actor will increase the greater the responsibilities it takes. At the same time, it emphasises the need of civilian instruments in the area of crisis management and post-crisis reconstruction: "In almost every major intervention, military efficiency has been followed by civilian chaos. We need greater capacity to bring all necessary civilian resources to bear in crisis and post-crisis situations" (ESS, 2003: 12). The 2008 Implementation Report reminds further that the "threat or use of military force cannot be allowed to solve territorial issues – anywhere" (p. 2).

The type of intervention the EU is ready to perform or at least to consider as acceptable is characterised by three constraints. First, military force is regarded as 'last resort'. Therefore, EU interventions have more frequently taken the form of economic and political reconstruction and peacekeeping through presence on the ground.

Second, the area of intervention is limited to the EU's neighbourhood as evidenced by both actual performance and the European Security Strategy. Third, intervention should only take place in a legal framework or more specifically if authorised by the UN Security Council. Taken these elements together convey the image of a reluctant security actor that is further restraint by limited European military capabilities and dependant on the peculiar institutional structure of EU foreign policy, dominated by intergovernmental decision-making.

Jan Techau wrote in 2013, that "Europeans are not per se unwilling to use force to achieve political goals. They only seem to be unwilling to do so in the framework of the EU." Reasons for member states' reluctance towards joint military operations are seen in the absence of a common threat, in the different strategic cultures, the lack of military capabilities but also of trust and ambition as well as the economic pressures related to the Euro crisis since 2009 (Techau, 2013). However, the EU's stated intention to increase its military capabilities since the 1990s sends the signal that military force is still seen as a useful foreign policy tool and that it might be used to further the EU's interests (Smith, 2000: 28).

2.4 From humanitarian intervention to the responsibility to protect – what to expect?

The analysis of the French, German and British discourse on the Kosovo intervention has shown that there was agreement on the policy of military intervention within Europe. Even Germany who is traditionally averse to the use of force (see chapter 3) was in favour of the Kosovo intervention. France and Britain justified their participation in the bombing campaign over Kosovo on the basis of national security interests. France, particularly, warned of the refugee's flows that would reach Europe if the crisis could not be contained. At the same time, French President Chirac emphasised that the decision to intervene in Kosovo was grounded in moral reasons and not in economic or strategic interests. Germany on the other hand justified its participation in the military intervention by referring to its historic responsibility.

Tony Blair's presentation of the humanitarian intervention norm shows both the difference and similarities with the emerging norm of the RtoP. The first four out of these five criteria are reflected in the development of the RtoP, in the aftermath of the Kosovo intervention. The biggest difference becomes apparent in the fifth criteria. While humanitarian intervention seems to be contingent upon national interests and state security, the RtoP is designed to address the people's needs and is based on human security.

The EU's role in the Kosovo crisis has been heavily criticised for lacking bolder action and an integrated strategy (Greek Prime Minister Costas Simitis cited in Peterson, 2003: 89). Others argued that the EU acknowledged its responsibilities as foreign policy actor during and after the Kosovo crisis (idem). Then Belgian Prime Minister Guy Verhofstadt claimed that "one of the most serious dents to the EU's legitimacy in the eyes of its own citizens had derived from the EU having 'to wait for the Americans' to intervene in Kosovo" (quoted in Youngs, 2004: 418).

The developments outlined in this chapter demonstrated that arguably reaching the climax of the humanitarian intervention dilemmas of the 1990s, the Kosovo crisis constitutes not least timely a juncture in the EU's history. The violent dissolution of former Yugoslavia contributed to the transformation of the EU's international role and its foreign policy ethos. Almost half a decade later, the EU has taken many steps in improving its security capabilities, particularly in conflict management. It now has a CSDP, political and military decision-making structures, battlegroups, military and civilian force catalogues, a security strategy, strategic headquarters, an operational planning cell, access to a gendarmerie force and a European Defence Agency. It has also undertaken a number of civil, military and civil-military crisis management operations.

Furthermore, the development of the RtoP in the aftermath of the Kosovo crisis aimed at shifting the focus of intervention from national interests to human security as well as from military action to the prevention of mass atrocities. With the goal of protecting civilians, the emerging norm introduced a range of non-coercive instruments that should be exhausted before the use of military force is considered. However, due to the RtoP's indeterminacy it remains unclear to what extent there is a collective understanding of what the emerging norm means and entails. Divergent interpretations might be reflected in an inconsistent application of the RtoP in practice.

The question that arises from this chapter is whether the development of the CSDP and the RtoP actually make a difference in whether and how Europe responds to mass atrocities in its neighbourhood since the Kosovo crisis in 1999. While this chapter traced the emergence of the RtoP and creation of the CSDP from a historical perspective, the following chapter places the emphasis on the CSDP and RtoP in practice. Chapter 3 will therefore review four cases of RtoP implementation and non-implementation in the period from 2005 until 2011, while scrutinizing the European interpretation of the emerging norm and the role of the EU as security actor.

Chapter 3: RtoP and CSDP in practice – implementing a collective understanding?

Having looked at the historical development of the RtoP and institutional evolution of the CSDP in the previous chapter, the focus of the following sections will be on the RtoP and the CSDP in practice. By picking up the historical narrative from the previous chapter, the main aim of this chapter is two-fold. First, the chapter seeks to reveal the extent to which there is a collective European understanding of what the RtoP means and entails. Second, it scrutinises the extent to which the RtoP has had an influence on the EU as a security actor.

Due to the RtoP's indeterminacy it is assumed that there are diverging understandings of and different levels of commitment to the RtoP. Furthermore, as an emerging international norm the RtoP has to work its way not only through the EU but also through national structures. While the EU's understanding of the RtoP has been addressed in the previous chapter, this chapter starts by looking at the member state's interpretations of the emerging norm.

Being among the most important players in the area of European security and defence, the focus throughout this thesis will be on the 'Big 3'[68]. The following section therefore briefly reviews the security strategies of France, Germany and the United Kingdom (UK) in order to establish the respective general understandings of the RtoP. The second and third part of this chapter will analyse the four most prominent 'RtoP cases' (see Bellamy, 2010) – two cases of RtoP implementation and two instances of non-implementation or misuse – with an emphasis on the European responses therein. Comparing the French, German, British and the EU discourse within and across the four 'RtoP cases', in the fourth part of this chapter, will reveal to what extent the RtoP has been applied consistently and whether there is a collective European understanding of when and how to apply the emerging norm.

68 For a more detailed justification of the choice of units of analysis, see chapter 4.

3.1 Member states' responsibility (to protect)

While all member states subscribed to the protection of human rights as part of the EU's *aquis communautaire*, they differ widely with regard to the means of protection. At one end of the spectrum there are countries whose colonial histories accustomed them to interventionist practices – namely France and the UK, who consistently supported both a militarily meaningful CSDP and an interventionist interpretation of the RtoP. At the other end of the spectrum there are member states with a neutral or non-interventionist tradition, like Germany, that emphasise the preventive and peace-building aspects of both the CSDP and the RtoP.

France: sovereignty as responsibility

France builds its international responsibility on its permanent membership of the UN Security Council since the UN's creation in 1945. In addition to that it assumes an essential role in the maintenance of peace in Europe as a founding member of NATO and the EU. France has therefore always held a central position in defining the scope and the ambition of EU foreign policy. The underlying philosophy of French engagement in this area has been a belief in the primacy of national foreign policy as a core element of state sovereignty (Lehne, 2012). At the same time, France commits to "work for a more unified, stronger European Union, with a greater presence in the fields of security and defence" (French White Paper, 2008: 75[69]).

The overall aim of France's security policy is to defend the French population and territory:

> *Protection and intervention are expected to enable the State first to ensure, primarily on the national soil, the security of its citizens, of society and the economic life of the country* (idem: 61).

69 The French government published a new version of the White Paper in 2013. As the empirical focus of this study is on European responses to mass atrocities in the Libyan and the Syrian crisis since 2011, the analysis draws on on the 2008 version of the White Paper.

Therefore, France will ensure that it "remains a major military and diplomatic power, ready to take on the challenges congruent with our international obligation" (idem: 9).

From the French perspective, intervention within the framework of humanitarian action can be intended to avert wider conflict and continues to be one of France's "essential mode[s] of action" for its armed forces: "Our intervention capability should be such as to guarantee our strategic interests and enable us to shoulder our international responsibilities" (idem: 67). Most interventions take place within a multilateral framework – either the UN, the EU or NATO. According to the "principle of concentration on priority geographical axes" and due to its colonial ties, the external dimension of France's security policy focuses particularly on countries in North Africa.

The use of military force is only envisaged in the case of "a sufficiently grave and serious risk or threat" (idem: 68). But France may also take part in an intervention directed towards the preservation of peace and international security. The *Guidelines for the commitment of French armed forces abroad* state that prior to the use of armed force, other possible measures have to be considered "without prejudice to the urgency of legitimate defence of the responsibility to protect" (idem). Moreover the democratic legitimacy of a military intervention is crucial. According to the White Paper "legitimacy will be all the greater if, for each engagement, the objectives are transparent and if it has the explicit support of the national community, as notably expressed through its representatives in Parliament" (idem: 69).

The French security strategy defines sovereignty as responsibility and affirms that fundamental principles such as non-interference in internal matters of a state cannot be superior to mass atrocities:

> ... *human rights are no more incompatible with State sovereignty than they are with the pursuit of our interests. The sovereignty of the State consists in the first place in protecting its population. Neither the principle of non-interference in domestic affairs of a State, nor that of the sovereignty can therefore be invoked to defend atrocities such as massacres and other massive violations of international humanitarian law* (idem: 115).

Germany: shared responsibility

According to the 2006 *White Paper on German Security Policy and the Future of the Bundeswehr*, German foreign policy is based on a comprehensive concept of security and is inseparably linked to the political development of Europe. The White Paper states that "Germany stands by its international responsibility for freedom and peace and, in doing so, strives for the long-term protection and welfare of its citizens" (idem: 14). Moreover, German security policy "is guided by the values enshrined in the Basic Law and by the goal of safeguarding the interests of [the] country" (idem: 20).

The main aims of Germany's security policy are in particular the protection of its own citizens, ensuring its sovereignty and territorial integrity but also to help uphol-ding human rights and strengthen the international order on the basis of internati-onal law. The comprehensive approach to security includes the use of diplomatic, economic, development policies, policing measures and military means. However, the White Paper stresses that security cannot be guaranteed with armed forces only (idem: 19). Germany thus commits itself to multilateralism and international law but has in contrast to France and due to its history developed a distinct aversion to the use of military force.

In accordance with the stated goals in the White Paper, the main tasks of the German *Bundeswehr* is to maintain national security and provide assistance in the defence of Germany's allies (idem: 51). Germany's commitment to its allies (*Bündnisverpflichtung*) forms an important part of its foreign policy strategy. The German armed forces can take part in international conflict prevention or crisis management mission only since 1994. The deployment of the *Bundeswehr* has subsequently been integrated into the constitutional structure of Germany's basic law and has to be democratically legitimised by the German *Bundestag* accordingly.

Regarding the RtoP, Germany "accepts its share of the responsibility to protect to strive for world peace and international security within the framework of the United Nations" (idem: 44). At the same time the White Paper emphasises that Germany "remains prepared to accept greater responsibility, also by assuming a permanent seat on the UN Security Council" (idem: 45). It also predicts that the RtoP will increasingly affect the mandating of international peace mission by the UNSC and will serve as legitimation under international law particularly when the use of force is implied (idem: 44). In comparison to France, Germany seems more reluctant in its commitment to the RtoP. This might be mainly related to its aversion of the use of military force and its interpretation of the RtoP, as being increasingly linked to the issue of military intervention.

The United Kingdom: collective responsibility

While Germany wants to be part of a European foreign policy and France aims to lead it, the UK's most important foreign policy relationship remains with the US (Lehne, 2012: 16). The 2010 *National Security Strategy* states that "in order to protect our interests at home, we must project our influence abroad" via a network of alliances – "principally with the United States of America, but also as a member of the European Union and NATO" (p. 5). The main aim of Britain's foreign policy is "to use all [its] national capabilities to build Britain's prosperity, extend our nation's influence in the world and strengthen our security" (idem: 9) by applying a "'whole of government' approach". Resembling the concept of comprehensive security, the British approach goes beyond the mere use of military means. It emphasises the importance of domestic resilience but also a stable global environment.

In order to shape a stable world, the UK might address causes of instability overseas in order to prevent them from manifesting themselves in the UK (idem: 10). Furthermore, securing these "strategic interests and responsibilities overseas could in some circumstances justify the threat or use of military force". In this context, there might be occasions when it is in the British national interest "to take part in humanitarian interventions" (idem: 23). Committing itself to multilateralism, the document states further that British interests can be best pursued in a system of collective security.

The RtoP is not explicitly mentioned in the 2010 British security strategy. However, Ambassador Michael Tatham stated at the UN General Assembly in September 2012 that "the United Kingdom is fully committed to implementing the Responsibility to Protect" (Tatham, 5 September 2012). Moreover, the 2006 White Paper on *The Future of the United Kingdom's nuclear deterrent*, emphasises the UK's identity as protector (Duncanson and Eschle, 2008: 554). In the White Paper's foreword,

Tony Blair states that "the primary responsibility of any government is to ensure the safety and security of its citizens" (White Paper, 2006: 5). In comparison to France and Germany, the British foreign policy strategy rarely mentions altruistic reasons. Reflecting the old norm of humanitarian intervention the overseas deployment of the British military would therefore only be considered if it also involved national security interests directly or indirectly by constituting a threat to international peace and security.

A common European perspective?

From the diversity of European security strategies, based on different national experiences and traditions, derives the difficulty to forge a common European security policy (Hyde-Price, 2004: 327). Accordingly, there is disagreement among member states about the means and ends of security policy (Baun, 2005). As nation states, all three – France, Germany and the UK – give priority to national security and state interests. France and the UK both seem willing (and able) to defend their national interests at home and abroad. However, while the UK makes its participation in a military intervention overseas contingent upon national security issues, France sees its sovereignty as responsibility and would thus also take part if security and safety of others were at stake.

In fact, France is the only one among the three that prioritises human rights over the fundamental principles of territorial integrity and non-interference in case of grave violations. Germany, on the other hand, appears much more reluctant to the use of military force and is the only country where the deployment of the armed forces is constrained by its constitution. It however accepts its shared responsibility and emphasises commitment to its alliances.

In order to see how these different security strategies and understandings of the RtoP play out in practice, the following sections will review two cases before the Libyan and the Syrian crises in 2011, in which the RtoP has been applied – the Darfur crisis and the post-electoral violence in Kenya – and two cases in which it has arguably been misused – the French attempt to invoke RtoP after the cyclone

Nargis in Burma and the Russian-Georgian war.[70] The analysis of these four cases will focus particularly on the French, German and British discourse as well as the role of the EU.

70 The four cases are among those most cited for the application of the RtoP by media commentators, diplomats, policy makers and scholar (see Bellamy, 2010).

3.2 RtoP and CSDP in practice

The Darfur crisis

Before the Libyan crisis, two of the most prominent cases in which the UN has invoked the RtoP doctrine were the Darfur crisis and the post-electoral violence in Kenya. The crisis in Darfur was the first to be seen through an RtoP prism and became a "primary test case" (Bellamy, 2010 153) for the nascent doctrine. The conflict that started in 2003, when two rebel groups, the Sudan Liberation Movement / Army (SLM / A) and the Justice and Equality Movement (JEM), attacked Sudanese government posts in response to decades of political and economic marginalisation and neglect. It has been labelled one of the world's worst humanitarian crises.[71] Until spring 2004, mass atrocities and crimes against humanity were widely known to be occurring in Darfur, and the number of 'war affected'[72] came close to one million. Until June the next year, the number had reached 2.9 million (Prunier, 2007: 148-152).

Before supporting an AU-led peace operation in Darfur, the UN regarded the possibility of a multilateral intervention in Darfur as unfeasible (Badescu and Bergholm, 2009: 295). The government in Khartoum rejected any UN presence in Darfur. In July 2004 the AU deployed sixty observes and 300 troops to Darfur as the African Union Mission in Sudan (AMIS), and in August 2004 it started the Abuja negotiations for inter-Sudanese peace talks. In March 2005, the UNSC referred Darfur to the International Criminal Court (ICC) and established the UN Mission in Sudan (UNMIS) with the task to reinforce AMIS and implement the Comprehensive Peace Agreement (CPA), intended to end the conflict in Southern Sudan.

In August 2006, the UNSC passed resolution 1706 recalling resolution 1674 and expanding the mandate of UNMIS authorising it to use "all necessary means … to prevent attacks and threats against civilians" (UNSC, 2006a). This was the first time that the UNSC invoked the RtoP to authorise the use of force. However, the resolution made deployment conditional on the consent of the Sudanese government. It assigned a 26,000-strong UN peacekeeping force to replace the AU mission. In July

71 According to the Darfur Consortium (2011), 300,000 civilians died in the course of the conflict and 2,5 million Darfurians had to flee their homes.

72 The UN's term for those killed, raped, displaced, malnourished etc.

2007, UNSC resolution 1769 established the African Union / UN Hybrid Operation in Darfur (UNAMID). UNAMID officially took over from AMIS in December 2007. In July 2008, the UNSC extended UNAMID's mandate for another year, followed by another extension in August 2009 for one more year until July 2010.

On the European side, Germany formally proposed the deployment of UN peacekeepers to Darfur in May 2004. However, inside the UNSC, Pakistan, China and Russia believed that the scale of human suffering in Darfur was insufficient to provoke serious reflections on whether Sudan was fulfilling its responsibilities to its citizens. Initially, France, Germany and the UK saw the responsibility primarily with the Sudanese government and emphasised that their crisis response would not go beyond the application of sanctions. On the adoption of Resolution 1556 the French Representative to the UN stated, "the primary responsibility of the government of Sudan is to protect its population" (Jean Marc de la Sablière, quoted in UNSC, 2004). Germany stressed that "the government of Sudan must now act rapidly and decisively for the sake of its very own population – to which it has ... a sacred obligation to protect. Otherwise ... further Council deliberations could lead to the imposition of sanctions" (Gunter Pleuger, 2004, quoted in idem). Similarly, the UK affirmed that "the best way to deliver security to the people of Darfur is to get those with primary responsibility for it to do it ... the government of Sudan" (quoted in Bellamy, 2006: 45).

When the UNSC met to pass Resolution 1706 in July 2006, Germany amongst others invoked the language of RtoP but without suggesting that the responsibility ought to pass from the Sudanese government to the UNSC. They referred to the AU as bearing the primary responsibility for action should Sudan fail in its responsibilities. The intervention debate crystallized around the question of who had the responsibility to protect the Darfurian population (Bellamy, 2006: 43). France expressed that there was a "collective responsibility" at least to implement the resolution (Jean-Pierre Lacroix, 2007, quoted in UNSC 2007b) but not to go any further. Merely the British Representative indicated a shift of the responsibility from the Sudanese government to the UN Security Council. At the same time the UK reminded to respect the sovereignty and territorial integrity of Sudan:

> *The test before the Council today was whether it was prepared to act to mandate that United Nations mission and assume its responsibilities towards the people of Darfur. The adoption of the resolution shows it is. The text also states clearly and categorically that the Council remains committed to the sovereignty and territorial integrity of the Sudan, which will be unaffected by the transition to a United Nations Operations.* (Karen Pierce quoted in UNSC, 2007b)

Finally, by referring to the RtoP the UK highlighted that it was "very pleased that this is the first Security Council resolution mandating a United Nations peacekeeping operation to make an explicit reference to this responsibility" (UNSC, 2007b).

The EU's assessment of and its response to the crisis in Darfur were equally reluctant. After having completed a fact-finding mission in Darfur in August 2004, the advisor to the EU High Representative states that there was "no situation of genocide" (Carroll, 2004). However, the EU expressed considerable doubts as to the willingness of the Sudanese government to assume its responsibility to protect its civilian population from attacks. Yet, by the end of the year, the European Parliament declared "that the actions of the Sudanese government in Darfur were 'tantamount to genocide'" (Bock and Miller, 2004). Furthermore, EU minister threatened sanctions "if no tangible progress was achieved" in meeting UN demands to halt the killing (idem).

Despite an AMIS support operation, further direct intervention by the EU in Darfur proved to be difficult, due to both objections of the Sudanese government, which opposed any additional intervention, but also from a lack of willingness of the member states (Gya, 2010: 9). The EU also had to consider the risk of jeopardising the UN mission and the need to coordinate international efforts. Most of the EU member states were not keen on a long-term commitment in Darfur and therefore preferred a 'bridging' operation, which would see the mission pass to the UN eventually.

Pushed by France, which underlined the connection between Sudan and Chad, the EU turned its attention in October 2007 to the collateral issue thrown up by the Darfur conflict, namely 170.000 internally displaced persons (IDP) in Chad, and 230.000 refugees from Sudan. In 2007, it was again the European Parliament that made the strongest statement issuing a resolution, invoking the RtoP and calling for action in Darfur. Member states, however, merely signalled their "readiness to consider further measures" (Waging Peace, 2007).

To deal with the IDPs on the border of Sudan and Chad, French President Nicolas Sarkozy and the EU High Representative, Javier Solana, met to discuss a possible EU mission to Chad. The President of Chad, Idriss Déby, would not accept a UN force but was persuaded to allow a EU mission (Natsios and Scott, 2012: 251). Despite little enthusiasm amongst EU member states for a mission, with resources stretched by several CSDP and other operations already, EUFOR Tchad was established in January 2008. In accordance with UNSC Resolution 1778 the mission was mandated to uphold security and protect aid corridors for the refugees and the UN.

EUFOR was criticised at the outset. It was described as yet "another French initiative to strengthen its influence in the region, and above all in Chad" (FRIDE, 2008). During the deployment, the mission was criticised further by its lack of potential to make a significant difference due to its size, equipment, capabilities and mandate (Gya, 2010). EUFOR's negative assessment was coupled with deteriorating security situations in Chad and in Darfur (Seibert, 2008).

Some argued that the case of Darfur constitutes a gradual step towards the consolidation of the RtoP as an international norm. According to Max Matthews (2008), the fact that the UNSC explicitly invoked the RtoP in its resolutions on Darfur, while deciding on implementing measures, added legal weight to the principle and foretold a trend towards the development of the RtoP into binding international law. By contrast, Alex Bellamy (2010) argued that both advocates and opponents of intervention used the RtoP language to legitimise their actions. RtoP allowed opponents of intervention to replace traditional arguments on the absolute validity of sovereignty against intervention in the case of humanitarian emergencies with arguments about who had the primary responsibility to protect civilians in Darfur.

While Germany emphasised the responsibility of the Sudanese government, France eventually spoke of a collective security towards the people in Darfur. Only the UK admitted that the responsibility had shifted from the Sudanese government to the international community. The EU's response remained very reluctant on a rhetorical as well as on a practical level. The RtoP was merely invoked by the European Parliament which was demanding a stronger EU response but does not have much of an influence in EU foreign policy-making. EUFOR Chad was eventually deployed to Sudan's neighbouring country on a demand by France but achieved only limited success. On the EU level the RtoP had only limited influence in the case of the Darfur crisis, which revealed different interpretations among the member states. Accordingly, the RtoP failed to activate the EU's responsibility to use the CSDP in its crisis response.

Post-election violence in Kenya

The second case that was viewed through the RtoP prism was the reaction to post-electoral violence in Kenya in 2007. Presidential elections were held on 27 December 2007. The announcement of the victory of incumbent President Mwai Kibaki against opposition candidate Raila Odinga triggered allegations of electoral fraud leading to violent demonstrations, causing over 1,000 casualties and 300,000 displaced persons (United Nations, 2008). Desmond Tutu and Francis Deng, the UN Special Adviser on the Prevention of Genocide were the first to make references to RtoP in relation to the 2007 post-election violence in Kenya (UN News, 2008). The UN Secretary-General reminded the Kenyans of their legal and moral responsibility to protect the lives of their citizens but did not repeat this reference to RtoP in subsequent statements (Strauss, 2009: 118). In early 2008, a UN-supported mediation effort by the AU Panel of Eminent Personalities, led by former UN Secretary General Kofi Annan, conduced Kibaki and Odinga to agree on a power sharing agreement. This mediated solution is said to have prevented a campaign of mass atrocities (Bellamy, 2010: 154).

In Europe, it was France that was at the forefront of calling for an international response on the basis of the RtoP. French Foreign Minister Bernard Kouchner stated that "in the name of the responsibility to protect, it is urgent to help the people of Kenya. The United Nations Security Council must take this question and act" (Tutu, 2008). However, when the UNSC took up the matter on 6 February 2008, the Presidential Statement took note of the violence and its impact on the region, but stopped short of referring to the RtoP (UNSC, 2008).

France pointed towards the role of Europe in the response to the Kenyan crisis. On 7 February 2008, State Secretary Jean-Pierre Jouyet affirmed further that he would prefer Europe to intervene in Kenya than the US as Europe still had to progress in terms of its international influence (Jouyet, 7 February 2008)[73]. At the same time, the French Foreign Minister noted that an outside military intervention was not a solution but that it was necessary to put on a certain pressure (Kouchner, 15 January 2008)[74]. France expressed its trust in Kofi Annan's mediation efforts and called on the UNSC – in the name of the RtoP – to open ways for delivery of humanitarian aid to the Kenyan population (idem)[75]. However, Kouchner also acknowledged that the crises in Darfur and Chad, as well as the one in Kenya have showed the limits of the RtoP (idem)[76].

Without making any reference to RtoP, Germany called for an immediate end to the violence and for a peaceful solution to the conflict between the government and the opposition in January 2008 (Steinmeier, 1 January 2008). German Foreign Minister Franz-Walter Steinmeier expressed concerns that the political crisis in Kenya was causing extensive human suffering and that it challenged the economic success and political success of Kenya over the past years (Steinmeier, 27 January 2008)[77]. Only when Annan's mediation efforts started to gain ground at the beginning of February, the German government stressed that the protection of the civilian population was the highest priority (Steinmeier, 2 February 2008)[78]. Thus the focus of Germany's crisis response seemed to be initially on Kenya as an economic and political actor. Germany's approach became more people-centred only, once a solution to the crisis seemed to be in sight.

While the RtoP was almost absent in the German response, the British discourse reflects the emerging norm to a greater extent but also with a stronger focus on the first pillar. The UK Foreign Secretary David Miliband stated on 10 January 2008 that "Kenya's leaders must live up to their responsibilities, end this violence, and

73 "Je préfèrerais que ce soit l'Europe qui soit intervenue au Kenya plutôt que la secrétaire d'Etat américaine. Nous avons encore de progrès à faire en termes d'influence européenne au niveau international."

74 "Bien sûr, nous n'interviendrons pas militairement mais il faudrait quand même avoir la possibilité de peser d'un certain poids."

75 "Au nom de la responsabilité de protéger, il est urgent de venir en aide aux population du Kenya. Le Conseil de sécurité des Nation unies doit se saisir de cette question et agir."

76 "... responsabilité de protéger. On en voit les limites, au Darfour comme au Tchad, et on les voit au Kenya ..."

77 "Die politische Krise in Kenia verursache großes menschliches Leid und stelle die Erfolge der wirtschaftlichen und politischen Entwicklung Kenias der letzten Jahre in Frage."

78 "Oberste Priorität hat der Schutz der Zivilbevölkerung."

work for the security and safety of the people of Kenya". When asked whether the UNSC should get involved in the political crisis in Kenya, the Foreign Secretary reiterated that a role of the international community cannot be a substitute for the responsibility of the Kenyan leaders:

> *I think we … need a strong international response but we shouldn't let that become a substitute for the fact that this still remains an issue where Kenya's own leaders need to show a lot more statesmanship than they've shown so far …* (Miliband, 1 February 2008).

At the invitation of the government of Kenya, the EU established a mission to observe the general elections there on 27 December 2007. On behalf of the EU the French Presidency condemned the violence in Kenya and urged the political leaders to refrain from any further violence (Council of the EU, 4 January 2008). Resembling the language of the RtoP, the EU stressed the responsibility of all parties to immediately end the violence and to find a political and democratic solution that benefits the Kenyan people (Council of the EU, 11 January 2008). Despite this rhetorical response the EU's role in response to the Kenyan crisis remained fairly insignificant. Ultimately, it was Kofi Annan's mediation that led to an end of the conflict.

Due to the successful prevention of further atrocities and its non-coercive character, the Kenyan intervention has been praised as the most successful case of RtoP implementation and a "high watermark" (Evans, 2011a) for the use of the concept. Gareth Evans has argued that "Kenya in early 2008 is probably the best example we have so far of the responsibility to protect appearing to play an important energising role in stimulating an effective response …" (quoted in Preston-McPhie and Sharma, 2012: 279). However, the Kenyan case also uncovered questions and limitations regarding the practical implementation of the RtoP. The international agreement was facilitated by host-country consent and the limitation of the intervention to diplomatic tools. It is far from clear how the international community would have reacted, had these tools failed. There is little evidence to suggest that the UNSC would have been prepared to adopt a more robust stance if it had been required (Bellamy, 2010: 154-55).

The two cases reveal a consensus that the international community has a legitimate role to play in the case of humanitarian emergencies. However, although the RtoP was utilized in both cases, in neither did the emerging norm provide a catalyst for decisive common action. The capacity or incapacity of RtoP to serve as catalyst for collective action can be further tested by reviewing cases of mass atrocities in which RtoP has been misused or not considered at all. Two prominent cases of non-implementation and misuse are the cyclone Nargis in Burma and the Russian-Georgian war.

Cyclone Nargis in Burma

When cyclone Nargis hit Burma's Irrawaddy Delta in 2008, and the Burmese authorities at first denied access to foreign aid workers, French Foreign Minister Bernard Kouchner called on the UNSC to invoke the RtoP to grant humanitarian access without the consent of the Burmese generals. He stated that

> *we are seeing at the United Nations if we can't implement the 'responsibility to protect' given that food, boats and relief teams are there, and obtain a UN resolution which authorises the delivery [of aid] and imposes this on the Burmese government* (Mydans, 2008).

The Foreign Minister warned that not helping the Burmese people could increase the risk of crimes against humanity and therefore called on the international community to assume their 'responsibility to protect' (Le Figaro, 17 May 2008).

Akin, the German government considered the delivery of humanitarian aid even against the will of the Burmese government. The Minister of Development Heidemarie Wieczorek-Zeul affirmed that "the international community has the responsibility and the right to assist people in emergencies even if the government is resisting" (Frankfurter Allgemeine Zeitung, 10 May 2008)[79]. Germany supported Kouchner's initiative to put pressure on the Burmese government. Furthermore, Germany together with France and the UK asked for a UNSC resolution that would force the military government in Burma to let in international aid workers (FAZ, 13 May 2008).

79 "Die internationale Gemeinschaft hat die Verantwortung und das Recht, Menschen in Not zur Seite zu stehen, auch wenn die eigene Regierung sich dagegen sträubt ..."

The UK saw the responsibility primarily with the Burmese government. British Prime Minister Gordon Brown described the crisis as one that was

> *being made into a manmade catastrophe by the negligence, the neglect and the inhuman treatment of the Burmese people by a regime that is failing to act and to allow the international community to do what it wants to do.* (Gordon Brown quoted in McKinnon and Tran, 2008)

However, Brown added that "the responsibility lies with the Burmese regime" (idem).

The EU High Representative Javier Solana, again, took the view that the UN Charter opened 'certain paths' to bring help to a country affected by a natural disaster, even if the political leadership did not allow swift and effective support (FAZ, 13 May 2008). The EU met to discuss its response to the cyclone and the French proposal to invoke the RtoP. Although, EU ministers failed to reach a consensus on the French proposal, Solana declared that the international community "should use all possible means to get aid through to the victims of Myanmar's cyclone" (O'Neill, 2008).

The special advisor on issues related to the RtoP, Edward Luck claimed that "linking the 'responsibility to protect doctrine' to the situation in Burma is a misapplication of the doctrine" (BBC News, 2008). Conversely, some argued that Burma could have been an RtoP case (see for example Cohen, 2009) because the natural disaster turned into a human-made disaster, as also argued by the UK. The refusal of the Burmese authorities to allow external support after the cyclone did not, in itself, trigger the application of the RtoP. If such actions had led to massive deaths and displacements, then RtoP would have been relevant. The French proposal was therefore finally rejected due to the limitation of the RtoP to genocide, war crimes, crimes against humanity and ethnic cleansing

The Russian-Georgian War

Another misuse of the RtoP doctrine was the invocation in the context of the 2008 Russian-Georgian war. After a forceful intervention in the breakaway province of South Ossetia, President Dmitry Medvedev and Prime Minister Vladimir Putin argued that the use of force was aimed at preventing genocide against the separatists. On 9 August, foreign minister Sergej Lavrov told the BBC "that the laws of the Russian Federation make it absolutely unavoidable to us to exercise the responsibility to protect" (quoted in Bellamy, 2010: 151). Western governments broadly rejected Moscow's arguments on the grounds that the claim of genocide was exaggerated and the use of force disproportionate. Critiques also argued that there was no legal authority for unilateral RtoP intervention in Georgia since Russia lacked UNSC authorisation (Vlasic, 2012: 171).

Moscow used the RtoP internationally to legitimise its intervention, but the public discourse less reflected humanitarian rhetoric than a forceful stance against the Georgian President Mikheil Saakashvili (Badescu, 2011: 143). Further evidence of Russia's false humanitarian claims emerged from a similar operation in Abkhazia. Russia argued that sending additional forces into another breakaway region was a preventive act to reassure the local population that the situation in South Ossetia would not be repeated (Kendall, 2008). Within days, Russian troops had expelled Georgian forces and controlled both South Ossetia and Abkhazia. In August 2008, Russia officially recognised both provinces as independent states and implemented a ceasefire mediated by the French President at the time holding the presidency of the EU. This episode fuelled the criticism of RtoP as being used as a 'Trojan horse' for state interests.

On 8 August 2008, France emphasised the respect for Georgia's sovereignty and territorial integrity within the internationally recognised borders (Point de presse, 8 August 2008)[80]. Moreover, the French Foreign Minister stressed the role of the EU in working towards ending "this vicious war, like all wars elsewhere, but this particularly brutal one taking place on Europe's doorstep" (Kouchner, 10 August 2008).

80 "La France réitère son attachement à la souveraineté et à l'intégrité de la Géorgie dans ses frontières internationalement reconnues."

He added that he did not "understand why Europe did not get involved in trying to achieve an immediate cease-fire"[81] (idem).

Similarly to France, Germany called for respect of the territorial integrity of Georgia and highlighted that the principle of non-interference is at the core of Germany's response to the conflict. At the same time Steinmeier indicated that by attacking and invading Georgian territory, Russia had crossed a line (Steinmeier, 11 August 2008). However, Germany did not specify further whether Russia's behaviour would have any further consequences and remained very reluctant in assigning blame, let alone responsibility to one party or another (Steinmeier, 27 August 2008).

Speaking in the Georgian capital Tbilisi on 8 August 2008, the British Foreign Secretary warned Russia that it should expect a response for its actions and that the international community would not forget the invasion of Georgia (Blomfield, 2008). Prime Minister Gordon Brown confirmed that "there is no justification for continued Russian military action in Georgia, which threatens the stability of the entire region and risks a humanitarian catastrophe" (Brown quoted in BBC News, 2008b). He claimed that "there is a clear responsibility on the Russian government to bring this conflict quickly to an end" (idem). Furthermore, he emphasised that Russia had clearly breached international law by violating Georgia's territorial integrity. In comparison to Germany, the UK directly accused Russia of a disproportionate use of force and of disregarding international law.

Under the French EU Council Presidency the EU played a surprisingly high-profile role in the Russian-Georgian War (Halbach, 2009: 113). For the first time it was the EU, not the US, that led the process of ending a conflict in the EU's neighbourhood. The EU condemned the violence and the disproportionate use of force by the Russian government but did not directly blame Russia nor did it indicate any consequences for Russia's behaviour. However, the EU committed itself "including through a presence on the ground, to support every effort to secure a peaceful and lasting solution to the conflict in Georgia" (European Council, 1 September 2008). The EU contributed to the OSCE observer mission in South Ossetia and decided to send a fact-finding mission with the "task helping to gather information and defining the modalities of increased

81 "La mission de l'Union européenne, est d'essayer de mettre fin à cette guerre odieuse, comme toutes les guerres d'ailleurs, mais celle-là particulièrement brutale qui se déroule aux portes de l'Europe. On ne comprendrait pas que l'Europe ne s'implique pas à essayer d'obtenir un cessez-le-feu immédiat."

EU commitment on the ground, under the ESDP" (idem). Following the ceasefire agreement initially negotiated by the Nicolas Sarkozy, in his function of Presidency of the EU, the EU deployed the monitoring mission EUMM Georgia with the objective to contribute to the post-war stabilisation process in Georgia and the surrounding region.

While the unilateral misuse of the emerging norm can serve to test the limits of its applicability, the failure to invoke the doctrine when a trigger is actually present is the type of inconsistency that is arguably more detrimental to the credibility of the RtoP as a universal norm. There are several cases where one or more of the four RtoP crimes were committed but where the RtoP norm was not invoked. According to Bellamy (2010: 150) these cases include Afghanistan (2001-ongoing), Iraq (2003-ongoing), Somalia (2006-ongoing), and Sudan (north-south, 2008-ongoing). Depending on whom you ask, more cases can be identified.[82]

The selectivity and double standards in applying the RtoP were indeed one of the areas of concern during the 2009 UN General Assembly debate on the implementation of the RtoP. Some member states countered these concerns noting that "no principle had withstood perfect application and that it would be wrong to conclude that because the international community might not act everywhere, it should therefore act nowhere" (Global Centre for the RtoP, 2009: 2). However, the decision rules in the UNSC provide for very few countries to determine in which cases to act.

82 An actualised list of eligible cases can be found on the website of the International Coalition for the Responsibility to Protect: http://www.responsibilitytoprotect.org/index.php/crises.

3.3 RtoP as a European norm

The first aim of this chapter was to answer whether there is a collective European understanding of what the RtoP means and implies. A comparison of the positions of France, Germany and the UK on the four above reviewed RtoP cases shows that there is agreement on the first pillar – the responsibility of each state to protect its own population. However, there seems to be much less agreement on when the responsibility moves from the state to the international community. Diverging views also surfaced regarding the question of whether the RtoP also applies to cases beyond the four crimes mentioned in the 2005 Outcome Document. And finally different understandings regarding the use of force under the RtoP could be detected.

France made the strongest arguments for the application of the RtoP in the case of Burma after the cyclone Nargis in 2008, by proposing a military intervention with the aim of securing the delivery of humanitarian aid to the Burmese people. During the post-election violence in Kenya France emphasised that the crisis showed the limits of the RtoP while at the same time advising against any use of military means. In case of the Darfur crisis, France did not explicitly promote the application of the RtoP and therefore spoke rather of a collective responsibility. Against this background it seems as if the French interpretation of the RtoP is strongly linked to the use of force and the question of military intervention.

By contrast, Germany rarely referred to the RtoP explicitly and was not in favour of considering the use of military means in any of the four cases. Germany seems to subscribe merely to the first pillar of the RtoP as in the case of the Darfur crisis as well as to the second pillar (the responsibility to assist) in the case of the Kenyan crisis. RtoP was absent in the German discourse on the Kenyan crisis and on the Russian-Georgian war. In case of the latter, Germany moreover took a more neutral position than France and the UK.

The UK discourse reflected the RtoP more frequently. In case of the Darfur crisis the UK committed to both the first pillar and the third pillar (the responsibility of the international community) of the RtoP. At the same time the UK emphasised its respect for the principles of sovereignty and territorial integrity. Furthermore the UK made clear that in some cases – as in the instance of Kenya – the responsibility of the state cannot be replaced by the responsibility of the international community. During the Russian-Georgian war, the UK openly accused Russia of breaching international law.

The review of the four RtoP cases reveals a mixed picture regarding the collective understanding of the RtoP. Agreement among France, Germany and the UK does not seem to go beyond the first pillar of the emerging norm. Despite that, member states seem divided on the meaning of pillar two and three as well as on the actions these components entail.

The second aim of this chapter was to assess to what extent the RtoP and the CSDP have an influence on the EU's role as a security actor. The EU was able to show the strongest commitment in its response to the Russia-Georgia war by contribution to the ceasefire agreement (in form of the French EU Presidency), as well as by supporting the peace process with presence on the ground (EUMM Georgia). However, the RtoP is rarely reflected in the EU official discourse and does not seem to serve as a catalyst for a decisive EU response. Furthermore, the EU's role in the ceasefire agreement has to be attributed mainly to the efforts of French EU Presidency under Nicolas Sarkozy.

In case of the Darfur crisis, the EU expressed doubts on the willingness of the Sudanese government to assume its responsibility and the European Parliament invoked the RtoP. However, member states could not agree on a common response going beyond civilian means and support to AMIS. Similarly, EU member states were unable to reach an agreement on the French proposal to invoke the RtoP in the case of cyclone Nargis in Burma. Finally, in case of Kenya, the EU had established – on invitation of the Kenyan government – an election observation mission, the conflict between the government and the opposition was, however, mainly solved due to Kofi Annan's mediation efforts. In combination with the RtoP, the CSDP seems therefore to have only a limited influence on the EU's role as a security actor. However, this might also be related to the fact that three out four RtoP cases analysed above were geographically outside the EU's neighbourhood.

RtoP	France	Germany
In general	Intervention as essential mode of action to guarantee strategic interests and shoulder international responsibilities Intervention as preservation of international peace and security Importance of democratic legitimacy Sovereignty as responsibility	Aversion to the use of military force Protection of own citizens ensuring sovereignty and territorial integrity Comprehensive approach to security Share of the RtoP within the UN
Darfur crisis	2004: responsibility of the Sudanese government 2007: collective responsibility	Responsibility of the Sudanese government Sanctions
Post-election violence in Kenya	RtoP of the international community/the UNSC European intervention rather than US to increase Europe's influence Limits of the RtoP No military intervention but political solution Responsibility of the Kenyan leaders	RtoP absent
Cyclone Nargis in Burma	RtoP due to risks of crimes against humanity	Responsibility of the international community to assist Burmese people Call for UNSC resolution
Russia-Georgia war	Respect of Georgia's sovereignty and territorial integrity Importance of the EU's role in crisis in its neighbourhood	Territorial integrity RtoP absent Neutral position

Table 6: Overview of European interpretations of the RtoP

The United Kingdom	The EU
Protect own interests and people Build Britain's prosperity, extend its influence in the world and strengthen security 'Whole of government' approach Fully committed to implement the RtoP	Comprehensive security Supporting the UNSC 'Robust intervention' Shared RtoP regarding the four RtoP crimes Respect for fundamental principles of international law such as sovereignty, non-interference and territorial integrity
2004: Responsibility of the Sudanese government 2007: Responsibility of the international community, but emphasis on Sudanese sovereignty and territorial integrity	Doubts about Sudanese government's willingness to assume its responsibility European Parliament invoking RtoP Disagreement among member state Initiated by France, military CSDP mission in Chad (EUFOR Chad)
Responsibility of the Kenyan leaders Role of the international community cannot substitute a state's responsibility	Responsibility of the Kenyan leaders
Responsibility of the Burmese government	No agreement on French proposal to invoke RtoP
Responsibility of the Russian government Disproportionate use of force Breach of international law	Disproportionate use of force Peace agreement negotiated by French EU Presidency Support to peace process with EUMM Georgia

3.4 Reassessing RtoP as (emerging) international norm

Since the 2005 World Summit, the RtoP has slowly but steadily made its way into the international discourse. However, the inconsistent implementation of the RtoP has raised questions with regard to its development as emerging international norm. The case of Darfur showed that there is no consensus on the legal weight of the RtoP in relation to other norms such as non-interference and about what ought to be done. The implicit use of the RtoP in the case of Kenya was possible because engagement was limited to diplomacy and host-state consent. Finally, the broader use (or misuse) of the RtoP does not feature a collective understanding of what RtoP means and entails. The review of the four RtoP cases shows that there is no international consensus, not even among supporters of the RtoP, on how to operationalise it. Therefore, the implementation of the RtoP remains a work in progress.

However, the choices that are being made both at the UN and by individual governments shape the development of the emerging norm. Normative development should not be seen as a precursor to implementation, but it continues throughout the process of application. When comparing the normative development of the RtoP since its creation in 2001 with its practical application until 2011, four conclusions can be drawn:

1. RtoP is used by proponents and opponents of the norm. As suggested by the Darfur crisis it has been invoked to justify action as well as inaction. Moreover, the Russian invasion of Georgia confirms the concerns that the RtoP can also be abused to fit the interests of the powerful.
2. The scope of the RtoP is limited to the four crimes as stated in the 2005 World Summit Outcome Document (genocide, war crimes, crimes against humanity and ethnic cleansing). The rejection of France's proposal to invoke RtoP in case of the natural disaster after the cyclone Nargis in Burma and of Russia's claim of having prevented genocide in Georgia affirmed this limitation of the norm.
3. The 'toolbox' of instruments implied by the RtoP remains unclear. Reaction under the RtoP should not be tantamount to military intervention but should

at first exhaust less coercive measures, such as political and diplomatic pressure as well as economic sanctions or referrals to the International Criminal Court (ICC).

4. The implementation of the RtoP and of the CSDP is challenged by the lack of political will from powerful states, especially those that have declared their support for the RtoP, to commit military forces in ways that would challenge the traditional meaning of sovereignty.

This chapter has highlighted the importance of the RtoP's practical application for its evolution starting from the millennium up until 2011. Building on the historical narrative traced in chapter 2, this section has provided a broad overview of the most prominent cases of RtoP application, while emphasising the evolving role of the EU as a security actor. The historical background (chapter 2) and the practical application (chapter 3) of the RtoP and the CSDP have also informed the theoretical and analytical framework presented in chapter 1. The approach developed to assess the influence of the RtoP on European responses to mass atrocities will now be applied to two case studies ten years after the creation of the RtoP and the CSDP. The outbreak of the Arab Spring in late 2010 and the Libyan crisis in particular have essentially revived the debate on Europe's responsibility to protect. The following two chapters provide an in-depth case study analysis of the Libyan crisis from February to October 2011 (chapter 4) and the Syrian crisis from March 2011 to September 2013 (chapter 5).

PART II

Chapter 4: The Libyan crisis – protection vs. intervention?

On 22 February 2011, only days after violence erupted in Libya, the members of the United Nations Security Council (UNSC) called on the Libyan government to "meet its responsibility to protect its population ..." They underscored the need to hold those accountable for attacks, including by forces under their control on civilians (UNSC, 2011a). Faced with escalating violence and something increasingly resembling a civil war, the UNSC identified Libya as a "threat to international peace and security" and adopted a range of measures on the basis of the Responsibility to Protect (RtoP). Within weeks the UNSC imposed an arms embargo and sanctions, referred the situation to the International Criminal Court (ICC), established a no-fly zone and authorised the UN member states to "take all necessary measures ... to protect civilians and civilian populated areas under threat of attack in the Libyan Arab Jamahiriya" (UNSC, 2011b). This was the first time that the UNSC had taken such quick and decisive action, explicitly based on the RtoP and without government consent.

Following the decision of the UN Security Council to impose a no-fly zone over Libya in response to the escalating violence against civilians, proponents of the RtoP have elevated the concept from notable development to triumphant achievement (Bolopion, 2012; The Economist, 2011). UN Secretary General Ban Ki-moon (quoted in ICRtoP, 2011) declared that the decision to authorise a military intervention "affirm[ed], clearly and unequivocally, the international's community's determination to fulfil its responsibility to protect civilians from violence perpetrated upon them by their government". One of the main proponents of the RtoP norm, Gareth Evans, announced in an article entitled *End of Argument* (2011) that the world had reached an "overwhelming consensus, at least on basic principles" of the RtoP.

The European Union (EU) clearly supported the RtoP in its discourse. Accordingly, the protection of civilians had been declared as being the main aim in the EU's response to the Libyan crisis (Gottwald, 2012a). However, the EU remained incapable of reacting with military means and of contributing to the military intervention due to disagreement among the member states and the lack of capabilities. While France together with the United Kingdom (UK) and the United States (US) took the lead in implementing the no-fly zone in Libya, Germany as another core member state abstained in the voting on Resolution 1973. Despite the UN and the EU acting as norm entrepreneurs, the Libyan crisis revealed different perspectives on how best to respond to the crisis. Furthermore, it has been claimed that the military operation went beyond the mandate by extending air strikes to non-military areas in order to achieve a regime change. The presumed overstepping of the UNSC mandate raised questions about whether the decision to use force in Libya was a manifestation of the international community's commitment to the emerging norm of the RtoP, or whether it was a military intervention based on a hidden agenda.

This chapter focuses on the influence of the RtoP on European responses to the Libyan crisis from February 2011, marking the outbreak of the violent conflict, to October 2011, flagged by Muammar Gaddafi's death and a de-escalation of the conflict. According to the previously developed research design, the analysis starts with the UN and the EU responses to the Libyan crisis and their potential roles as norm entrepreneurs for the RtoP. Furthermore, this chapter analyses the French, German and British official discourses in terms of their crisis perception, the discussed foreign policy options and the actual policies implemented. The final part of this chapter will draw some preliminary conclusions on the influence of the RtoP and on the role of the EU as a security actor in the Libyan crisis.

4.1 The role of norm entrepreneurs

The UN response

Based on the RtoP, the UNSC has taken quicker and more decisive action than in any previous situation of mass atrocities. One week after the outbreak of violence in Libya, the UNSC issued a press statement calling "on the government of Libya to meet its responsibility to protect its population" (UNSC, 2011a). On 26 February, the UNSC unanimously adopted Resolution 1970 condemning "the violence and use of force against civilians", and recalling "the Libyan authorities' responsibility to protect its population". Acting under chapter VII of the UN Charter, the resolution referred the situation to the ICC, and imposed an arms embargo and targeted sanctions. On 17 March, the UNSC passed Resolution 1973 reiterating "the responsibility of the Libyan authorities to protect the Libyan population". It authorised the member states under chapter VII "to take all necessary measures ... to protect civilians ...while excluding a foreign occupation force of any form on any part of the Libyan territory" (UNSC, 2011b). Furthermore, Resolution 1973 established a no-fly zone "in order to help protect civilians". This was the first time that the UNSC authorised the use of military force for the protection of civilians against a functioning *de jure* government.

Pillar three of the RtoP states that in situations where a state has manifestly failed to protect its population from the four crimes it is the international community's responsibility to take action, first through peaceful means and if necessary through forceful means. A number of statements issued by Gaddafi demonstrated his intention to trigger large-scale and systematic massacres. He labelled the protesters "cockroaches", stated his intention to "cleanse Libya house by house" and called on his supporters to attack protesters (quoted in ICRtoP, 2011). The evidences of an evolving case of crimes against humanity were also confirmed ex-post by the 27 June decision of the ICC to issue an arrest warrant for Gaddafi, his son Saif Al-Islam, and Abdullah al-Senussi for crimes against humanity (murder and persecution).

Almost from the outset of the crisis, senior UN officials warned of the imminent threat of mass atrocities and framed their responses in the RtoP language. On 22 February, the UN's High Commissioner for Human Rights, Navi Pillay (2011), emphasised the need to protect civilians and called on the authorities to stop using violence against demonstrators, which "may account to crimes against humanity". On the following day, the Secretary General framed the ensuing debate as one about the prevention of mass atrocities and protection of vulnerable populations.

On 26 February, the UNSC voted unanimously to pass Resolution 1970. Among other things, it condemned "the widespread and systematic attacks against civilians, which it suspected 'may amount to crimes against humanity'". It welcomed the earlier criticisms of the Libyan government's actions by the League of Arab States (LAS), the African Union (AU), and the Organisation of Islamic Conference (OIC) and underlined the Libyan government's responsibility to protect its population.

On 12 March, the LAS (2011) called on the UN Security Council

> *to take the necessary measures to impose immediately a no-fly zone on Libyan military aviation and to establish safe areas in places exposed to shelling as a precautionary measure that allows the protection of the Libyan people and foreign nationals residing in Libya, while respecting the sovereignty and territorial integrity of neighbouring States.*

It moreover urged the international community to

> *cooperate and communicate with the Transitional National Council (TNC) of Libya and to provide the Libyan people with urgent and continuing support as well as the necessary protection from the serious violations and grave crimes committed by the Libyan authorities, which have consequently lost their legitimacy.* (LAS, 2011)

It was in this context, that the Security Council members debated whether to authorise the use of force to establish a no-fly zone and to protect civilians. One of the central arguments made in the Council, and outside, was that the situation in Libya was both an ongoing threat to international peace and security and a humanitarian crisis that was likely to get significantly worse without urgent and decisive action. On 17 March Resolution 1973 passed with ten votes in favour (Bosnia and Herzegovina, Colombia, France, Gabon, Lebanon, Portugal, Nigeria, South Africa, the

United Kingdom, and the United States), zero votes against, and five abstentions (Brazil, China, Germany, India and Russia).

The resolution initially reiterated the Council's concern that crimes against humanity may have been committed, deplored the ongoing humanitarian crisis, and took note of the criticisms of Gaddafi's regime made by a variety of international organisations, particularly the LAS call for a no-fly zone and safe areas to protect civilians. Once again, it defined the situation in Libya as a threat to international peace and security and, acting under Chapter VII of the UN Charter, demanded, among other things, an immediate cease-fire and intensified efforts to find a political solution to the crisis. In paragraph 4, the Council authorised the use of "all necessary measures ... to protect civilians and civilian populated areas under threat of attack ... while excluding a foreign occupation force of any form on any part of the Libyan territory." In paragraph 6, it established a "ban on all flights in the airspace of the Libya Arab Jamahiriya in order to help protect civilians." The only exceptions were those flights necessary to enforce the no-fly zone and those "whose sole purpose is humanitarian" (paragraph 7). It also refined the arms embargo and asset freezes detailed in Resolution 1970, in part by creating a panel of experts to assist in their implementation.

UN Resolution 1973 stated explicitly that the primary goal of the intervention is the protection of civilians. There was however a discrepancy between the goals stated in the resolution and the political call for regime change issued by those implementing them. In May 2011, the International Coalition for the Responsibility to Protect (ICRtoP) warned "not to undermine RtoP by confusing civilian protection with other motives such as regime change or resource control" (ICRtoP, 2011).

Although Resolution 1973 would not have been issued if it was not for the existence of several political factors that were unique to the situation in Libya, the analysis of the UN discourse shows that the RtoP was taken into consideration and thus guided political decision-making on the international level (Williams and Bellamy, 2012). Remarkably, Resolutions 1970 and 1973 referred merely to Libya's responsibility to protect and did not explicitly mention the responsibility of the international community to protect the Libyan population. The application of the RtoP by the UN in the case of the Libyan crisis therefore emphasised the most commonly accepted part of the emerging norm – the responsibility of each state to protect its own citizens. The other components of the RtoP norm – pillar 2 and 3 – were left open for interpretation. The analysis of the EU and its member states responses to the Libyan crisis throughout the next sections will show that pillar 2 and 3 of the RtoP are – as in previous instances – not interpreted consistently across different cases. While diverging interpretations of the RtoP do not necessarily impede its influence, they certainly impede the development of the RtoP into a collective international norm.

The EU response

Representing the common position of the EU member states, the High Representative of the EU for Foreign Affairs and Security Policy (HR), Catherine, Ashton, reacted to the unfolding events in Libya on 20 February 2011. A declaration was issued stating that the EU "condemns the repression against peaceful demonstrators and deplores the violence and death of civilians" (Ashton, 20 February 2011). The EU moreover urged the Libyan "authorities ... to immediately refrain from further use of violence" (idem). On 23 February, President of the European Council, Herman Van Rompuy, stated that the EU

> *should not be patronizing, but should also not shy away from using its political and moral responsibility. While the decision on the future of Libya should be made by its citizens, the EU's ... responsibility is to help.*

A few weeks later, on 11 March, the extraordinarily convened European Council declared that

> *the safety of the people must be ensured by all necessary means. The European Council expresses its deep concern about attacks against civilians, including from the air. In order to protect the civilian population, Member States will examine all necessary options, provided that there is a demonstrable need, a clear legal basis and support from the region. Those responsible will be held accountable and face grave consequences.*

The EU welcomed the adoption of Resolution 1973 and stressed that the main aim of the resolution was the protection of the Libyan civilians: "Resolution 1973 provides a clear legal basis for the members of the international community to provide protection to the civilian population" (Van Rompuy and Ashton, 17 March 2011). In line with other voices in the international community, the EU agreed that the Gaddafi regime had lost all its legitimacy and that he had to relinquish power. The EU described the situation as a "humanitarian emergency", to which it was committed to respond (idem). Catherine Ashton emphasised that it "is key for the European Union that we look at what we can do to strengthen economic sanctions and to intensify our humanitarian support for the people of Libya" (Ashton, 18 March 2011).

The Foreign Affairs Council confirmed a couple of days later that "while contributing in a differentiated way, the EU and its Member States are determined to act collectively and resolutely ... to give full effect to these decisions [taken by the UNSC]" (FAC, 21 March 2011). It underlined that "the Council and the EU Member States will support actions provided for by UNSCR 1973 necessary to protect civilians and civilian populated areas under threat of attack" (idem). Finally, the Council declared that "the EU is ready to provide CSDP support to humanitarian assistance in response to a request from OCHA[83] and under the coordinating role of the UN" (idem).

Sven Biscop claimed in March 2011 that "... the EU, as a distinctive actor waging a value-based foreign policy, has a moral responsibility to protect civilians against violence" (Biscop, 2011a: 1). However, the Libyan crisis proved not to be the EU's finest hour. While the EU officially supported the adoption of Resolution 1973 and the authorisation of the use of force, the actual action taken on the EU level was nevertheless limited to civilian means of crisis management (Gottwald, 2012a).

The European Commission reacted by putting into effect two of its disposable crisis management instruments: the civil protection mechanism, by which approximately 5,800 EU citizens have been brought back to their home countries, and humanitarian assistance, under which the Commission together with some member states had provided over €144.8 million for humanitarian aid and civil protection until 30 May (European Commission, 2011). Additionally, EU field experts in humani-

83 The United Nations Office for the Coordination of Humanitarian Affairs (OCHA).

tarian aid and civil protection have been deployed inside Libya and on its borders with Tunisia, Egypt, Algeria and Chad (idem). Regarding the migrant influx from North Africa, the EU responded to Italy's formal request for support and launched FRONTEX Joint Operation Hermes 2011, mandated to assist Italian authorities in coping with ongoing and prospective migratory flows (FRONTEX News, 2011).

The EU implemented the sanctions authorised by the UN Security Council and went even further. Council decision 2011/137/CFSP aimed at implementing UNSC resolution 1970 requesting an arms embargo and targeted sanctions. Council decision 2011/137/CFSP was amended according to UNSC resolution 1973 with the aim of implementing the no-fly zone and extending the asset freeze to additional persons as well as to the Libyan National Oil Cooperation and five of its subsidiaries. These restrictive measures had been extended further on 12 April and on 7 June 2011.

On 1 April the European Council issued the decision to set up a military mission, called EUFOR Libya. Tied to a request made by the UN Office for the Coordination of Humanitarian Affairs (OCHA), EUFOR Libya would be deployed with the aim of contributing to the safe movement and evacuation of displaced persons and of supporting the delivery of humanitarian aid (Official Journal of the EU, 2011). In April 2011 the EU decided to offer EUFOR Libya in support of the UN's efforts in its humanitarian work. Although "human security has been the primary motive for setting up EUFOR Libya, it was legally created very quickly and thus not very concretely defined" (Interview with Finnish Civil Servant, 8 July 2011). In response to the offer made by the EU, UN humanitarian chief Valerie Amos expressed concerns about the "blurred lines" between military and humanitarian action and said that EUFOR Libya was considered a measure of last resort (EuBusiness, 2011).

A Concept of Operations (CONOPS) for EUFOR Libya was developed during an extraordinary meeting of the EU Military Committee on 11 April, but the Foreign Affairs Council on 12 April approved neither the CONOPS nor an Operation Plan for a potential EUFOR mission, since Sweden was opposed to making such a decision during the Council meeting. Significantly, Sweden was the framework nation of one of the two 'battlegroups' on stand-by, whose deployment was considered in the context of Libya (Bloching, 2011). As part of the Nordic battlegroup Finland also expressed concerns about the deployment of ground troops. Finnish Foreign Minister Alexander Stubb warned of getting into a "stalemate" leading to "more of a Kosovo situation ..." (Marsden, 2011). The EU's response in setting up EUFOR Libya was not supported by all member states, nor did it seem to fulfil the UN's needs and thus appeared to be rather a symbolic gesture (Koenig, 2011).

The fact that there was disagreement concerning the practical implementation of the RtoP with military means cannot only be seen in the diverging opinions about setting up EUFOR Libya but moreover in Germany's abstention from the UNSC voting on Resolution 1973 and its reluctance to participate in the military intervention in Libya. Although the EU officially fully supported the RtoP approach taken by the UN and aimed explicitly at ensuring the protection of civilians throughout its crisis response, disagreement among the member states on the actual implementation of the RtoP revealed different interpretations of the emerging norm. Heads of state and governments eventually agreed on the need for Gaddafi to cede power but the EU member states remained at odds with each other on how best to respond to the crisis. Significantly, the three biggest EU member states – France, Britain and Germany – openly opposed each other in the UNSC voting on the no-fly zone over Libya. On the one hand, the differing European responses to the Libyan crisis revealed once more the difficulties the EU faces in having a *common* foreign and security policy. On the other hand, the apparent weakness in the EU's crisis response has been linked to the lack of leadership, with the HR being pulled in different directions by national leaders, as well as with the still premature institutional set-up of the EEAS (Gottwald, 2012a).

Furthermore, Lady Ashton has emphasised that her vision for Europe's role in the world is primarily civilian. On several occasions throughout the crisis she repeatedly insisted that the EU should confine itself to humanitarian issues (Brattberg, 2011: 3). The ambitions of the EU to become a fully-fledged power with military capabilities have thus experienced another setback in the Libyan crisis. During a speech in February, Ashton declared that the EU "is not a traditional military power ... it cannot deploy gunboats or bombers" (quoted in Brattberg, 2011: 4). Similarly, Joe Coelmont (2011: 3) concluded that "Europe has now passed the Rubicon of engaging in a military intervention ...".

Although the EU's response was clearly influenced by the RtoP, when comparing the EU's rhetoric to the practical implementation of its crisis response, a gap between discourse and action appears. The EU openly supported a people-centred approach in its crisis management and backed the UN's application of the RtoP. However, it remained unable to translate this support into action due to disagreement among the member states and a lack of capabilities. The analysis of the EU's actual crisis response reveals the imbalance between military and civilian crisis management and moreover the lack of an integrated civil-military approach. While the EU was successful in the area of civilian crisis management, a response using its military capabilities remained virtually non-existent.

4.2 National perceptions of the Libyan crisis

The way the Libyan crisis is perceived in the official discourses of France, Germany and the UK is assumed to lay the ground for later justifications of the actual policies proposed and adopted. The analysis of the member states' discourse starts by looking at how the situation in Libya was depicted and whether and at what stage it was influenced by the RtoP. In general, the better the later proposed policy fits the type and amount of information at the beginning of the crisis the higher the legitimacy will be. This means, in this case specifically, that – according to the scale of measuring the RtoP's influence in chapter 2 – the legitimacy of the RtoP increases if it is not only used to frame the crisis but also as basis for the later adopted policy.

France

On 21 February 2011, the French government raised serious concerns about the development of the situation in Libya vis-à-vis the severe repression that had been taken place throughout the previous days (Point de presse, 21 February 2011). The French President, Nicolas Sarkozy, condemned the use of force of the Libyan government against its own people and called for an end of the violence through a political solution (Communiqué de la Presidence, 21 February 2011). At the same time, France seemed initially occupied primarily with the security and the repatriation of French citizens resident in Libya: "Our real preoccupation is to ensure the security of the French in Libya" (Wauquiez, 21 February 2011)[84].

The events in Libya were described as "massacres" for the first time in the French discourse on 22 February. However, when asked for more concrete information on the situation in Libya in general and the massacres specifically, the official answer remained vague (Point de presse, 22 February 2011). The spokesperson of the French Foreign Ministry referred to a press statement given by the French President in which he had condemned the disproportionate use of violence in Libya but remained unable to provide a precise number of (civilian) victims. The claim by the Italian Foreign Minister, Franco Frattini, that the repression in Libya had already caused 1000 victims, was not confirmed by the French government. The French Foreign Minister explained that the situation in the country was too confusing to be able

84 "Notre vraie préoccupation c'est d'assurer la sécurité des Français en Libye."

to provide a reliable number of victims (Point de presse, 24 February 2011). At the same time the French *porte-de-parole* emphasised that the repressions of the Libyan government against the protesters had caused "too many" victims.

The description of the events in Libya changed from "massacres", to "massive human rights violations" to "alleged crimes of humanity". On 23 February, the French President called on the international community to not to merely stand aside and watch the massive human rights violations that were committed in Libya. One day later the French Foreign Minister, Michèle Alliot-Marie, claimed that the violence in Libya "could constitute crimes against humanity" (Alliot-Marie, 24 February 2011). Gerard Araud, the French Permanent Representative to the UN, accused the Libyan government further of a "systematic, planned and massive repression of their own population" (Araud, 25 February 2011)[85]. He stated further that the severity of the situation was further confirmed by "menacing declarations from the Libyan direction" (Araud, 26 February 2011)[86].

More precise information on the conflict in Libya was firstly presented to the *Assemblée Nationale* on 2 March. According to the Libyan Human Rights, almost 6000 people had died until the beginning of March 2011 as "victims of the organised terror by the Libyan Dictator M. Gaddafi, who, after having organised assassinations in the world, is now killing his own people" (Ayrault, Assemblée Nationale, 2 March 2011)[87]. On the same occasion, Sarkozy affirmed that the Libyan crisis was of exceptional seriousness and that the Colonel Gaddafi had lost all his legitimacy (Sarkozy, Assemblée Nationale, 2 March 2011).

Recalling UNSC Resolution, France referred to the RtoP for the first time on 26 February. The French Ambassador reminded that it is the Libyan authorities' responsibility to protect all citizens on their territory. At the same time he emphasised that Resolution 1970 implied both "the responsibility of each state to protect its own citizens as well as the responsibility of the international community to intervene

85 "Les autorités libyennes répriment de manière systematique, massive et planifiée leur propre population."
86 "Déclaration menaçantes de la direction libyenne."
87 "Nous venons effectivement d'apprendre de la ligue libyenne des droits de l'homme que déjà près de 6000 personnes sont mortes, victime de la terreur organise par le dictateur libyen M. Kadhafi, qui, après avoir organisé des attentats dans le monde, est en train d'assassiner son propre peuple."

if a state fails to comply with the first responsibility" (Araud, 26 February 2011)[88]. In a joint press conference with British Foreign Secretary, William Hague, French Foreign Minister, Alain Juppé, reiterated that the international community had to step in and assume its responsibility since "all the mediation directed towards letting Gaddafi be succeeded was not welcome (Juppé, 3 March 2011)[89]. From the beginning, the responsibility to protect the Libyan people of the international community seemed therefore to be linked to the goal of regime change.

On 10 March, Nicolas Sarkozy and David Cameron agreed that

> *the world is witnessing an unacceptable prosecution of violence and repression in Libya. Ignoring the exigencies of Resolution 1970 and the appeals of regional organisations and the whole international community, Gaddafi continues to attack its population with airplanes and helicopters"* (Sarkozy and Cameron, 10 March 2011)[90].

On 15 March, Laurent Wauquiez, Secretary of State for European Affairs, described the situation in Libya as "extremely worrying". Gaddafi's forces were taking over more and more ground from the opposition forces and were moving towards Benghazi. Due to the increasing number of air raids the threats for the civilian population were perceived as ever more important (idem). In the French Parliament, the situation was described in similar terms: "Gaddafi's forces were quickly taking over ground at the cost of massacres and attacks of the civilian population" (Assemblée Nationale, 15 March 2011)[91]. Finally, on the day of the adoption of UNSC Resolution 1973, Juppé depicted the conflict as "murderous offensive of Gaddafi against his civilian population" (Juppé, 17 March 2011)[92].

88 "Ce texte … rappelle la responsabilité de chaque Etat à protéger sa population et de la communauté international à intervenir lorsque les Etats manquent à leur devoir."

89 "Les Nation unies, je vous rappelle, ont adopté il y a quelques années un nouveau concept qui est la responsabilité de protéger – 'the responsibility to protect' – les gouvernements doivent protéger les populations contre les crimes de guerre et quand ils ne le font pas, la communauté internationale est fondée à se substituer à eux. On en est là aujourd'hui et donc toute médiation visant à permettre au colonel Kadhafi de se succéder à lui-même n'est évidemment pas la bienvenue."

90 "Le monde est témoin quotidiennement d'une poursuite inacceptable de la violence et de la répression en Libye. Ignorant l'exigence de la résolution 1970 du Conseil de sécurité des Nations unie, les appels des organisations régionales et de toute la communauté internationale, le régime de Kadhafi continue à attaquer sa population, y compris avec des avions et de hélicoptères."

91 "Les forces du colonel Kadhafi regagnent rapidement du terrain, aux prix de massacres et de bombardements de la population civile."

92 "L'offensive meurtrière de Kadhafi contre ses populations civiles."

Although struggling to provide any detailed information and precise numbers on the crisis in Libya, France described the violence from the outset as disproportionate and unacceptable. In line with the worsening of the conflict and the increase in violence, the French discourse became stronger in its description of the crisis. Initially perceived as a brutal and bloody repression, then as massacres possibly constituting crimes against humanity and finally as murderous offensive of the Libyan government against its own population. Against this background the French government argued that the international community had the responsibility to step in. However, the RtoP appeared in the French discourse only after the UNSC had issued Resolution 1970. The reason given for the shift of responsibility from the Libyan government to the international community was that Gaddafi refused to step down. France, thus, framed the crisis in Libya as an RtoP case inspired by the UN but mixed the aim of protection with the objective of regime change.

Germany

The German Foreign Minister referred to the RtoP at an earlier point of time in the Libyan crisis than France but interpreted it differently. On 22 February 2011, Guido Westerwelle, called on the UNSC to assume its responsibility to protect the Libyan people and to react by authorising sanctions against the Gaddafi regime at the international level (Westerwelle, 22 February 2011). In contrast to France, Germany referred particularly to the responsibility of the UNSC and not of the international community as a whole. Furthermore, Germany indicated that the RtoP should be restricted to political and economic measures.

Due to the limited amount of precise information on the situation inside Libya, Germany appeared more reluctant than France in describing the evolving conflict. On 24 February, State Minister Hoyer described the Libyan crisis as the "opposite of what we define human, ethical and responsible …" (Hoyer, 24 February 2011)[93]. Referring to a recent media address by Gaddafi, the Minister further expressed doubts about the Libyan leader's sense of reality. He portrayed the situation in Libya as "dangerous" and "confusing" (idem). As in the case of France, Germany's initial primary concern was the repatriation of German and other European citizens.

93 "Wenn wir in diesen Tagen auf Libyen schauen, dann sehen wir dort genau das Gegenteil dessen, was wir als human, ethisch und verantwortbar bezeichnen ..."

On 25 February, Guido Westerwelle described the situation in Libya as a "war of the regime against his own people". He acknowledged that massive human rights violations and atrocities were taking place in Libya and emphasised at the same time the need of an emergency meeting of the UNSC in order to agree on a range of political and economic sanction, such as visa bans and asset freezes (Westerwelle, 25 February 2011). Asked by a journalist whether the claim made by Jean Asselborn that a genocide was taking place in Libya would imply considering a military intervention in Libya, the Foreign Minister denied that claim. Faced with a civil war rather than genocide, Westerwelle argued, the international community should find a political solution to the crisis not a military one (idem). Instead of accepting that the Libyan government has failed in its responsibility to protect its own people, Germany emphasised that the perpetrators of the violence will be held accountable "if necessary ... before the International Criminal Court" (Westerwelle, 28 February 2011).

Similarly to the French discourse, Germany reported the occurrence of gross human rights violations and atrocities in Libya without initially being able or willing to provide any precise numbers of victims. From the outset, Germany labelled the crisis in Libya as an RtoP case and emphasised the responsibility of the UNSC to respond with non-coercive means. Whereas France seemed to avoid the use of war attributes, Germany described the crisis in Libya as war and civil war. The appropriate answer to such a crisis was, according to Germany, to find a political solution and not to become a warring party itself by the use of military force.

The United Kingdom

Even before Germany and France, the British Foreign Secretary, William Hague, expressed his concern about the "unacceptable violence used against protesters in Libya" on 19 February 2011. However, similarly lacking a concrete assessment of the situation on the ground Hague vaguely referred to alarming "reports of large numbers of people being killed or attacked by Libyan security forces" (Hague, 20 February 2011). On 21 February 2011, the UK called on the Libyan government "to take responsibility for the safety of its people" (idem).

Differing from German and French descriptions of the situation in Libya, William Hague, portrayed the crisis as "a danger to the people" that "could have serious implications for the wider region" (Hague, 22 February 2011). Although initially prioritising the "safety of British nationals in Libya" the Foreign Secretary expressed concerns "about the loss of life in Libya and their government's failure to protect its own people" from the beginning (Hague, 23 February 2011).

The descriptions of the conflict and the hostilities were much more detailed in the official UK discourse than in the French or the German documentation. In a statement to the House of Commons on 7 March, William Hague described at full length, in which part of Libya what kind of atrocities were committed. The Foreign Secretary concluded that there was a clear risk of a protracted conflict and "an extremely dangerous and volatile situation in large parts of the country" (Hague, House of Commons, 7 March 2011).

> *The Quadhafi regime is launching military counter-attacks against the opposition forces. There has been intense fighting in the East and centre of the country along the coastal strip between the opposition-held Ras Lanuf and the Quadhafi stronghold of Sirte. There are credible reports of the use of helicopter gunships against civilians by government forces, and unconfirmed reports of a helicopter and jet shot down over Ras Lanuf… In Tripoli there have been disturbing reports of hostage taking and large military deployments around the city designed to consolidate Quadhafi's position and intimidate his opponents. His forces remain in control of Tripoli, Sebha and Sirte; but his authority is contested in large swathes of the country where local tribes have withdrawn their support* (idem).

On the adoption of Resolution 1973, Sir Mark Lyall Grant, UK Ambassador to the UN, explained that "the situation in Libya is clear. A violent, discredited regime which has lost all legitimacy is using weapons of war against civilians." Besides having ignored UNSC Resolution 1970,

> *it is now preparing for a violent assault on a city of one million people that has a history dating back 2500 years. It has begun airstrikes in anticipation of what we expect to be a brutal attack using air, land and sea forces. Gaddafi has publicly promised no mercy and no pity* (Grant, 17 March 2011).

The UK labelled the crisis in Libya as an RtoP case and in contrast to France and Germany acknowledged that the Libyan government was failing in its responsibility to protect. However, initially it did not indicate who was supposed to assume the responsibility if not the Libyan government. Moreover, the UK was the first to point out the potential consequences of the Libyan crisis to the wider region. France Germany and the UK seemed to agree that the RtoP applied to the Libyan crisis. However, the emphasis ranged from the RtoP of the international community (France), to the RtoP of the UNSC (Germany) to the failure of the Libyan government to assume its RtoP (UK). The ambivalences within Europe on the exact meaning of the RtoP in practice were exposed even more in the decision-making processes on the actual policy response and leading up to the military intervention.

National perspectives on the role of the EU

The role of the EU as a security actor depends not only on the availability of crisis management capabilities but also on what kind of role the member states envisage for the EU to play in the crisis response. According to Nicolas Sarkozy, the response of the European Council was strongly determined, particularly in comparison to previous crises such as in Bosnia that had revealed the complete lack of a European response. Laurent Wauquiez emphasised in a similar comparison that Europe has come a long way: "Considering its inability to respond to Srebrenica the EU has proven its ability to respond to events in Libya" (Wauquiez, 12 May 2011)[94]. At the same time the French President noted that a strong European response does not imply that there are no differences in the member states' approaches to the crisis (Sarkozy, 11 March 2011). Alain Juppé emphasised further that convening an extraordinary meeting of the European Council to talk about Libya already constituted a very important step for the role of the EU as a security actor (Juppé, 17 March 2011).

Since the European Council acknowledged that Resolution 1973 "contributed significantly to protect the Libyan people and the civilian areas threatened by attacks and helped save lives of civilians"[95] in the aftermath of the UNSC voting, the decisi-

94 "Toutefois, il convient, là encore, de mesurer le chemin parcouru entre une Europe qui avait révélé son impuissance à Srebrenica et, à l'inverse, une Europe qui s'est montrée malgré tout capable de réagir face aux événements survenus en Libye."

95 "... contribué à protéger les populations et les zones civiles menacées d'attaques et ont contribué à sauver la vie de civils."

on to implement the Resolution was taken unanimously by the European countries. According to France, this agreement has significantly strengthened Europe (Juppé, 24 March 2011). Furthermore, the European Council defined the conditions that were set out in Resolution 1973 to end the military intervention as proposed by France (idem). When civilians are safe and the objectives of Resolution 1973 are met, the military operation will be completed.

Finally, the French Foreign Minister affirmed that the role of the EU in finding a solution to the crisis in Libya mainly relates to the use of peaceful measures (Juppé, Assemblée Nationale, 30 March 2011). First, the EU should continue to increase pressure on Gaddafi's departure through sanctions, followed by its readiness to support the Libyan people in their transition to democracy. Furthermore, it should continue to support humanitarian and civil protection also by maritime means. Finally, with regard to the EU's security and defence policy, Le Monde reported on 22 March 2011 Juppé passing a shattering assessment: "The common security and defence policy of Europe? It is dead."[96] (Stroobants, 2011)

Responding to the criticism that the EU's High Representative Catherine Ashton had been completely absent in the Libyan conflict, Juppé countered that Lady Ashton had been very active in the preparation of the "day after" (Juppé, 29 August 2011). She was responsible of the EU's involvement in humanitarian action and will take care of building the rule of law and of monitoring new elections. Juppé clarified further that it was 'normal' that during the period of military intervention, the focus has been put on NATO rather than the EU.[97] At the same time, the Foreign Minister noted that in case a 'peace building' mission was to be deployed to Libya in the aftermath of the military intervention, this task should be shouldered by the UN rather than the EU.

96 "La politique de sécurité et de défense commune de l'Europe ? Elle est morte."

97 "Elle n'a pas été tout à fait absente. À chaque réunion du Conseil Affaires étrangères, sous sa présidence, nous avons discuté de la Libye. Elle est très active sur la préparation du 'jour d'après', l'implication de l'Union européenne dans l'action humanitaire, dans la construction d'un État de droit, et dans la surveillance des élections : l'Union européenne sera très présente. Il était normal que dans la période militaire, le projecteur ait été mis sur l'Otan, plus que sur l'Union européenne."

In August 2011, the French President concluded that there are lessons to be learned particularly for Europe:

> *In this crisis, through the initiative of the United Kingdom ... the Europeans have demonstrated for the first time that they were able to intervene decisively in a conflict on Europe's doorstep – because Libya is in the Mediterranean, and the Mediterranean is primarily the business of Europe rather than an America affair ... Again this is a remarkable improvement since the wars in Bosnia and Kosovo, where Europe was going to beg for help from the Americans to do a job Europe did not have the courage to do at its doorsteps.* (Sarkozy, 31 August 2011)[98]

At the beginning of February, just before the violent outbreak of the Libyan crisis, the German Foreign Minister, Guido Westerwelle, set out his perspective of the EU's CSDP and its role as a security actor:

> *An essential element in the global role of the European Union is a powerful security and defence policy. As the largest economic area and trade power, as a community of values and merger of liberal democracies, the European Union has an interest in stable and peaceful conditions in the world. The necessary engagement for that cannot be left to the U.S. and other countries. The development of the Common Security and Defence Policy – to protect against terrorism, to secure trade and shipping routes or to manage crises – will essentially decide to what extent Europe will participate shaping world affairs.* (Westerwelle, 4 February 2011)

However, with regard to the EU's role in the Libyan crisis Westerwelle continuously emphasised that the EU should respond with economic sanctions, asset freezes and humanitarian aid. At the same time, the German Foreign Minister noted that the EU needed to revise its neighbourhood policy in order to be able to address problems such as in Libya. Also advising against a military role of the EU, David

98 "Elle n'a pas été tout à fait absente. À chaque réunion du Conseil Affaires étrangères, sous sa présidence, nous avons discuté de la Libye. Elle est très active sur la préparation du «jour d'après», l'implication de l'Union européenne dans l'action humanitaire, dans la construction d'un État de droit, et dans la surveillance des élections : l'Union européenne sera très présente. Il était normal que dans la période militaire, le projecteur ait été mis sur l'Otan, plus que sur l'Union européenne."

Cameron stated at the beginning of March 2011 that "in terms of the European Council, of course, the EU is not a military alliance. And there is always a hesitation discussing military options" (Cameron, 14 March 2011). Still, he advocated for a strong response in the international community – "Europe included" (idem).

After the establishment of the no-fly zone over Libya, William Hague, pointed towards the role of the EU as a normative power in its response to the Libyan crisis:

> *It is very important that not only in Libya, but in north Africa as a whole, the UK and the European Union . . act as a magnet for positive change – for civil society, open political systems, the building up of small and medium-sized enterprises, and all the other building blocks of democracy – but we cannot guarantee the outcome, of course. That is why we must make sure Europe provides a very big and effective magnet for those changes.* (Hague, House of Commons, 30 March 2011)

Neither France, Germany nor the UK saw a substantial role of the EU going beyond the application of civilian means. Although France defended the contribution of Europe in general and the HR specifically, it was made clear that the EU's task was "to clean up the dishes" in the sense that it was responsible to support the reconstruction of and democratic transition in Libya. Juppé even stated that the CSDP could be buried after Libya. While Germany was against the use of military force altogether, the UK naturally preferred to rely on NATO as military alliance and not the EU. It was acknowledged that the EU's role as a security actor has increased substantially since the Kosovo crisis in 1999 and that Europe was able to respond decisively to the Libyan crisis. However, large parts of the European response took place outside the EU institutional framework and would not have been possible without US support. The EU's role as a security actor in case of the Libyan crisis was therefore if anything, a reluctant one.

4.3 National responses to the Libyan crisis

While all three member states included in this analysis framed the Libyan crisis as a RtoP case, the following sections will focus on whether the RtoP was used further in the decision-making process and in the implementation of actual policies in response to the Libyan crisis. According to the scale developed in chapter 2 of this study, the influence of the RtoP will be the highest if it is present in the discourse on the proposed policy, if it is used as basis for the choice of the actual policy and if this policy is then implemented accordingly. The previous section has shown that the main aim of European and international responses to the Libyan crisis was the protection of Libyan civilians, as also stated in UNSC Resolution 1973. At the same time, there was agreement that Gaddafi had lost all its legitimacy and was therefore urged to step down. However, the objective of regime change was neither compatible with Resolution 1973 nor with the RtoP and was therefore potentially undermining the influence of the latter.

France

On the outbreak of the Libyan crisis, France emphasised that its foreign policy was based on two principles: "non-interference into a state's internal affairs and respect of universal values, human rights, freedom and democracy" (Point de presse, 17 February 2011)[99]. Yet, only a few days later, the French Foreign Minister mentioned for the first time the option of a military operation in Libya (Alliot-Marie, 25 February 2011). In this context, François Fillon, affirmed that the establishment of a military no-fly zone would be considered as an option only under two conditions: First, there would have to be a decision by the UN Security Council (which seemed unlikely at the end of February, according to the First Minister). Second, a military intervention could only take place in cooperation with "other big countries" because no European state had the means to realise such an operation on its own (Fillon, 28 February 2011).

Laurent Wauquiez expressed further concerns about how a military operation implemented by NATO would be perceived by neighbouring countries in Libya and

99 "La politique de la France demeure fondée sur deux principes : la non-ingérence dans les affaires intérieures des Etats et l'attachement à des valeurs universelle, le respect des droits de l'Homme, la liberté et la démocraties."

whether such a venture was feasible at all. The Secretary of State supposed that a NATO operation would stir criticism, that the West is intervening because of Libya's crude oil resources and would thus send the wrong political signal. Moreover, he doubted whether France had the capabilities to establish a no-fly zone over a country four times larger than France itself. France, although strongly in favour of intervention, was thus initially reluctant to give NATO a major role.

At the beginning of March, Nicolas Sarkozy stated that the international community had developed a strategy to put pressure on the Gaddafi regime in the "spirit" of the RtoP (Sarkozy, 2 March 2011). He emphasised that on a Franco-British initiative and based on the RtoP, the UNSC had adopted Resolution 1970 imposing not only sanctions but also including a referral to the ICC (idem). Sarkozy argued that a military option did not (yet) fit the context but affirmed that France would pay close attention to further decisions that might be taken in the UNSC (idem).

Moving forward quickly, only a day later, the French and the British Foreign Minister announced that they agreed to start working on the planning of a no-fly zone which would be implemented if the use of force by the Libyan regime against the civilian population became "more concrete" (Juppé, 3 March 2011). Juppé explained further that the conditions for the implementation of the Franco-British plan would be a "clearer situation" on the ground as well as the support of other countries in the region (idem). He emphasised that it should not be an intervention of Western countries only.

Accordingly, the demand of the League of Arab States (LAS) for a no-fly zone over Libya from 4 March 2011 changed the dynamic in the international community's response to the crisis (Araud, 4 March 2011). The French Ambassador to the UN, Gerard Araud, underlined that the logic of the UN was based on the principle of non-interference mainly "because the Western countries are always suspected of wanting to intervene" (idem). Although the Libyan crisis was clearly an internal affair, he argued, Arabic and African countries were the ones asking for an intervention by UN Security Council. Therefore this was not a case of Western countries trying to impose "a certain number of values" but it was the Arabic and the African countries that "conducted this assault" (idem).

Ahead of the Extraordinary European Council on 11 March, Sarkozy and Cameron agreed that there were three conditions for the implementation of a military operation in Libya: (1) A demonstrable need (which was already given since the Libyan population was being attacked from the air); (2) a clear legal basis (in the form a UNSC Resolution); and (3) regional support (by the LAS and the African Union). Sarkozy reminded further that the situation in Libya could not be compared to the events in Tunisia and Egypt due to the different levels of repression and brutality:

> *Acts of war crime are taking place in Libya. I believe that war crimes were also committed in Egypt and in Tunisia. A political revolution is carried out with violence, naturally, but in Libya we are confronted with bombed villages, bombed oil platforms, this is not comparable.* (Sarkozy, 11 March 2011)[100]

At the same time, Sarkozy stressed that considering the option of a military intervention in the case of Libya did not constitute a change in France's diplomacy or even a new doctrine and affirmed that he was among the first to express reservations about the use of force. However, the French President saw a difference between "refusing a military intervention and letting people be massacred by fighter jets while they were demonstrating"[101] (idem).

Trying to persuade the other members of the UNSC to follow France's lead, Sarkozy wrote a letter requesting the heads of state and government to assume their responsibility and to support the proposed initiative on the day before the historical voting on Resolution 1973. On 17 March, Alain Juppé also called on to the international community to stop the incitement of war by supporting the civilian population and not letting international legality and moral be jeopardised (Juppé, 17 March 2011). When asked whether the intervention was to be a war against Colonel Gaddafi, the Foreign Minister replied that it was not a war but an operation designed for the protection of the civilian population. Gerard Araud described Resolution 1973 as a historical moment, in which "the UN got involved into a state's internal affairs on

100 "Il y a des actes de guerre en Libye. Je ne pense qu'il y ait eu des actes de guerre en Égypte ou des actes de guerre en Tunisie. Il y a eu une révolution politique avec de violences, naturellement, mais là on est dans des villes bombardées, des terminaux pétroliers bombardées, cela n'a rien à voir."

101 "Mais, entre refuser une intervention militaire et laisser des gens massacrés par des avions de chasse alors qu'ils manifestent, il y a peut-être à réfléchir sur ce que l'on fait ..."

behalf of the RtoP, on behalf of our duty to help people in danger"[102] (Araud, 23 March 2011).

However, doubts about the legitimacy as well as the aim of the military intervention were raised not only by French journalists but also within the French Parliament. On the question of how France was able to reconcile its policy of non-interference with a military intervention aimed at removing Gaddafi from power, the answer was merely that "it should not be forgotten that Gaddafi soldiers were massacring the Libyan people"[103] (Point de presse, 18 March 2011). Furthermore, the question posed in *Assemblée National* on whether the military intervention in Libya was established to protect the Libyan people or the Libyan oil, remained unanswered (Assemblée Nationale, 8 March 2011).

After the implementation of Resolution 1973, Sarkozy argued that the international community was able to prevent a "massacre" from occurring in Libya. He highlighted the events in Srebrenica 1995 where "... 8000 people were killed ... because the international community did not adopt the measures to prevent the massacre ... Imagine if the coalition had not acted, what would have happened in Benghazi"[104] (Sarkozy, 24 March 2011).

In line with its perception of the Libyan crisis as massacres possibly constituting crimes against humanity, France was among the first countries calling for a military intervention. Although also emphasising the principle of non-interference, France took the view that a military intervention would still be legitimate if based on (1) a clear legal basis, (2) a demonstrable need and (3) regional support. Acting as norm entrepreneur, France actively persuaded the other members of the UNSC to assume their responsibility to protect the Libyan civilians. While simultaneously calling on Gaddafi to step down, France confirmed after the adoption of Resolution 1973, that the UNSC decision provided the right measures to protect the people in Libya. At the same it was argued that a military intervention was better than doing nothing also with regard to the credibility of the UN and the validity of international law.

102 "L'ONU s'implique dans les affaires intérieures d'un État au nom de la responsabilité de protéger, au nom de notre devoir d'assistance à peuple en danger."

103 "Il ne faut pas s'oublier que les Libyen se font massacrer par la soldatesque de Kadhafi."

104 "... à Srebrenica en 1993, 8000 personnes ont été assassinée ... parce que la communauté internationale n'avait pas pris à l'époque les mesures pour empêcher ce massacre ... Imaginez, si la coalition n'avait pas agi, ce qui se serait passe á Benghazi."

Germany

The decision by the UN Security Council from 26 February to issue Resolution 1970, based on the RtoP, was welcomed by the German government. The imposition of sanctions, an arms embargo, an asset freeze and the referral of Gaddafi to the ICC for alleged crimes against humanity, were clearly in line with Germany's approach to the conflict. In the face of ongoing and increased violence in Libya and in line with its major Western partners, the German government was in favour of regime change in Libya and of protecting the Libyan people, but preferred addressing both aims with the use of peaceful means.

Accordingly, Germany remained openly sceptic of the creation of a no-fly zone over Libya, both regarding its operationalisation and its consequences. On 9 March, Foreign Minister Guido Westerwelle argued that it should be avoided so as not to be drawn into a civil war in Libya. He raised further concerns that a military intervention in Libya would provide 'fuel' for those arguing that the revolts in Libya were controlled by the West (Westerwelle, 9 March 2011). Westerwelle reiterated that it was crucial to have a mandate of the UNSC as well as the support of the LAS for the establishment of a no-fly zone (idem).

> *A no-fly zone is an option, but the German government remains reluctant because one has to consider the outcome of such decisions. We do not want to become delinquent in the sense that Germany becomes a permanent warring party. We should have learned from the experiences in Iraq. Everything that goes beyond targeted sanction requires a UN mandate. And it is compelling that neighbouring countries and the Arab League support or even participate in such measures.* (Westerwelle, 12 March 2011)[105]

On 16 March, the German Foreign Minister raised further concerns about whether a military intervention in a country like Libya, whose territory is four times bigger than Germany, would be the appropriate response. Westerwelle stated that "a no-

105 "Eine Flugverbotszone ist eine Option, aber die Bundesregierung ist hier zurückhaltend, denn man muss bei solchen Entscheidungen auch das Ende bedenken. Wir wolle nicht auf eine schiefe Ebene gerate, an deren Ende Deutschland dauerhafte Kriegspartei ist. Wir sollten aus den Erfahrungen insbesondere Irak gelernt haben. Alles, was über gezielte Sanktionen hinausgeht, braucht ein Mandat der Vereinten Nationen. Und: Es ist zwingend notwendig, dass die Nachbarländer und die Arabische Liga das nicht nur unterstützen, sondern sich gegebenenfalls an solchen Maßnahmen auch beteiligen."

fly zone is nothing like a traffic regulation ...". He argued further that a military intervention could lead to more violence instead of freedom and peace. In terms of the consequences of such an operation Westerwelle asked: "And what happens if the attacks continue on the ground? Would we then have to continue fighting Gaddafi's tanks from the air? Or would we have to send ground troops?"[106] (Westerwelle, 16 March 2011). At the same time he acknowledged that

> *the decision on the right approach towards the inhuman violence in Libya is not easy. As a member of the Security Council, Germany is particularly responsible in this difficult situation. We respect and welcome the resolution of the Arab League last week. However, we see the responsibility for further action on the side of the international community first of all with the countries in the region.* (Westerwelle, 15 March 2011)[107]

In the UNSC vote on Resolution 1973, mandating amongst other measures the establishment of a no-fly zone over Libya, Germany abstained. Germany, nevertheless, supported the reinforcement of the restrictive measures imposed by Resolution 1973 and underlined the importance of Gaddafi's referral to the ICC (Westerwelle, 17 March 2011). After the voting, Westerwelle explained that Germany did not want to "wage a war that would take place in Libya, even with international involvement. Therefore German soldiers will not participate in a war in Libya"[108] (idem). He argued further, that history has proven that war is not a solution.

On Germany's abstention in the UNSC, Ambassador Peter Wittig elaborated further that

106 "Aber was geschieht, wenn die Angriffe am Boden weitergehen? Müssen wir Gaddafis Panzer dann aus der Luft bekämpfen? Und wenn das nicht reicht, müssen wir dann Bodentruppen schicken?"

107 "Die Entscheidung über den richtigen Weg im Angesicht menschenverachtender Gewalt ist alles andere als einfach. Als Mitglied des Sicherheitsrates trägt Deutschland in dieser schwierigen Lage eine besondere Verantwortung für die internationale Sicherheit. Wir respektieren und begrüßen den Beschluss der Arabischen Liga vom vergangenen Wochenende. Aber wir sehen die Verantwortung für das weitere Handeln der international Staatengemeinschaft zuerst bei den Staaten in der Region."

108 "Die Frage ist aber, ob wir Deutschland in einen Krieg führen, der dann in Libyen stattfinden würde, auch mit internationaler Beteiligung, und dagegen habe ich mich gewendet. Ich möchte nicht, dass deutschen Soldaten in Libyen ein Krieg geführt wird."

> *if the steps proposed turn out to be ineffective, we see the danger of being drawn into a protracted military conflict that would affect the wider region. We should not enter a military confrontation on the optimistic assumption that quick results with few casualties will be achieved* (Wittig, 17 March 2011).

In the aftermath of the implementation of Resolution 1973, Germany officially recognised the legitimacy and the validity of the UNSC decision. However, the German Foreign Minister expressed concerns that the intervention in Libya could serve as a precedent for solving conflicts namely through the use of military force. "The injustices in North Africa cannot be solved by means of military intervention wherever a conflict arises", he argued. Furthermore, Westerwelle claimed that "Germany could not intervene anywhere in the world, where injustice happens, with military means"[109] (Westerwelle, 18 March 2011). At the same time, Germany's abstention was further justified with the fact that Germany "assumes worldwide a lot of responsibilities". While being militarily engaged in other arenas, such as Afghanistan, Germany did not see it as its responsibility to participate in a military intervention in Libya.

In a statement in front of the German Bundestag, Westerwelle emphasised that Germany

> *is on the side of all the people anywhere in the world that defend their freedom. We are on the side of all those that are repressed, tortured and murdered because they defend their freedom. We as a democracy are a community of values and therefore we argue worldwide for liberal and democratic values.* (Westerwelle, 18 March 2011)[110]

The Foreign Minister argued that when deciding whether to participate in a military intervention there are humanitarian aspects and the risk of civilian casualties that have to be considered (idem). Therefore the lessons from Iraq and Afghanistan

109 "Ich bitte auch ... immer zu bedenken, dass wir Deutsche nicht mit deutschen Soldaten überall in Ländern der Welt eingreifen können, wo Unrecht geschieht."

110 "Wir stehen an der Seite von Menschen, die für ihre Freiheit wo immer auf der Welt eintreten. Wir stehen an der Seite derjenigen, die wegen ihres Eintretens für demokratische Prinzipien unterdrückt, gequält, gefoltert, gemordet werden. Wir sind als Demokratie eine Wertegemeinschaft, und deswegen treten wir auch weltweit für freiheitliche und demokratische Werte ein."

should not be forgotten. Westerwelle reiterated his understanding for the "honourable motives" of those that voted in favour of international military engagement in Libya (idem). He assured, that his decision to abstain Germany had received respect and understanding among its partners.

As elaborated in the previous section, Germany has described the crisis in Libya as a civil war from the beginning. Accordingly its main argument against a response to the crisis with military means was to not to become a warring party in a protracted conflict. Germany's position on the Libya intervention reflected its general aversion against the use of force. Therefore its crisis response focused on non-coercive measures. Germany agreed that the Libyan people needed to be protected but saw the responsibility to protect primarily with the countries in the region. In contrast to France and in line with the UK, Germany emphasised the potential risks of a military intervention for the wider region. Finally, Germany expressed concerns that the international action in Libya might serve as a precedent for further military interventions.

The United Kingdom

On 28 February 2011, British Prime Minister David Cameron stated that

> *for the future of Libya and its people, Colonel Gaddafi's regime must end and he must leave. To that end we are taking every step possible to isolate the Gaddafi regime, deprive it of money, shrink its power and ensure that anyone in Libya will be held account. ... And we do not rule out the use of military assets.* (Cameron, 28 February 2011)

From the outset, the British response to the Libyan crisis seemed to be directed towards the removal of Gaddafi rather than the protection of the Libyan population. At the same time, William Hague acknowledged in front of the British Parliament that the UN had a responsibility to protect, which had to be balanced against the principle of non-interference (Hague, House of Commons, 7 March 2011). Therefore, the UK affirmed that the establishment of a no-fly zone over Libya would need international support, a clear trigger and a legal basis (Hague, 10 March 2011).

When updating the Parliament on the special European Council from 11 March 2011, Prime Minister Cameron emphasised that British national interests were at stake in the Libyan crisis:

> *Do we want a situation where a failed pariah state festers on Europe's southern border, potentially threatening our security, pushing people across the Mediterranean and creating a more dangerous and uncertain world for Britain and for all our allies as well as for the people of Libya? My answer is clear: this is not in Britain's interest. And that is why Britain will remain at the forefront of Europe in leading the response to the crisis.* (Cameron, 14 March 2011)

The Foreign Secretary argued along the same lines that a failed Libyan state could provide "a potential source for terrorism in the future, that would be a danger to the national security interest of this country" (Hague, 15 March 2011). In the run up to the voting on Resolution 1973, the UK justified the proposal of a military intervention in Libya mainly with national security reasons. At the same time, Cameron emphasised the urgency of the situation in Libya: "The clock is now ticking, and we now need a sense of urgency, because we do not want to see a bloodbath in Benghazi, and further repression and taking of innocent civilian life in Libya" (Cameron, House of Commons, 18 March 2011). He added that "the stronger argument is that it is better to act than to stand back and do nothing and witness the slaughter of civilians, when that is so clearly not in our national interest" (idem.)

In the UK's explanation on its vote in favour of Resolution 1973, UK Permanent Representative, Sir Grant, affirmed that the UK was willing to assume its responsibility. However, the aim of protecting the Libyan civilians seemed to be deeply linked to the objective of regime change in the British discourse:

> *We, along with partners in the Arab world and in NATO, are now ready to shoulder our responsibilities in implementing Resolution 1973. … The central purpose of this resolution is clear: to end the violence, to protect civilians, and to allow the people of Libya to determine their own future, free from the tyranny of the Qadhafi regime.* (Grant, 17 March 2011)

When asked whether the Prime Minister could assure that the military intervention made a "real difference" to the people in Libya (Miliband, House of Commons, 18 March 2011), Cameron's answer remained vague. He underlined that the objective of Resolution 1973 was to save lives and to protect people and not to choose the government of Libya (Cameron, idem). At the same time, Cameron admitted that the international community had agreed that Gaddafi needed to go and that it was almost impossible to envisage a future that included him. Nevertheless, he stressed, that the aims were those stated in Resolution 1973 (idem).

A further justification for Britain's participation in the military intervention in Libya was its role as an international actor:

> *We are one of the world's leading military powers, and we also have a huge strength in diplomacy, soft power and development. We should not play a disproportionate part, but I think that we should play a proportionate part alongside allies such as France, America and the Arab World. To say that we should pass such a resolution but then just stand back and hope that someone, somewhere in the Arab world will bring it about is profoundly wrong.* (Cameron, idem)

The previous section revealed that the UK described in detail the use of military force by the Libyan government against its civilians and stressed the government's failure to protect. Britain's participation in the military intervention was justified with the argument that a failed Libyan state would be against the UK's national interest. Alongside a demonstrable need, regional support and a clear legal basis, the presence of national security interests seems to constitute a fourth condition for British involvement in the Libyan intervention. In the UK discourse the aim of protection seemed therefore not only blurred with the objective of regime change but also raised questions regarding the compatibility of national interests and a people-centred approach to intervention. To what extent the RtoP was actually reflected in the actual implementation of Resolution 1973 or whether it was rather seen as a 'classical' humanitarian intervention will be the focus of the next section.

Assessing the application – protection vs. intervention?

Five days after the establishment of a no-fly zone over Libya, France justified its participation by claiming that the international coalition "has saved Benghazi", it has stopped Gaddafi's offensive and has re-established the equilibrium between the opposition and the Gaddafi regime. On the question of whether the objective of the military operations in Libya was the removal of Colonel Gaddafi, the French Foreign Minister confirmed that the aim of regime change was not included in Resolution 1973. Yet, Juppé expressed doubts whether "after what has happened and what is happening in the Arab world that such a regime governed by such a person could persist" (Juppé, 24 March 2011). The objective of protecting the Libyan civilians seemed, therefore, from the French perspective, only possible in combination with Gaddafi resignation of power. At the same time, France stressed that it was up to the Libyan people to decide how Libya would be governed in the future (idem).

At the *Assemblée Nationale*, it was emphasised that France is not a "liberator" since it did "not have the mandate to intervene on the ground" (Ayrault, Assemblée Nationale, 22 March 2011). Furthermore, it was claimed that a no-fly zone can "never win a war or get rid of a dictator. The Libyans themselves have to design their liberation and victory" (idem).

At the end of March 2011 Sarkozy and Cameron confirmed in a joint statement:

> *... we do not envisage any form military occupation of Libya, which would violate the requirements of the resolution. We strongly reaffirm our engagement to the sovereignty, independence, territorial integrity and national unity of Libya. Military action is not an objective in itself. There is no other sustainable solution than a political one, and the latter belongs to the Libyan people.* (Sarkozy and Cameron, 28 March 2011).[111]

111 "Nous soulignons le fait que nous n'envisageons aucune occupation militaire de la Libye, ce qui enfreindrait les conditions prévues par la résolution. Nous réaffirmons notre engagement le plus ferme en faveur de la souveraineté, de l'indépendance, de l'intégrité territoriale et de l'unité nationale de la Libye. L'action militaire n'est pas un objectif en soi. Il n'y a de solution durable que politique, et cette dernière appartient au peuple libyen."

In terms of the execution of the military operation, Alain Juppé assured that France that it had "formally requested that there would be no collateral damage on the civilian population, which made the intervention obviously more difficult because Gaddafi's troops ... tend to approach the civilian population" (Juppé, 6 April 2011)[112].

In mid-April, the French Foreign Minister reaffirmed that France's policy was not directed towards achieving a regime change:

> *We do not intend to decide on the nature and distribution of internal competences of independent countries. We express ourselves, we condemn, we intervene solely on the basis of international law and, in particular, the implementation of the new principle, adopted in 2005 by the UN and registered for the first time in a resolution of Security Council, I mean the principle of responsibility to protect ...* (Juppé 16 April 2011)[113]

However, presumably acting within the strict framework set out in the respective UNSC resolution, did not prevent France from demanding the departure of Gaddafi whose regime, as argued by France, appears no longer consistent with the protection of the Libyan citizens (idem). Furthermore, Juppé asserted that "the fate of Benghazi" would have been ten times worse than in Srebrenica. The French Ambassador to the UN, Gerard Araud, affirmed that "when serious violations of international humanitarian law and human rights, war crimes, crimes against humanity are committed, it is indeed the duty of the Security Council to intervene to prevent them. This is what we did in Libya" (Araud, 10 May 2011).

In June 2011 Nicolas Sarkozy reminded again of the lessons learned from history:

112 "... nous avons demandé formellement qu'il n'y ait pas de dommages collatéraux sur les populations civiles; cela rend les interventions évidemment plus difficiles parce que les troupes de Kadhafi ... ont tendance à se rapprocher des populations civiles."

113 "Nous n'avons pas l'intention de décider de la nature et de la répartition des compétences internes de pays qui sont indépendants. Nous nous exprimons, nous condamnons, nous intervenons sur le seul fondement du droit international et, en particulier, de la mise en œuvre du principe nouveau, adopté en 2005 par l'organisation des Nations unies et inscrit pour la première fois dans une résolution du Conseil de sécurité, je veux parler du principe de responsabilité de protéger ..."

> *I would like to recall that in Srebrenica 8,000 people, who should be protected by democracies but that were not, were murdered, 8000. Is there anyone who thinks that in Benghazi, a million inhabitants, Gaddafi would have killed merely 8000? So the operation in Libya has saved lives and will continue until the Libyans can build their democracy.* (Sarkozy, 24 June 2011)

Furthermore, the French Foreign Minister stressed that oil was not the reason for France's intervention in Libya (Juppé, 26 June 2011).

A day after Gaddafi's death on 20 October 2011, France announced that the end of the Libyan conflict "... was an illustration of the strength of the principle of responsibility to protect, endorsed by the UN, and which formed the basis of Resolution 1973"[114] (Point de presse, 21 October). Gaddafi's defeat was described as a success for the international community and the values enshrined in the UN Charter, on the basis of which the UN were able to protect the Libyan population and prevent the bloodbath announced by Gaddafi himself (idem.)

Since its abstention in the voting on Resolution 1973 in the UN Security Council, Germany's position has been widely criticised not only but especially from parts of the opposition. Former Foreign Minister Joschka Fischer referred to the abstention as "scandalous mistake". The core allegations of the criticism were that Germany had isolated itself politically and had breached the solidarity to his allies (*Bündnissolidarität*) (Westerwelle, 24 March 2011).

In order to compensate for the abstention, Germany offered on 23 March to send further AWACS to Afghanistan "to relieve those NATO members that were ... participating in the implementation of the no-fly zone" (Westerwelle, 23 March 2011). Despite that, Germany assured that its different opinion on the Libyan crisis did not harm the Franco-German relationship nor did it question its solidarity towards its allies (idem). Furthermore, Westerwelle expressed concerns about how quickly the call for a military intervention came up in the German public debate. He warned to be careful not to lower the threshold for military interventions and the use of force can only be a last resort (Westerwelle, 30 April 2011).

114 "La fin du conflit en Libye, dont nous attendons la proclamation ... est une illustration de la force du principe de la responsabilité de protéger, consacré par les Nations unies, qui a été le fondement de la résolution 1973 ..."

Finally, the German Foreign Minister concluded:

> *We have made our contribution to change with political means. The sanctions and the international isolation were of great importance ... We have set up a comprehensive sanctions policy that has isolated the dictator. Ultimately, the decisive factor was the will of freedom of the Libyan people.*[115] (Westwerwelle, 24 August 2011)

Though Germany has been criticised for its abstention on Resolution 1973, this criticism was not directed at Germany's compliance with the RtoP as applied by the UN. It was rather a question of solidarity with its European and transatlantic allies. Germany was thus excluded from further consultations on Libya and exposed on the international scene. Among domestic critiques, it was also not the principle of RtoP but Germany's well-established foreign policy doctrine of 'never alone' that was at the centre of the debate. Germany's abstention has shown that diverging understandings of the RtoP can lead to different positions on its implementation.[116]

After the adoption of Resolution 1973, the UK assured that "all missions are meticulously planned to ensure every care is taken to avoid casualties" (Foreign Office press statement, 20 March 2011). Furthermore, William Hague affirmed at the House of Commons that "operations have been directed against [Gaddafi's] military forces and control of those forces" and that "the greatest care" would be taken "to avoid civilian casualties" (Hague, House of Commons, 24 March 2011). He emphasised that the "action is saving lives and is protecting hundreds of thousands of civilians in Benghazi and Misrata from the fate that otherwise awaited them" (idem).

At the end of March, the Foreign Secretary stated that "so far, the action we have taken has been successful in protecting countless civilians from Qadhafi's forces ..." (Hague, 29 March 2011). He further underlined the speed with which "NATO has moved to put in place the planning and launch of the ... demanding operations, more quickly than was the case for Bosnia or Kosovo" (Hague, 30 March 2011).

115 "Wir haben unseren Beitrag zum Umbruch mit politischen Mitteln geleistet. Die Sanktionen und die internationale Isolierung waren von großer Bedeutung. Dadurch ist Gaddafis Regime von Nachschubquellen. Wir haben auf eine umfassende Sanktionspolitik gesetzt, die den Diktator isoliert hat. Entscheidend war am Ende der Freiheitswille des libyschen Volkes."

116 At the same time it has also been suggested that Germany abstained because of the critical local elections taking place at the end of March 2011 and unpopularity of military action in Libya in the German public.

The NATO Foreign Ministers agreed in April that the NATO mission in Libya has three military objectives: (1) the end to all attacks and threat of attacks against civilians; (2) the withdrawal of all regime forces to bases; and (3) immediate humanitarian access. They emphasised that "NATO is absolutely determined to continue its operation for as long as there is a threat against Libyan civilians and it is impossible to imagine that the threat will disappear with Qadhafi still in power" (Press release on NATO's Foreign Minister meeting, 19 April 2011).

After the Libyan opposition forces managed to take over Tripoli at the beginning of September, David Cameron stated at the House of Commons:

> *It is the Libyan people who have liberated their country; there was no occupying army. This has been a Libyan-led process, assisted by the international community … It was a unique set of circumstances and not something that we can or would wish to repeat all over the world, but I have never accepted the argument that because you can't do everything, you shouldn't do anything. Removing Gaddafi from power was a major achievement.* (Cameron, House of Commons, 5 September 2011)

On the death of Gaddafi, David Cameron remarked: "I'm proud of the role that Britain has played in helping them to bring that about and I pay tribute to the bravery of the Libyans who have helped to liberate their country" (Cameron, 21 October 2011).

In comparison with previous cases of mass atrocities the Prime Minister concluded that "on this occasion a coalition of nations across the Western and Arab World had the will to act. In so doing, they stopped Benghazi from joining Srebrenica and Rwanda in history's painful roll call of massacres the world failed to prevent" (Cameron, 22 September 2011).

Making its participation contingent on the presence of national interests, the UK government followed very much the old norm of humanitarian intervention as laid out by Tony Blair during the Kosovo war in 1999. At the beginning of September 2011, Cameron confirmed that "this was a practical, liberal, Conservative intervention" (Cameron, House of Commons, 5 September 2011). At the same time, the

Prime Minister underlined that Britain "had a moral obligation to try to deal with [the Libya crisis] because [it] could prevent a massacre", however, there was not only "an'ought', there was also 'a could'" (idem).

While the initial strikes were implemented by the US, NATO took over military operations from the US-led coalition ten days after. The majority of the missions were then carried out by France and Britain, with the support of a few smaller allies, including Belgium, Denmark and Norway (Chivvis, 2012). Subsequently, US military and political power would play a major role behind the scenes, but the US would not play a larger role in the succeeding air strikes. According to US President Barack Obama it was Europe's role to assume the major part in Libyan crisis response: "the Mediterranean is your inner sea, not ours – we will help you with the things you can't do but we won't do the things that you can do for yourselves" (quoted in Brown, 2011).

However, in April, the US agreed to reintroduce *Predator* drones to strike (they had been removed when the US retrieved its strike aircraft at the end of Odyssey Dawn) (Chivvis, 2012: 8). In June, France and the UK introduced attack helicopters. Although both these military instruments increased the risk of Allied and civilian casualties, they offered the possibility for even more precise strikes. In seven months of military operations, NATO achieved all of its stated strategic objectives: it upheld an arms embargo, provided for humanitarian relief, established a no-fly zone and helped to protect the Libyan civilian population from further destruction by Gaddafi and his forces (idem: 10).

On the other hand, Varun Vira and Anthony Cordesman (2011) argued that protecting civilians according to Resolution 1973 has proven to be difficult in its implementation. Moreover, what began as an operation that was initially closely aligned with the RtoP, expanded considerably into something resembling an air war aimed at forcing regime change. By mid-June, NATO forces expanded the scope of the air strikes, which reinforced the suspicion that they may be seeking a forceful regime change by deliberately targeting Gaddafi and his allies. However, France and the UK have continuously denied that military operations are targeting Gaddafi personally and maintained that NATO attacks aim at degrading Gaddafi's military forces, destroying their ability to maintain communications or logistical and supply chains, as well as at increasing the pressure within Gaddafi's inner circle (idem).

Similarly, Geir Ulfstein and Hege Føsund Christiansen (2013) put forward the argument that NATO actions to protect Libyan civilians were clearly within the mandate of Resolution 1973. However, military strikes intending to overthrow Gaddafi, including support to the rebels' advancement, violated the mandate given by the UN Security Council and constituted an illegal use of force (idem). In this context, Ulfstein and Christiansen (2013: 162) argue further that the overstepping of the mandate may have undermined the credibility of the RtoP for future crises involving the commitment of mass atrocities.

The explanation given by those conducting the military operation in Libya was ambiguous. In a joint statement together with Barack Obama, Nicolas Sarkozy and David Cameron argued on the one hand that Resolution 1973 did not mandate the removal of Gaddafi. On the other hand, they stated that NATO was to maintain its operations and increase pressure on the regime as long as Gaddafi is in power. By providing close air support for the rebels' advances into cities held by Gaddafi's forces, NATO helped to destroy Libyan military forces loyal to Gaddafi. Moreover, NATO air strikes arguably assisted the rebels also in conquering new areas and in finally bringing down the Gaddafi regime. The implementation of the military operation raises question of whether the aerial support for rebel manoeuvres on the ground in Libya was legally in line with Resolution 1973 or whether the coalition was overstepping the mandate (Ulfstein and Føsund, 2013: 168-169).

Resolution 1973 did not cover regime change or general human rights protection in Libya. The UNSC mandate explicitly only authorised a coalition of the willing to protect 'civilians and civilian populated areas' under 'threat of attack'. Clearly, the areas held by Gaddafi were not under threat of attack by him. By contrast, when the opposition forces advanced on cities held by Gaddafi's troops it was the rebels themselves who posed a threat to civilians and civilian populated areas (Akande, 2013).

The basis for NATO air strikes on areas held by Gaddafi was arguably the consent by the rebels rather than Resolution 1973. But neither the UN mandate nor consent would provide a legal basis for NATO's use of force to support the rebels in their offensive against Gaddafi (Ulfstein and Føsund, 2013: 169). While there were military and political reasons for NATO wanting to put an end to the conflict between Gaddafi and the rebels, the air support for the Libyan opposition forces to advance on Gaddafi-held territories went beyond the mandate of Resolution 1973 and thus violated the prohibition against the use of force as stated in Article 2(4) in the UN Charter. As in the case of the Kosovo intervention in 1999, the implementation of the military intervention in Libya raises important questions on its legitimacy and legality despite the existence of a UN mandate. These issues will also be crucial for the further normative development of the RtoP.

4.4 Preliminary conclusion

The analysis of the Libyan crisis has shown that the RtoP did have an influence on European responses to the crisis in the sense that it was used to legitimise their positions. Yet, France, Germany and the UK referred to the RtoP in different ways and justified partly different approaches towards the Libyan crisis on the basis of the emerging norm. Therefore, the 'Big 3' disagreed on whose responsibility it was to respond to the crisis and with what means. While France and the UK shared the understanding that a military intervention on the basis of the RtoP was legitimate, Germany was opposed to the use of means other than political and economic pressure.

At the same time, Europe seemed to agree that Gaddafi had lost all his legitimacy as leader of Libya and that he had to step down. Although France and Britain strongly emphasised in their discourses that the sole objective of the military intervention was the protection of the Libyan civilians, achieving this aim seemed to be possible only if linked to Gaddafi's removal. The lines between the goal of protection and regime change, which was not authorised by Resolution 1973, became therefore unclear. Furthermore, the UK legitimized its participation in the military operation in front of the national audience mainly on the basis of national security interests.

Thus, the application of the RtoP in the case of the Libyan crisis appeared to a certain extent more like a 'classical' intervention. While in previous RtoP cases the emphasis was on non-coercive means, the Libyan crisis stressed the use of force component of the emerging norm. During the Libyan intervention, concerns were expressed, such as in Germany, about the Libyan case serving as a precedent for the use of force against the will of a *de facto* government. The international community in general and Europe specifically might thus be twice as shy after Libya to respond to further cases of mass atrocities.

For the EU, although it supported the application of the RtoP in its discourse, the protection of the Libyan civilians seemed possible only with civilian means. In its actual crisis response, the EU has certainly been successful not only in protecting EU citizens but also in the delivery of humanitarian aid and the implementation of restrictive measures against the Libyan regime. In some respects the Libyan crisis was tailor-made for the EU's CSDP but a lack of capabilities, internal discord and personalities undercut the EU's chances of playing any significant role in military operations (Chivvis, 2012).

Although the EU has constantly tried to increase its military power by merging military and civilian means into a Common Security Defence Policy, it has mostly failed to implement military methods and concentrated more on humanitarian crises and natural disasters. The Libyan crisis has shown once more that the EU's response has mainly focused on 'soft' security actions, such as civil protection and humanitarian assistance. At the same time, the EU has emphasised in its discourse that it is primarily its responsibility to help and to assist. While there might still be a gap between expectations and capabilities in the area of the CSDP the EU's understanding of responsibility as well as its security role envisaged by France, Germany and the UK seem to actually match with its available capabilities.

Some have argued that the Libyan crisis and the UN's reaction to it constituted a "breakthrough" for the RtoP as an emerging international norm (Cotler and Genser, 2011; Evans, 2011b; Ischinger, 2011) and another step towards its recognition. In comparison to previous RtoP cases, the reaction to the Libyan crisis was marked by forceful political commitment to the emerging norm. The UNSC was quick to condemn the violence and call on the Libyan authorities' responsibility to protect. The clarity of the language of the UNSC was unprecedented: UNSC Resolution 1970 and 1973 clearly stated that their primary goal was the protection of civilians. It was the first time that the UNSC evoked the RtoP doctrine to authorise the use of force without host government consent. Finally, the decisions at the level of the UNSC entailed speedy and decisive implementation. The fact that the crisis has been linked to the RtoP from the beginning and that there was broad consensus on the UNSC's application of the emerging norm is of important symbolic value (Geiß and Kashgar, 2011: 101). Furthermore, it strengthened the role of the UNSC as the legal and legitimate authoriser of the use of force under the RtoP (Van Landingham, 2012).

The Libyan case study shows that the RtoP has clearly influenced the decision-making process on the European crisis response but that the RtoP's legitimacy was undermined by the actual military operations going beyond the mandate given in Resolution 1973. According to the scale developed in chapter 4, the influence of the

RtoP remains moderate. The fact that the RtoP was not implemented accordingly point towards the fact that the crisis response was motivated by other reasons and that the RtoP has merely been used superficially. Furthermore, the fact that there are (still) different understandings of the RtoP at work and the fact that RtoP in the case of Libya was linked to the use of military force, might create new barriers for the development and the application of the emerging norm. The Western-led intervention has arguably increased the scepticism vis-à-vis the RtoP by some countries, namely Russia, China and India. When looking at international and European responses to the Syrian crisis, it could be argued that the way the RtoP was implemented in Libya constituted – despite all the praise – a setback for the emerging norm itself.

Chapter 5: The Syrian crisis – responsibility to protect or to punish?

"Syria is not Kosovo" titled the New York Times on 4 September 2013 and wrote further:

> *The United States and Europe are at odds with Moscow, the Security Council is deadlocked, NATO has stayed on the sidelines, and the Arab League has been ineffectual. There is no strategy to achieve a stable endgame in which peacekeepers would be deployed and rebels would be disarmed, and the promised Geneva peace conference has been delayed indefinitely. As a matter of international law, Kosovo is no precedent either.* (Rubin, 2013)

This devastating assessment summed up two and half years of the international community's effort in conciliating the Syrian crisis.[117] While the option of a military intervention was initially very quickly put off the table, it became a matter of the international debate only after the alleged attacks on the Syrian civilian population by the Assad government using chemical weapons of mass destruction in August 2013. Arguments brought forward in favour of a military intervention seemed to be based on the need to punish the Assad government rather than to protect the Syrian population. Furthermore, the Libyan intervention was used to delineate the two crises from each other and to argue against a military intervention. An international military intervention with or without UNSC mandate was ultimately averted due to an agreement between the US, Russia and the de facto Syrian government on the destruction of its chemical weapons arsenal and its admission of the Chemical Weapons Convention (CWC). However, the fighting between opposition and government forces and the suffering of the civilian population continues at the time of writing.

Significantly, the RtoP was considered as a legitimate basis to act upon only once the option of a military intervention was put back on the table by the US. Arguments in favour of a military intervention were based on the need to punish the Syrian government for the use of chemical weapons, which have been prohibited

117 By the time of writing the crisis in Syria was still ongoing.

by international law since 1997, rather than the need to protect the Syrian civilian population. The following analyses examines the influence of the RtoP on European responses to the Syrian crisis under the question of whether the RtoP is applied to protect the Syrian people or whether it is misused to punish the regime of Bashar al-Assad.

This chapter analyses the influence of the RtoP on international and European responses to the Syrian crisis from March 2011 to September 2013. The next section starts by giving a brief overview of the development of the Syrian crisis during the chosen time frame. The following section focuses on the role of norm entrepreneurs and the UN and EU responses to the Syrian crisis. Member states responses will be investigated in sections three and four before drawing some preliminary conclusions on the RtoP influence in the case of the Syrian crisis since 2011 and its status as an emerging international norm.

Summary of the Syrian crisis

The Arab Spring hit Syria on 15 March 2011 with popular demonstrations that grew nationwide by April. Similar to other Arab countries, the crisis initially started off as civil uprising from initially minor protests in January 2011, as a response to the regional Arab Spring, government corruption and human rights abuses. Large-scale unrest began on 15 March in the southern city of Daraa, where about fifteen children had been arrested and reportedly tortured for writing on a wall, the well-known slogan of the uprisings in Tunisia and Egypt: "The people want the downfall of the regime" (International Crisis Group, 2013). Citizens carried out a peaceful protest, demanding the release of the children. The protesters also called for democracy and freedom. The government responded to the protests with large-scale arrests, torture of prisoners, police brutality and censorship of events. As in Libya, the protesters in Syria have demanded their leader to step down. In response, Syrian president Bashar al-Assad has not only stated he has no intentions of stepping down, but he has also rejected allegations that Syrian security forces have committed crimes against humanity (Buckley, 2012).

Following military crackdowns in June 2011 many soldiers defected to protect protestors. At the same time, many protestors began to take up arms (International Crisis Group, 2013). On 29 July, a group of defected officers announced the formation of the Free Syrian Army opposition (FSA), an umbrella group, which would later represent the main opposition army. The establishment of the FSA formally marked the beginning of armed resistance to the Assad government (Boxx, 2013). The FAS gained in size but remained without centralised leadership until December 2011. In early November 2011, clashes between the FSA and government security forces in Homs escalated. November and December saw increasing rebel attacks, as opposition forces grew in number. In January 2012, Assad began using large-scale artillery operations against the insurgency leading to the destruction of many civilian homes due to indiscriminate shelling. By this time, daily protests had almost disappeared and were eclipsed by the spread of the armed conflict (MacFarquhar, 2012).

The situation in Syria deteriorated rapidly since February 2012, with one UN report indicating "the death toll often exceeds 100 civilians a day, including many women and children" (BBC News, 2013). In the same month, the UN Secretary-General Ban Ki-moon appointed Kofi Annan as the UN-Arab League Joint Special Representative for Syria. Annan's peace-plan provided for a ceasefire, but even as the negotiations for it were conducted, Syrian armed forces attacked a number of towns and villages and summarily executed scores of people. Incommunicado detention, including children continued (Amnesty International, 2012). In March 2012, the UN reported that over eight thousand people had died as a result of the conflict in Syria (Buckley, 2012).

Assad responded to Annan, sounding like Gaddafi, that a political dialogue could not succeed while "armed terrorist groups" were in operation in his country (idem). In April 2012, Assad began deploying attack helicopters against the rebel forces (idem). On 12 April both sides, the Syrian government and rebels of the FSA, entered a ceasefire period mediated by Kofi Annan. Unfortunately, the agreement failed with infractions of the ceasefire by both sides resulting in several dozen casualties. Acknowledging its failure, Annan subsequently called for Iran to "be part of the solution", though the country had initially been excluded from the Friends of Syria initiative[118] (Al Arabiya, 2012). Annan's peace plan practically collapsed by early June and the UN mission was withdrawn from Syria (The Times of India, 2012). The Special Representative officially resigned on 2 August 2012. A few weeks after, Lakhdar Brahimi was appointed the new UN-Arab League peace envoy for Syria. Following consultations with the Syrian President Assad, as well as with Russian and Chinese officials, a second cease-fire attempt was announced towards late October 2012. As both rebels and the Syrian Army resumed large-scale operations, the cease-fire quickly collapsed. (Matthew, 2012)

In November 2012, opposition forces came together to create a new coalition to be more inclusive and representative of the Syrian opposition (Al Arabiya, 2012). The new body was named the National Coalition for Syrian Revolutionary and Opposition Force, and has steadily gathered international recognition as the legitimate representative of the Syrian people. The Coalition was first recognised by the Arab League on 12 November 2012, then joined by France on 13 November, the EU on November 19, the UK on 20 November, the US on December 12, and then others such as Germany. However, the fighting continued and increased for almost another year culminating in summer 2013. On 21 August 2013, a chemical attack took place in the Ghouta region, Damascus countryside, leading to thousands of casualties and several hundred in the opposition forces (Dagher and Fassihi, 2013). The attack was followed by a military offensive by government forces into areas, which have been strongholds of the opposition since the beginning of the uprising.

On 31 August, the President of the United States, Barack Obama, announced that he "decided that the United States should take military action against Syrian regime targets" for its use of chemical weapons but that he would ask Congress to vote to authorise military action (Obama, 2013). He further affirmed that "the attack [on 21 August] is an assault on human dignity" and that "it also presents a serious danger to our national security" (idem). President Obama explained further that "we should not put boots on the ground ... but I'm confident we can hold the Assad regime accountable for their use of chemical weapons, deter this kind of behaviour, and degrade their capacity to carry it out" (idem).

118 The Group of Friends of the Syrian People or simply Friends of Syria is an international group of countries meeting periodically to discuss the events in Syria outside the UN Security Council. The collective was created in response to the second Russian and Chinese veto on a Security Council resolution condemning Syria in February 2012. The group was initiated by then-French president Nicolas Sarkozy and its first meeting took place on 24 February 2012 in Tunisia.

Obama's appeal triggered a wide-reaching debate particularly among European states on whether or not to intervene militarily in Syria. While France and the UK promptly signalled their willingness to support the US, the latter had to withdraw from the proposal after David Cameron lost a vote on British participation in the House of Commons. As usual, Germany remained sceptical on the usefulness of a military intervention. Since a UNSC mandate was unlikely to be issued, national and international debates crystallised around questions of legitimacy and legality of a possible intervention. Furthermore, questions about the purpose of a military intervention came up: Was the proposed action a military strike to punish the Syrian government or a necessary intervention to protect the Syrian civilian population from further atrocities? Assad eventually agreed to give up its chemical weapons and to sign the CWC. A military intervention was therefore averted. Yet, analysing international and European responses and the role of the RtoP therein can provide valuable insights on the motivations behind the crisis response in general and for the proposal to make use of force particularly.

5.1 The role of norm entrepreneurs

The UN response

As the protests in Syria gradually turned into an armed conflict between the government forces and the protesters, the UN became the focus of international reactions and interactions. Although the UN Security Council was not able to take immediate steps to halt the conflict in Syria, it has debated the crisis on a number of occasions (Eminue and Dickson, 2012; see table 7). On 27 April 2011, the UNSC held a public debate on Syria. On 9 May 2011, the Secretary-General called for an end to the violence and mass arrests, for an independent inquiry into the killings and for a UN team to enter Syria to assess the humanitarian situation. Then, in August 2011, the UNSC issued a presidential statement expressing "its grave concern at the deteriorating situation in Syria, and … profound regret at the death of many hundreds of peopled" (UNSC, Media Release, 3 August 2011). It further condemned "the widespread violations of human rights and the use of force against civilians by the Syrian authorities" and called "for an immediate end to all violence and urged all sides to act with utmost restraint, and to refrain from reprisal, including attacks against state institutions" (idem).

The Security Council reminded "the Syrian authorities to fully respect human rights and to comply with their obligations under applicable international law. Those responsible for the violence should be held accountable" and reiterated "its strong commitment to the sovereignty, independence, and territorial integrity of Syria" (idem). Finally, the UNSC stressed that the only solution to the crisis in Syria is through an inclusive and Syrian-led political process, with the aim of effectively addressing aspirations and concerns of the population, which will allow the full exercise of the fundamental freedoms for its entire population, including that of expression and peaceful assembly (idem).

On 4 October 2011, France, the UK, Germany and Portugal tabled a draft resolution (UN Doc. S/2011/612, hereinafter, Draft Resolution) for consideration by the UNSC. The European Draft Resolution repeated many points from the August Presidential statement, though in stronger terms, condemning the "continued grave and systematic human rights violations and the use of forces against civilians by the

Syrian authorities". The Draft Resolution had initially imposed sanctions, but was watered down during the negotiations preceding the vote. It ultimately only warned of the Security Council's "intention ... to consider its options", including measures under Article 41 of the UN Charter, thus only hinting at the prospect of mandating sanctions in the future (Mohamed, 2012). Despite these revisions, there were nine votes in favour (Bosnia-Herzegovina, Colombia, France, Gabon, Germany, Nigeria, Portugal, the UK and the US), two votes against (Russia and China) and four abstentions (Brazil, India, Lebanon and South Africa). The European sponsored Draft Resolution thus failed to pass.[119]

In a bid to further discuss and find a lasting solution to the Syrian crisis, the UN began a meeting on 31 January 2012, which continued until 4 February, when finally another draft resolution, this time sponsored by a large number of Arab States and Western countries, was put to vote. However, once again the draft resolution was vetoed by Russia and China with all other members voting in favour. As part of his efforts to find a solution to the Syrian crisis, Special Envoy Kofi Annan presented his six-point peace plan to the UN in mid-March 2012. Anna's plan called on everyone involved in the conflict to

> *address the legitimate aspirations and concerns of the Syrian people, stop fighting, pull back military concentrations from towns while simultaneously the Envoy would seek similar commitments from the Syrian opposition and other 'elements'.* (Annan, 2012)

The Syrian government accepted Annan's peace plan (see box 1) on 25 March and on 2 April Annan reported to the UNSC that the Syrian regime had agreed to a ceasefire to come into effect on 12 April. Two days later, the UNSC adopted Resolution 2042, which condemned the "widespread violations of human rights by the Syrian authorities", as well as "any human rights abuses by armed groups". The resolution authorised the initial deployment of 300 unarmed military observes as part of the Annan peace plan. Before being adopted, the draft had been amended in order to avoid further Russian and Chinese vetoes. Russia's representative stated

119 In a related development on 27 October 2011, Russia and China proposed a draft resolution, according to them, designed to encourage a peaceful process to help the Syrian government deal with both its desired reforms and with the extremist violence against the Syrian government that was making such reforms difficult (Mohamed, 2012). However, the Russian and Chinese proposal was not even put to a vote at the Security Council.

at the UNSC that "the initial draft underwent substantial changes to make it more balanced, appropriately reflect realities and take into account the prerogatives of the Syrian government in receiving the Observer Mission on its territory" (Churkin, UNSC, 14 April 2012).

On 21 April, the UNSC adopted Resolution 2043, which mandated the deployment of a further 270 unarmed military observers to Syria. The resolution formally created the UN Supervision Mission in Syria (UNSMIS), whose official mandate was to "monitor a cessation of armed violence in all its forms by all parties and to monitor and support the full implementation of the Envoy's [Kofi Annan] six-point proposal" (see box 1; UNSC, 2012a). However, violence again increased and the UN reported that both sides had violated the ceasefire agreement.

The peace plan calls on the Syrian authorities to:

1. Commit to work with the Envoy in an inclusive Syrian-led political process to address the legitimate aspirations and concerns of the Syrian people, and, to this end, commit to appoint an empowered interlocutor when invited to do so by the Envoy;

2. Commit to stop the fighting and achieve urgently an effective United Nations-supervised cessation of armed violence in all its forms by all parties to protect civilians and stabilise the country. To this end, the Syrian government should immediately cease troop movements towards, and end the use of heavy weapons in, population centres and begin pullback of military concentrations in and around population centres. As these actions were being taken on the ground, the Syrian government should work with the Envoy to bring about a sustained cessation of armed violence in all its forms by all parties with an effective United Nations supervision mechanism. Similar commitments would be sought by the Envoy from the opposition and all relevant elements to stop the fighting and work with him to bring about a sustained cessation of armed violence in all its form by all parties with an effective United Nations supervision mechanism;

3. Ensure timely provision of humanitarian assistance to all areas affected by the fighting, and to this end, as immediate steps, to accept and implement a daily two-hour humanitarian pause and to coordinate exact time and modalities of the daily pause through an effective mechanism, including at local level;
4. Intensify the pace and scale of release of arbitrarily detained persons, including especially vulnerable categories of persons, and persons involved in peaceful political activities, provide without delay through appropriate channels a list of all places in which such persons are being detained, immediately begin organizing access to such locations and through appropriate channels, respond promptly to all written requests for information, access or release regarding such persons;
5. Ensure freedom of movement throughout the country for journalists and a non-discriminatory visa policy for them;
6. Respect freedom of association and the right to demonstrate peacefully as legally guaranteed (Hamilton, 2012).

(As annexed to Security Council resolution 2042 (2012) of 14 April 2002)

Box 2: Text of Kofi Annan's six-point peace plan for Syria

On 27 May 2012, the UNSC affirmed that "such outrageous use of force against the civilian population constitutes a violation of applicable international law and of the commitments of the Syrian government under UNSC resolutions 2042 (2012) and 2043 (2012)" (UNSC, 2012a; 2012b). The Council called on the Syrian government "to cease all violence in all its forms, including the cessation of use of heavy weapons in population centres … and reiterated that all violence … by all parties must cease" (idem). On 20 July the UNSC adopted Resolution 2059, renewing the mandate of the UNSMIS for 30 days. In October, the Council pointed out "the grave impact the crisis in Syria has on the security of its neighbours and on regional peace and stability" and "called on the Syrian government to fully respect the sovereignty and territorial integrity of its neighbours" (UNSC, 2012c).

After the severe attacks in Aleppo on 5 October 2012, the Security Council expressed its "determination to combat all forms of terrorism, in accordance with its responsibilities under the Charter of the United Nations" (UNSC, 2012c). In response to the attacks in Damascus in March 2013, the UNSC reaffirmed its commitment to counter terrorism as it "constitutes one of the most serious threats to international peace and security" (UNSC, 2013a). The Council stated further that "any acts of terrorism are criminal and unjustifiable, regardless of their motivation, wherever, whenever and by whomsoever committed" (idem). This was the first time that the Security Council linked unfolding events in Syria to terrorism as a security threat.

In March 2013, Valerie Amos, UN Under-Secretary-General for Humanitarian Affairs and Emergency Relief Coordinator reported that there were as many as 4 million in need within Syria, including 2 million internally displaced persons and 650.000 Syrian refugees negatively influencing the economic and political situations in host countries. She also highlighted the indiscriminate nature of the violence, distressing reports of sexual violence and the need for unhindered humanitarian access. Navanethem "Navi" Pillay, UN High Commissioner for Human Rights, referred to findings of an independent study commissioned by her office that more than 60.000 people had died in the Syrian Conflict. (UN News, 2013)

In May 2013, the UN General Assembly adopted a resolution strongly condemning the Syrian government's use of indiscriminate violence against the Syrian civilian population and welcoming the establishment of the National Coalition for Syrian Revolutionary and Opposition Forces as interlocutors for the political transition. The resolution was adopted with 107 votes in favour, 12 votes against, and 59 abstentions. (UNSC, 2013b) A further GA resolution from June demanded that

> *The Syrian authorities immediately end all violations of international human rights law and meet their responsibility to protect the population and comply fully with their obligations under applicable international law, including international law applicable to the rights and protection of women and girls, and the Conventions on the Right of the Child.* (General Assembly, 2013)

This was the first time in two years since the Syrian crisis had started, that an official UN body referred explicitly to the RtoP. Similar to the GA, the UNSC called in June 2013 "upon all parties in Syria to do their utmost to protect civilians and avoid civilian casualties, recalling the primary responsibility of the Syrian government in this regard". The emphasis within the UN was thus merely on pillar 1 of the RtoP.

In July, António Guterres (2013), UN High Commissioner for Refugees, stated that there were nearly 1.8 million Syrian refugees in neighbouring countries with two-thirds of them having fled since the beginning of 2013 – a rate not seen since the Rwandan genocide. Ivan Šimonovi (2013), UN Assistant Secretary-General for Human Rights, confirmed that serious human rights violations, war crimes and crimes against humanity were now the rule in Syria as stated in several reports on massacres by the government and affiliated militias. Nevertheless, a decisive and collective response to the Syrian crisis by the international community seemed impossible until the US pushed for a military intervention after the chemical weapon attacks in August 2013. The peaceful agreement, under which Assad would give up its chemical weapons and sign the CWC, was made outside the UN framework. Still, the agreement between the US and Russia was later confirmed and put under the UNSC auspice in Resolution 2118 on the Syrian civil war and the Framework for Elimination of Syrian Chemical Weapons (UNSC, 2013c).

Type of document	Date	Document No.	Main points
UNSC Resolutions	14/04/2012	S/RES/2042	Authorising the deployment of 30 military observers.
	21/04/2012	S/RES/2043	Establishing UNSMIS.
	20/07/2012	S/RES/2059	Extending UNSMIS for a final period of 30 days.
	27/09/2013	S/RES/2118	Requiring the verification and destruction of Syria's chemical weapons stockpiles, calling for the convening of the Geneva II peace talks and endorses the establishment of a transitional governing body in Syria with full executive powers.
UNGA Resolutions	16/02/2012	A/RES/66/253	Condemning the violence in Syria, endorsing the Arab League's 22 January initiative on a Syrian political transition and requesting the Secretary-General to appoint a special envoy for Syria.
	03/08/2012	A/RES/66/253B	Deploring the UNSC's failure to act on Syria and calling for a political transition.
	15/05/2013	A/RES/67/262	Strongly condemning the Syrian government's indiscriminate violence against civilian populations and welcoming the establishment of the National Coalition for Syrian Revolutionary and Opposition Forces as interlocutors needed for a political transition.

Table 7: UN documents on Syrian crisis

The EU response

Referring for the first time to the unfolding events in Syria, the High Representative for the EU's Foreign and Security Policy stated on 18 March 2011 that she was "deeply concerned by the events in Damascus ... whereby peaceful demonstrators demanding the release of prisoners of conscience were violently dispersed by police and many of them arrested". Ashton called on "the Syrian authorities to ensure the protection of peaceful demonstrators and to uphold the right to freedom of expression and assembly" (Ashton, 18 March 2011). Concerns about the degree of violence in Libya were first expressed in June when the HR referred to "reports of torture and other violence being used against family members, including children, as a means to silence activists" (Ashton, 6 June 2011). In July, Lady Ashton "condemned the continual breakdown against peaceful protesters, including by means of large-scale deployments of the Syrian military" (Ashton, 8 July 2011). She affirmed that "this path of repression and violence discredits the promises by the Syrian leadership and its legitimacy and commitment to reform" (idem). At the end of the month, the HR cited reports from Syria, according to which "large numbers of civilians have been killed in a totally unjustified assault by Syrian security forces on the town of Hama, using tanks and other heavy weapons against citizens exercising their right to peaceful protest." (Ashton, 31 July 2011)

It was not until 2012 that the EU institutions referred to specific numbers of victims caused by the Syrian conflict. The most detailed account was brought forward by the European Parliament stating in February that

> "*The UN estimates that the death toll in Syria has exceeded 5400 in the course of the 11 month-long uprising, although up-to-date figures are very difficult to obtain because some areas ... are completely sealed off; whereas thousands have been injured, at least 69.000 have been detained, of whom about 32.000 have subsequently been released, and about 12.400 have fled to neighbouring countries ... the UN Children's Fund reports that hundreds of children have been killed and hundreds more arbitrarily arrested and tortured and sexually abused whilst in detention.*" (European Parliament, 16 February 2012)

The Foreign Affairs Council in March 2012 therefore condemned the

> "*continued brutal attacks and systematic human rights violations by the Syrian regime, including the use of heavy weaponry in civilian areas, which risk exacerbating further the spiral of violence, sectarian clashes and militarisation, and endanger the stability of the region*" (FAC, 22-23 March 2012).

The latter concern was reiterated in October 2012, when the Foreign Affairs Council stated that the EU "remains deeply concerned by the spill-over effects of the Syrian crisis in neighbouring countries in terms of security and stability".

In its discourse the EU described the different dimensions of the Syrian crisis in detail: the large-scale human rights violations, the level of violence also against children as well as the risks for stability and security in the region. At the same time the EU fell short of proposing a decisive response to the crisis. The EU initially saw the responsibility mainly with the Syrian government and the UN Security Council.

On 6 June 2011, Ashton urged the "Syrian leadership to fulfil its commitments and responsibilities to halt violence and intimidation against the Syrian people. In the same month the Foreign Affairs Council affirmed its commitment 'to ensure that the UN Security Council assumes its responsibility in relation to the situation in Syria and its regional implications'". In August, the EU however noted that the Syrian President Assad had lost "legitimacy in the eyes of the Syrian people" and should therefore step down (Ashton, 19 August 2011).

The EU's responsibility vis-à-vis the ongoing crisis in Syria was again pointed out merely by the European Parliament. In September, President Jerzy Buzek stated:

> *We cannot allow the Syrian regime to continue killing the Syrian people. Authorities in Damascus have lost all remaining legitimacy and must step aside immediately … We Europeans must assume our responsibility to protect civilians and our responsibility to protect democracy.* (European Parliament, 15 September 2011)

The EP's discourse and calls for action grew stronger towards the end of 2012. In a resolution from 15 December the EU emphasised that the crisis in Syria constituted "a threat to the stability and security of the entire Middle East region". It stressed that "the Syrian government has failed to meet its responsibility to protect its population, to immediately put an end to all human rights violations and to stop any attacks against civilians" (EP, 15 December 2012). The EP advised that "in light of this failure, the international community needs to take urgent and appropriate measures" (idem).

The Foreign Affairs Council, however, adhered to its approach of referring the main responsibility "to end the violence against the Syrian population" to the members of the UN Security Council while recalling the main findings of the report of the Independent Commission of Inquiry which stated that "crimes against humanity may have been committed in the country" (FAC, 14 May, 2012). The recognition of one of the RtoP crimes in the case of Syria did, however, not serve as a catalyst for more decisive EU action. Instead, the EU tried to appeal to the responsibility of the international community. In this context, Herman van Rompuy stated:

> *A swift reaction by the UN Security Council is urgently needed. I urge all members of the UN Security to assume their responsibilities in relation to the situation in Syria, and adopt steps long overdue in order to bring an end to the repression in Syria.* (Van Rompuy, 30 January 2012)

The EU emphasised further the need of accountability. In June 2012 Ashton called "for a full investigation of the horrendous crimes ... Those guilty of these atrocities must be brought rapidly to justice" (Ashton, 7 June 2012).

Although the EU in mid-2012 acknowledged the failure of the Syrian government to protect its citizens, it held on to the position that the main responsibility for the crisis lies with the Syrian authorities (Ashton, 18 June 2012; FAC, 23 July 2012). At the same time, the EU stressed that it "remains committed to the sovereignty, independence and territorial integrity of Syria" (FAC, 19 November 2012).

In terms of the EU's policy response to the Syrian crisis, the application of sanctions was discussed for the first time in April 2011 by the Foreign Minister of Hungary, then holding the EU Presidency. While proposing restrictive measures, Zsolt Németh affirmed at the same time that "the military intervention applied in Libya ... should serve as a warning" to Syria. He argued further that the intervention in Libya is not "analogous to Iraq, but rather to Rwanda or Kosovo, where the international community had to intervene, in an effort to protect the civilians" (Németh, 6 April 2011). At the same time, the European Parliament raised concerns that Europe could be accused of "applying double standards with regards to military intervention in Libya and the very different response to Syria" (Charles Tannock, EP, 30 May 2011).

Within the EEAS, the question whether a foreign intervention as in Libya would be considered in case of the Syria crisis was discussed in September 2011. In a press statement it was emphasised that no one was in favour of military intervention and that the Syrian people should "own" the developments and the future transition in Syria:

> *Unlike in the Libya case, neither the Syrian people, nor the countries in the region have been requesting outside military assistance for their protection. Therefore, an intervention would be illegitimate, harmful and counter-productive. It would neither help the situation within Syria nor the relations and stability in the regional framework. In addition, as it was the case for Libya, a military intervention would require a mandate of the UN Security Council, which is neither on the table nor foreseen.* (EEAS, 13 September 2011)

The EU Civil Protection Mechanism was activated twice, once in April 2012 to help Turkey cope with the influx of refugees and once in September 2012 to assist Jordan. In March 2013, the HR recognised the inability of the international community to find "a coherent, united way to respond to the horror that is being perpetrated and to act collectively to protect the people" (Ashton, 13 March 2013). She reiterated that without authorisation by the UNSC, as well as a clearer situation on the ground in Syria, military action would not be considered. Ashton recalled Commissioner

Kristalina Georgieva[120], in arguing that "from a humanitarian perspective there are no military fixes either. Humanitarian corridors, buffer zones and other ideas of the same kind are not viable solutions" (idem). By contrast, the European Commission and the HR advocated a comprehensive approach for the EU's response to the conflict and its consequences both in Syria and its neighbouring countries. Therein the EU's role is mainly

> *to support a political process that brings a sustainable solution to the crisis, prevent regional destabilisation from the spill-over of the conflict in neighbouring countries, address the dramatic humanitarian situation and assist affected populations, address the consequences of the conflict on and in the EU.* (EU Joint Communication, 24 June 2013)

According to the EU Factsheet on the Syrian crisis, the EU "has responded decisively to the violent repression and anti-government protests in Syria, which began in March 2011" (EU Factsheet, 1 March 2012). However, the previous analysis of the EU's discourse on the crisis suggests that EU has been rather reluctant in assuming responsibility in its crisis response to Syria. In terms of concrete action the EU has supported the resolutions adopted by the UN, implemented sanctions and restrictive measures and has provided humanitarian assistance.

The EU froze the draft Association Agreement that had been negotiated with Syria and suspended bilateral cooperation between the EU and the Syrian government under the MEDA[121], a European Neighbourhood Policy instrument. The European Investment Bank suspended all its loan operations and technical assistance to Syria. At the regional level, the EU coordinated actions with the League of Arab States in its political response to the crisis by: supporting the LAS observer mission since December 2011; commending imposition of LAS sanctions; supporting the Arab Plan of Action and welcoming LAS demands to Assad to end the violence and step aside (Fargues and Fandrich, 2012).

---

120 European Commissioner for International Cooperation, Humanitarian Aid and Crisis Response.

121 The MEDA programme serves "to implement the cooperation measures designed to help Mediterranean non-member countries reform their economic and social structures and mitigate the social and environmental consequences of economic development" (http://europa.eu/legislation_summaries/external_relations/relations_with_third_countries/mediterranean_partner_countries/r15006_en.htm, 18 December 2012)

The EU has been at the forefront in providing humanitarian assistance for Syrian civilians. It has continuously called for unhindered access for humanitarian organisations to assess the need of the civilian population and to provide humanitarian and medical aid where needed. It has provided humanitarian support for refugees and internally displaced persons in its response to the Syrian crisis. The bulk of EU aid was used to respond to the immediate needs of the hundreds of thousands of people affected by the Syrian crisis (Syrians, but also Palestinian and Iraqi refugees) through the provision of food, water, shelter and medical assistance (Fargues and Fandrich, 2012). Furthermore, the EU has allocated over €1.5 billion in humanitarian aid[122].

The EU has also called for a process of transitional justice. It has commended the work of the International Commission of Inquiry on Syria and its investigations into alleged violations of international human rights law with a view to holding accountable, those responsible for such violation, including those that may amount to crimes against humanity (Blockmans, 2012). Despite diplomacy and humanitarian assistance the EU has implemented 17 rounds of tightening sanctions (see box 3). The restrictive measures adopted by the EU included an arms embargo, economic sanction as well as freezing assets held within the EU and of persons associated with the Syrian regime.

122 €515 million from the EU humanitarian aid budget and over €1 billion from member states plus €428 million from other EU funding instruments such as for education and support to host communities and local societies. The biggest bilateral donors were the UK, Germany and Denmark (ECHO Factsheet, 7 November 2013).

- Embargo on exporting arms and equipment for internal repression to Syria
- Ban on exports of key equipment and technology to the Syrian and gas sectors
- Ban on participation in the construction of new power plants in Syria
- Ban on exports of equipment and software intended for use in the monitoring of internet and telephone communications by the Syrian regime.
- Ban on providing grants, loans, export credit insurance, technical assistance, insurance and reinsurance for exports of arms and of equipment for internal repression for Syria.
- Ban on trade in gold, precious metals and diamonds with Syrian public bodies and the central bank.
- Freeze on 52 entities' assets held within the EU, including the Syrian central bank, while ensuring that legitimate trade can continue under strict conditions
- Asset freeze and visa ban on 155 persons associated with the regime and / or responsible for violent repression or human rights abuses
- Prohibition on access to EU airports for cargo flights operated by Syrian carriers, with the exception of mixed passenger and cargo flights.

(Adapted from Blockmans, 2012: 2)

Box 3: EU sanctions on Syria

5.2 National perceptions of the Syrian crisis

France

At the beginning of 2012, France started to depict the crisis in Syria as involving the commitment of mass atrocities. In January 2012, France emphasised that the "international community cannot turn a blind eye to the atrocities in Syria"[123] (Joint declaration of France, Australia, the UK, South Korea and Luxembourg, 18 January 2012). In June, French Foreign Minister Laurent Fabius, described the situation in Syria as a "terrifying spiral of violence" becoming "a threat to the regional stability and security" (Fabius, 1 June 2012). The French Foreign Minister confirmed that the conflict in Syria clearly constituted a civil war (Fabius, 14 June 2012). It was stated further that while the Syrian regime was "sinking into horror, it continues to perpetrate massacre over massacre and now it is the children that are at the front line; they are used as human shields"[124] (Spokesperson of the French Foreign Ministry, 14 June 2012). In its official discourse France has thus described the Syrian crisis as a war since early 2012.

Gerard Araud highlighted that "the longer the international community waits, the more there will be violations of human rights, the greater the risk will be of chaos, civil war, or even an explosion of Syria with all the consequences this may have on the region"[125] (Araud, 1 August 2012). Further depicting the situation in Syria as "appalling", Araud argued that the members opposing action of the Security Council were equally responsible for the "humanitarian disaster" in Syria (Araud, 27 February 2013). The French government thus took note of the ongoing human rights violations and their consequences for the Syrian population.

In July the French Representative to the UNSC described in detail the large-scale atrocities committed in Syria, affirming that they constituted war crimes and crimes against humanity – both crimes included in the RtoP:

123 "… La communauté internationale ne peut fermer les yeux sur les atrocités commises en Syrie."

124 "Ce régime s'enfonce dans l'horreur, continue de perpétrer massacres sur massacres et maintenant, ce sont les enfants qui sont en première ligne ; ils sont utilisés comme bouclier humain."

125 "Plus nous attendons, plus il y aura des violations des droits de l'Homme plus il y aura des risques de chaos, de guerre civile, voire d'explosion de la Syrie avec toutes les conséquences que cela risque d'avoir sur la région."

> *Daily, the regime, its militia and their allies are guilty of gross and systematic violations of human rights ... These are war crimes and crimes against humanity: forced disappearances, torture, sexual violence, summary executions, deliberate attacks against schools and hospitals, repression by medical personnel. The government's use of ballistic missiles, cluster bombs and incendiary bombs against civilians intensifies. More than 100.000 people have died in the conflict, among them many children, and the pace is accelerating.*[126] (Araud, 29 July 2013)

Regarding who was carrying the responsibility in the Syrian crisis, France stated during the UNSC meeting on 31 January 2012 that the Syrian regime was not only not protecting its civilian population but was "shamefully" massacring its population "without restraint". Despite the atrocities committed by the Syrian government, France claimed that the regional consequences (flows of refugees and rising intercommunity tensions) provided enough reason to establish the UNSC's responsibility "even without referring to the responsibility to protect" (Araud, 31 January 2012). François Hollande stressed at the same time that France "must also assume [its] responsibility" (Hollande, 14 March 2012). The French President claimed that "we cannot allow people to be massacred ... by a regime that ... does not want a discussion and a political transition" (idem). While referring the main responsibility of responding to the Syrian crisis primarily to the UNSC, France also showed awareness of its share of responsibility.

During the following meeting of the UNSC in March 2012 the French representative referred more explicitly to the RtoP as the basis for the international community's response to the Syrian crisis:

126 "Quotidiennement, le régime, ses milices et leurs allies se rendent coupables de violations massive et systématiques des droits de l'Homme dans tout le pays. Celles-ci constituent des crimes de guerre et des crimes contre l'Humanité : disparitions forcées, torture, violences sexuelles, exécution sommaires, attaques délibérées contre des écoles et des hôpitaux, répression du personnel médical. L'utilisation par le gouvernement de missiles balistiques, de bombe à fragmentation et de bombes incendiaires contre les civiles s'intensifie. Plus de 100.000 personne ont déjà trouvé la mort dans ce conflit, parmi elles de nombreux enfants, et le rythme s'accélère."

> *In 2005, the evolution of our work led us to recognise that the [Security] Council had the obligation to act when the responsibility to protect was not assured and when gross violations of human rights took place before our eyes, and that governments were accountable for acts of commission and omission alike. That is the context in which we hold today's meeting …*

On the adoption of a resolution in the UN Human Rights Council confirming that crimes against humanity had been committed in Syria, Laurent Fabius declared that "this resolution … makes clear that the Syrian authorities have failed in their primary responsibility to protect the Syrian people"[127] (Fabius, 1 June 2012). Finally, the French Foreign Minister advocated for an alteration of the voting rules in the UN Security Council:

> *After all, this might mean that the rules of the Security Council should evolve because if two large countries, Russia and China say 'no', and consequently, the killing continues, then the public consciousness, you, me everyone reacts by saying that 'no' does not make sense.*[128] (Fabius, 24 September 2012)

Since the beginning of 2012, France clearly described the conflict in Syria as a commitment of mass atrocities, human rights violations and as a civil war that was endangering the Syrian population as well as regional security. Although referring the responsibility to act to the UNSC, France also acknowledged its own responsibility to respond to the Syrian crisis. France openly claimed that the Syrian government was failing in its responsibility to protect its own population as stated by the RtoP.

127 "Cette résolution … établit clairement que les au orités syriennes ont failli à leur responsabilité première de protéger le peuple syrien."

128 "Tout d'abord, cela signifie peut-être que les règles du Conseil de sécurité doive évoluer parce que, si deux pays, la Russie et la Chine disent « non », et par voie de conséquence, la tuerie se poursuit, alors la conscience publique, vous, moi, tout le monde, réagit en disant que ce « non » n'a aucun sens."

Germany

In a joint statement Germany, France and the UK from January 2012, agreed that Assad "who is resorting to brutal military force against his own people and who is responsible for the situation, has lost all legitimacy" and asked him to step down. This was one of the very few accounts of the German government on how it perceived the Syrian crisis. In comparison to the official discourse on the Libyan crisis, the Syrian crisis in terms of the dimension of the violence and the atrocities being committed, the German discourse remained predominantly silent. Significantly, the German discourse on the Syrian crisis did engage neither with the question of responsibility or the RtoP.

The United Kingdom

The British account of the crisis in Syria, was in comparison to the German discourse, much more detailed. Foreign Secretary William Hague expressed in July 2011 that he was "appalled by the continuing heavy violence in Syria and the murder of peaceful protesters". Hague stated further that "the regime has killed over 1500 civilians and has blood on its hands. In November Alistair Burt, Minister for the Middle East welcomed the publication of the Commission of Inquiry's report on human rights violations in Syria. He emphasised that the reports of the "abhorrent treatment of children, including sexual torture" were particularly disturbing and that the "widespread and systematic attacks against civilians may amount to crimes against humanity" (Burt, 28 November 2011). Up to the end of 2011, the UK did not explicitly refer to the commitment of mass atrocities, but acknowledged the killing and murdering of thousands of Syrian civilians.

In February 2012, Hague pointed out that "over the last 11 months, 6.000 people have been killed" in the Syrian conflict. He explained that "the Syrian regime has deployed snipers, tanks, artillery and mortars against civilian protestors and population centres, particularly in the cities of Homs, Idlib, Hama and Daraa" (Hague, 12 February 2012). On the other hand, the UK also drew attention to the fact, that "abuses are also committed by members of anti-government groups in Syria. Although it is clear that these are on a far smaller scale than … the violations perpetrated by the Syrian authorities" the UK called on all parties in Syria to refrain from violence (Brown, 27 February 2012). In contrast to France and Germany, the British government took note of the crimes committed by anti-government forces instead of merely highlighting violations perpetrated by the Assad government.

In March 2012, the Foreign Secretary referred to 10.0000 victims of the Syrian crisis allegedly killed by the Syrian regime as "part of the regime's campaign of terror" (Hague, 31 March 2012). The UK described Syria as being "on the edge of a collapse or of a sectarian civil war" (Hague, 11 June 2012) which "could lead to thousands more casualties, a humanitarian disaster and human rights violations on an even greater scale, and instability in the neighbouring countries" (Hague, 12 June 2012). Finally in May 2013, Hague declared that "with every week that passes we are coming closer to the collapse of Syria and a regional catastrophe, with the lives of thousands more Syrians at stake" (Hague, 20 May 2013). Although still refraining from calling the crisis in Syria an actual civil war, the UK frequently highlighted the number of victims.

In September 2011, the UK expressed the opinion that Assad had "lost all legitimacy" and could "no longer claim to lead Syria" (Cameron, House of Commons, 5 September 2011). With Assad ignoring the calls of the international community to stop the violence, William Hague affirms in January 2012 that there was a "growing consensus that the world must speak up for the people of Syria". He called on the members of the UNSC to act collectively to put an end to the killing in Syria (Hague, 28 January 2012). He emphasised further "to fail to do so would be to undermine the credibility of this institution, ... and fail in this Council's responsibilities" (Hague, 30 January 2012). The UK thus implicitly confirmed that the Syrian government was not holding up its responsibility to protect and called on the UNSC to step in.

Furthermore, the UK Representative to the UN claimed that Russia and China, in supporting the Assad regime had failed in their responsibility as permanent members of the UN Security Council (Grant, UNSC, 4 February 2011). In a similar context, the British Foreign Secretary argued in July 2012 that "the Security Council has not shouldered its responsibilities and so it is not going to try to bring a solution to this ..." (Hague, 20 July 2012). Speaking to the Syria Action Group Hague argued that "we face a heavy responsibility today. The world is looking for leadership to end the bloodshed and horror in Syria" (Hague, 30 June 2012). Therefore the "Security Council's responsibility to act is now even greater than before ... if it is not, the scene is set for months of greater bloodshed, greater suffering, and greater danger to international peace and security" (Hague, 29 August 2012).

Although describing the violence and crimes committed in Syria in great detail, the UK appeared hesitant to explicitly make use of the terms mass atrocities, human rights violations and war up until August 2012. It claimed that the Assad government had lost its legitimacy and called on the UNSC to act. Although highlighting Russia's and China's responsibility as UNSC members, the British government did not explain or refer to its own responsibility in responding to the Syrian crisis before September 2012.

National perspectives on the role of the EU

In case of the Syrian crisis, none of the three chosen member states seemed to have envisaged a particular role for the EU in the crisis response. In the official French, German and British discourses the EU was thus mainly absent. As one of few exceptions, the French Defence Minister stated in June 2012 that "for European defence, it is time to recover". He continued to elaborate that "Europe has to become a producer of security, in the sense that it assumes its own security". Although this ambition had not progressed in the previous years, according to Jean-Yves Le Drian, there was a shared conviction emerging from the 2012 NATO Summit in Chicago on "the importance of a stronger and more capable European defence" (Le Drian, 7 June 2012). Yet, neither France, Germany nor the UK mentioned the EU's role in managing the Syrian crisis in their official discourse.

5.3 National responses to the Syrian crisis

France

Since mid-2012, France seemed inclined to respond to the Syrian crisis with more coercive means. Signalling its willingness to participate in a military response to the Syrian crisis, the French Defence Minister, Jean Yves Le Drian, stated in June 2012 that "if there is a military intervention, France will take its place"[129] (Le Drian, 7 June 2012). Yet, in July, Gerard Araud affirmed that France's crisis response will be primarily political and emphasised that "there will be no military intervention, we will not help to add war to war"[130] (Araud, 29 July 2012).

In August 2013, after the chemical weapon attacks, France confirmed that its foreign policy was based on the respect of international law. The latter was, however, according to Laurent Fabius evolving over time. He argued that international law should not be an excuse to let mass murders be committed and affirmed that "this is why I recognise the principle of the 'responsibility to protect' civilians" (Fabius, 27 August 2013). Significantly, the French President François Hollande declared three days later that

> *the chemical massacre in Damascus cannot and must not go unpunished. Otherwise this would mean running the risk of an escalation that would trivialise the use of these weapons and threaten other countries* (Hollande, 31 August 2013).

At the same time, Hollande underlined that he was not in favour of an international intervention aiming to overthrow the Syrian "dictator" but that the Syrian regime must be stopped from bringing "irreparable damage" over its population. The President concluded that he "would not call it war but the sanction of a monstrous violation of the rights of the human being"[131] (Hollande, 31 August 2013). Revealing a certain indecisiveness, France switched its position from signalling its readiness to participate in a military intervention and from calling the Syrian crisis a civil war

129 "S'il y a une intervention militaire, la France tiendra sa place."

130 "Il n'y aura pas d'intervention militaire, nous n'allons pas ajouter la guerre à la guerre."

131 "Je ne suis pas favorable à une intervention internationale qui viserait … à renverser le dictateur, mais j'estime qu'un coup d'arrêt doit être porte à un régime qui commet l'irréparable sur la population … Je ne parle pas d'une guerre, mais de la sanction d'une violation monstrueuse des droits de la personne humaine."

in June 2012 to acting on the basis of the RtoP and sanctioning the Assad regime instead of making war in August 2013.

The calls for the necessity of punishment were repeated by French Prime Minister Jean-Marc Ayrault, who affirmed that "there has been a violation of a key international protocol established for 90 years, which prohibits the use of chemical weapons"[132] (Ayrault, Assemblée Nationale, 4 September 2013). Ayrault argued that the "crime of gasing a population" could not go unpunished if not there was the risk of an extension of the security threat not only to the whole region but in fact to the whole world[133] (idem). Laurent Fabius reiterated that the solution to the Syrian crisis will be political and not military but warned at the same time that "if we do not put a stop to such acts of the regime, there will be no political solution"[134] (Fabius, 4 September 2013). At the same time, a military intervention was dependent on the decision of the US. The Foreign Minister stressed that France would not intervene alone (Fabius, 8 September 2013). The use of military force thus aimed ostensibly at punishing the Assad regime and not at protecting the Syrian civilian population.

During the session of the *Assemblée Nationale* on 4 September 2011, members of parliament debated extensively and lively whether France should participate in a military intervention in Syria led by the US. Those arguing against the French contribution claimed that there was no conclusive evidence on who had committed the chemical weapons attack as well as no authorisation in form of a UNSC resolution. Furthermore, it was argued that it is France's "responsibility to protect French interests and French security"[135] (Jean-Louis Borloo, Assemblée Nationale, 4 September 2013). Those in favour of a military intervention on the other hand were of the opinion that the paralysis of the UN Security Council should not prevent France from taking action when universally accepted international law is violated (Élisabeth Guigou, idem). Prime Minister Ayrault argued further that it is France's responsibility to put a stop to the use of weapons of mass destruction and chemical weapons and warned that if not Iran might be the next in line to use them (Ayrault, idem). Although ex-

132 "… il y eu une violation d'un protocole internationale essentiel celui qui, établi il y a 90 ans, interdit l'usage des armes chimiques … ."

133 "… gazer une population, ce crime-là ne peut donc rester impuni sinon c'est le risque de la récidive, la menace de l'extension et c'est la sécurité – pas simplement des Syrien, pas simplement de la région – la sécurité du monde qui est en cause."

134 "… si nous ne mettons pas un coup d'arrêt à de tels agissements du régime, il n'y aura pas de solution politique."

135 "… notre responsabilité est de protéger les Français et les intérêts français."

plicitly referring to France's responsibility to protect, the notion was linked primarily to French security interests and the necessity to discipline the Assad regime.

At the same time Gerard Araud emphasised that the RtoP entails the prevention of the four RtoP crimes, including their incitement, through appropriate and necessary means. He affirmed that France accepts this responsibility and will act in accordance to it (Araud, 11 September 2013). Although underlining the importance of the first pillar of the RtoP, Araud explained further that prevention goes beyond the first RtoP pillar and can include further measures such as referrals to the ICC and the use of force if necessary (idem). The French Ambassador cited amongst others, the cases of Libya and Kenya as examples for the international community taking responsibility and being able to effectively prevent atrocities. Therefore Araud stated that

> *faced with such a massacre and at the risk of its repetition, we have a choice: a choice between resignation and action. No reaction would mean leaving the Syrian people to barbarism and the entire region to fall into chaos. It would protect a murderous regime using weapons of mass destruction. Action is needed to prevent further attacks and to trigger a political solution, if not the fine words – 'never again' – remain powerless to generate.*[136] (Araud, 11 September 2013)

Explicitly referring to the RtoP and signalling its willingness to assume its share of responsibility also with military force, France was in favour of a strong response to the Syrian crisis since mid-2012. Arguably acting on the basis of the RtoP and with aim of protecting the Syrian population and preventing the further use of chemical weapons, France called for a military intervention in Syria. At the same time, France demanded on several occasions that military force was necessary to punish the Assad government and sanction the use of weapons of mass atrocities. It therefore became unclear whether the primary objective was actual protection of the civilian population requiring a response going beyond military strikes or whether the aim was rather 'to teach Assad a lesson'.

136 "Face à un tel massacre et au risque de sa répétition, nous avons le choix : le choix entre la complicité résignée et l'action. Ne pas réagir, ce serait abandonner le peuple syrien a la barbarie et la région entière au chaos. Ce serait protéger un régime meurtrier ayant recours à des armes de destruction massive. L'action s'impose pour éviter une nouvelle attaque et pour provoquer une solution politique, que les belles formules – « Plus jamais ça » - resteront impuissantes à générer."

Germany

Unsurprisingly, Germany advised caution in response to the Syrian crisis, particularly with regard to the use of force. German State Minister Werner Hoyer warned in August 2011 to consider the question of a military intervention in Syria carefully. He reminded that despite legal arguments, there was also no regional support for coercive measures (Hoyer, 2 August 2011). Foreign Minister Westerwelle argued that the international community "can break the spiral of violence and avert the logic of war only if the Security Council acts united and agrees on a resolution ... that constraints Assad with strong non-military sanctions"[137] (Westerwelle, 17 July 2012). In January 2013, Westerwelle argued further that "Germany does not get engaged in speculations or in preparations of any intervention in Syria"[138] (idem, 14 January 2013). Germany was also essentially opposed to providing the Syrian opposition forces with arms. Westerwelle declared that "it is important to weigh all decisions not just by what seems appropriate in a short-term but by what ultimately helps the people of Syria and brings peace and stability to the whole region"[139] (Westerwelle, 28 August 2013). Despite its reluctance, Germany seems to have adopted a people-centred perspective toward the Syrian crisis.

After the chemical weapons attack in Syria in August 2013 and Obama's announcement on a military intervention in Syria, Germany affirmed that its military participation was neither requested nor considered (idem, 1 September 2013). Westerwelle argued that the international community should not interfere in Syria's civil war with the goal of 'regime change' or to force a military decision in favour of the rebels. The Foreign Minister, however, urged the international community to find the right response to the first use of chemical weapons of mass destruction in the 21st century.

137 "Wir können die Spirale der Gewalt nur durchbrechen und eine Logik des Krieges abwenden, wenn der Sicherheitsrat Geschlossenheit zeigt und sich auf eine Resolution einigt ..., die das Assad-Regime mit harten, nicht-militärischen Sanktionen belegt ..."

138 "Deutschland beteiligt sich weder an Spekulationen noch an Vorbereitungen für irgendwelche Interventionen in Syrien."

139 "Umso wichtiger ist es, alle Entscheidungen genau abzuwägen, nicht nur danach, was gerade kurzfristig geboten erscheint, sondern danach, was am Ende auch den Menschen in Syrien , dem Frieden und der Stabilität in der gesamten Region wirklich dient."

He claimed that

> *if the international community were to return to business as usual … this would mean a heavy burden for our future. Anyone who considers the use of such weapons must know that they will face the consequences of the international community*[140] *(idem).*

At the same time Westerwelle emphasised that it was important to await the report of the UN Chemical Weapons Inspectors before taking any further measures. The Foreign Minister justified Germany's position on the basis that the culture of military restraint had been a constant in his foreign policy approach since 2009. Seemingly well aware of the criticism Germany had received for this position, Westerwelle underlined that Germany's reluctance towards a military intervention in Syria was not affected by the then upcoming federal elections on 22 September 2013.

Confirmed in its approach to the Syrian crisis with exclusively non-coercive means, Westerwelle welcomed the agreement of the US, Russia and Syria on the destruction of the Syrian chemical weapons arsenal. He stated:

> *If the words are put into action now, the chances for a political solution increase considerably. There will be no lasting peace with military means but only through a political solution.* (Westerwelle, 14 September quoted in RP Online, 2013)

In line with its general aversion to deploy its military abroad, Germany was clearly against any kind of military intervention in Syria. The German discourse on how to respond to the crisis did not mention the RtoP or the more general term responsibility. Yet, even if unwilling to participate in any kind of military action against the Assad government, Germany still advocated the punishment of the regime for the use of chemical weapons against its own population.

140 "Würde die international Gemeinschaft zur Tagesordnung übergehen, wenn der Einsatz chemischer Massenvernichtungswaffen bewiesen ist, wäre dies eine schwer Bürde für unsere Zukunft. Jeder, der den Einsatz solcher Waffen in Erwägung zieht, muss wissen, dass er mit Konsequenzen der Weltgemeinschaft rechnen muss."

The United Kingdom

After the UNSC's failure to agree on a resolution on Syria in February 2012, the UK laid out a further plan for the British crisis response containing seven steps of action. First, the UK confirmed to continue to support the League of Arab States. Second, it aimed at widening the international coalition of nations seeking a peaceful resolution in Syria. Third, the British government planned to intensify its contacts with members of the Syrian opposition. Fourth, the UK committed to continue to raise the situation in front of the UNSC. Fifth, British officials agreed to increase pressure through the EU. Six, the UK committed itself to work with others to ensure that those responsible for crimes in Syria were held to account. And seventh, the UK would try to make clear to the Syrian regime that its use of violence is unacceptable to the civilised world (Hague, 12 February 2012). In early 2012, the UK did thus not consider or discuss a military solution to the Syrian crisis, but relied exclusively on political and legal measures.

William Hague reiterated on 11 June 2012 that the UK was "working intensively to find a peaceful means of resolving the crisis ... in close cooperation with our European partners". The British course of action was first to push for implementation of Annan's peace plan; second, to increase pressure and isolate the regime internationally; and third, to provide justice accountability and humanitarian assistance (Hague, 11 June 2012). However, Hague also declared that the UK would "not rule out any other option which could at any stage stop the bloodshed" (idem). The British government thus slowly moved from focusing on non-coercive means to also considering measures 'other' than peaceful ones.

Pushing for further action, the UK agreed with the US as early as June 2011 that there was sufficient evidence that chemical weapons, including the toxic gas sarin, had been used in Syria by the Assad regime (Hague, 14 June 2011). Therefore Hague called on the international community "to be prepared to do more to save lives ... and to stop the regime using chemical weapons against its people" (idem). After a third veto in the UNSC on a resolution on Syria, the Foreign Secretary declared that the UK will be "doing more outside the Security Council" and will therefore intensify its "work to support the Syrian opposition and to give humanitarian aid" (Hague, 20 July 2012).

In March 2013, the British government for the first time linked the Syrian crisis to its own security interests. Hague emphasised that the situation in Syria was vital to British national interest for three reasons. The first was the growth of extremism in Syria. The Foreign Secretary claimed that "we cannot allow Syria to become another breeding ground for terrorists who pose a threat to our national security" (Hague, 6 March 2013). The second ground was that the Syrian crisis was undermining the peace of the region and related to that the British government's concern about the Syrian regime's willingness to use chemical weapons. Hague also warned that Iran might be providing considerable military support to the Syrian regime. And the third reason was that British foreign policy is inseparably linked to upholding human rights, protecting lives and supporting international law. Therefore, Hague argued, the UK "must assist the genuine moderate and democratic forces in Syria who are in dire need of help and who feel abandoned by the international community" (idem). Almost as to prepare the British public but without specifying the kind of instrument the UK was intending to use in response to the Syrian crisis, the British government closely tied the fate of Syria to its own national interests.

Yet, not later than after the alleged chemical weapons attacks by the Syrian regime in August 2013, it was clear that something needed to be done. William Hague declared:

> *This is the first chemical warfare in the 21st century. It has to be unacceptable, we have to confront something that is a war crime, something that is a crime against humanity. If we don't do so, then we will have to confront even bigger war crimes in the future.* (Hague, 28 August 2013)

The subsequent debates on a British participation in a military intervention in Syria on 29 August 2013 in the House of Commons crystallised around the issues of legality, legitimacy and feasibility of a military intervention. David Cameron referred to Tony Blair's doctrine of humanitarian intervention according to which the international community could circumvent international law in the case of genocide. Furthermore, the RtoP was, for the first time, cited as a legitimate basis for action and an argument in favour of military intervention:

> *... did not the world leaders and the UN sign up unanimously in 2005 to the doctrine of the responsibility to protect, ... ? Syria has defaulted on its responsibility to protect its own citizens, so surely now the international community and ourselves have a responsibility to undertake what we agreed to do as recently as 2005.* (Sir Tony Baldry, House of Commons, 29 August 2013)

Furthermore, those in favour of a military intervention also argued that British national interests were at stake not only in terms of a stable Middle East in general but also in relation to the use of chemical weapons specifically (Cameron, idem). Finally, it was claimed that inaction would "make a complete mockery of the international norm of the responsibility to protect." (Lord Hannay of Chisnick, idem). While the norm had already been damaged a lot in Syria, the military intervention was seen as "a chance to honour it in the face of a massive breach of international humanitarian law" (idem).

Opponents on the other hand contended that there was a widespread scepticism among the British public about any further military involvement overseas (Liam Fox, idem). Furthermore, concerns were expressed about the outcome of a military intervention and to what extent it could be engineered. There was criticism regarding the lack of a legal basis which was also needed in case of the application of the RtoP:

> *The effort to achieve a resolution under Chapter VII is a vital component of the doctrine of the responsibility to protect, because if no such resolution is achieved ... we turn to what was once called humanitarian intervention and now is called responsibility to protect.* (Sir Menzies Campbell, idem).

In line with the RtoP, sceptics emphasised that it was fundamental to exhaust all political and diplomatic means before considering more coercive measures (idem). Furthermore, it was argued that the RtoP "could have been invoked 100.000 lives ago. Therefore the idea that it becomes relevant because chemical weapons have been used is a non-starter" (John Baron, idem). In addition, it was underlined that there is a difference between humanitarian intervention and RtoP. While humanitarian intervention "is specifically about boots on the ground", the RtoP is about protection and not about punishment (Lord Kerr of Kinlochard, idem). "It is about imposing ceasefires, separating warring parties and brining in aid. It is about a process of enforced pacification. It has nothing to do with punishment." (Idem)

Finally, opponents brought forward arguments on the feasibility of a military intervention in terms of Syria's military and political alliance with Iran and the Lebanese Hezbollah as well as its political cover from Russia. In this context, concerns were expressed that a military intervention could lead to a widening of the war particularly into Lebanon (Lord Williams of Baglan, idem). In the end, British MPs rejected the government motion on a possible UK military action against Syria by 285 votes to 272.

Significantly, the RtoP appeared in the official British discourse on the Syrian crisis only after the chemical weapons attack in August 2013 and in order to legitimise a military strike against the Assad regime Although both proponents and opponents of a military intervention in Syria referred to the RtoP, the emerging norm seemed to be linked very closely to the calls for a need to sanction the Assad government and to legitimise the use of force. The late prominence of the RtoP in case of the Syrian crisis and the connection to the aim of punishment via coercive means leave great doubts as to its actual influence.

Assessing the application – protection vs. punishment?

As in the Libyan crisis, international and European responses to the Syrian crisis revealed different interpretations of whether the RtoP applied and what it meant. While the RtoP was absent in the German discourse, France and the UK seemed to agree, after the use of chemical weapons of mass destruction in Syria, that it was their responsibility to punish the Syrian government for such a crime. The RtoP was well reflected in the French and the British discourse, but seemed to be ultimately linked to the need to sanction the Syrian government rather than to protect the Syrian civilian population responsibly.

France described the events in Syria as atrocities and massacres and emphasised that the crisis was becoming a threat to regional stability and security. In July, France referred to the Syrian crisis as humanitarian disaster. It was also confirmed that the large-scale atrocities constituted war crimes and crimes against humanity – two of the four RtoP crimes. In light of the increasing violence France signalled to be willing to assume its responsibility and stressed at the same time that the regional consequences of the crisis provided enough reasons to establish the UNSC's responsibility even without the RtoP. France also argued that the Syrian authorities had failed in their primary responsibility to protect the Syrian people. In light of Russia's and Chinas continuous use of their vetoes, the French government suggested an alteration of the voting rules in the UNSC. In terms of the actual crisis response, France seemed willing to participate in a military action since mid-2012. It also stated that international law should not stand in the way of protecting people from mass murder and confirmed its commitment to the RtoP. Moreover, the French government did not refer to the term war but advocated the sanctions of the gross human rights violations. It was reiterated more explicitly that the crime of using chemical weapons should not remain unpunished. In the debate on a French participation in a military intervention in Syria at the French Parliament, the RtoP was used for arguments in favour as well as against military action.

In the case of Germany, the Syrian crisis was almost absent in the official discourse. It was merely stated that the Assad regime was responsible for the crisis situation and that he had lost all legitimacy. As to the proposed military intervention, Germany showed itself even more reluctant than in case of the Libyan crisis. It was emphasised that there was no regional support and no legal basis for coercive measures. At the same time, Germany stressed the need to sanction the use of chemical weapons. Although Germany did not refer to the RtoP explicitly, the recommended focus of the crisis response, at least after the 2013 chemical weapon attacks, was not only on sanctioning the Syrian regime, but also on the protection of the Syrian civilians, adopting a people-centred approach to the crisis response.

In contrast to Germany's reluctance, the UK spoke in November 2011 about the widespread and brutal attacks against civilians in Syria. Moreover, the UK gave a detailed account on the number of victims and the alleged crimes committed. In March 2012 it was claimed that Syria was on the edge of a civil war. The UK government argued that inaction in the UNSC undermined the credibility of the body and constituted a failure in the institution's responsibility. After Russia and China's third veto in the UNSC on a Syrian Resolution, the UK declared that it would do more outside the UNSC framework. Furthermore, the UK legitimised its crisis response by arguing that the Syrian crisis was vital to national security interests in terms of terrorism, in terms of the use of chemical weapons and in terms of Britain's foreign policy principles such as protecting lives.

After the US call for support of a military intervention at the beginning of September, the UK claimed that the Syrian government had failed in its responsibility to protect and that therefore, the international community and Britain itself had to take over, as agreed in 2005 in the RtoP. The parliamentary debate on Britain's participation in a military campaign over Syria crystallised around questions of legality and the lack of popular support. Furthermore, it was argued that the RtoP could not be used to punish the Syrian government for the use of chemical weapons. It was emphasised that there was a difference between humanitarian intervention, meaning boots on the ground, and the RtoP aiming at protection and not punishment. Similar to France, the RtoP was used both by proponents and opponents of British military action in Syria.

Although member states agreed on the importance of a stronger European defence, this aspiration was not put into practice, at least not in the case of the Syrian crisis. While the EU was very active in implementing sanctions against the Syrian regime, as well as in providing humanitarian aid, a more decisive and robust action was not implemented. With the UNSC blocked by Russia's and China's veto and the EU's commitment to international law, the EU's options were limited. Until the chemical weapons attacks in August 2013 and the US demand for military action it seemed as if the whole world was unsure about how and with what means to react to the Syrian crisis.[141] Although the EU's profile as a security actor remained even lower than in the Libyan crisis, it should be noted that all other international players were equally unable to act as effective security actors in response to the Syrian crisis.

While the use of chemical weapons of mass destruction and the sanctioning of such an action are not included in the RtoP, the RtoP's application in case of the Syrian points toward a misuse of the norm. Possibly influenced by the US, the dominant European discourse was on punishment and not on protection. RtoP was further used to emphasise the evolving character of international law and that a vetoed UNSC and thus the lack of international legality would not necessarily impede the legitimacy of a military intervention.

141 The paralysis of the international community in its response to the Syrian crisis cannot only be explained by a blocked UN Security Council but further with a lack of information on what was happening on the Syrian ground. While in the case of Libya, the opposition movement seemed fairly united in their revolt against the Gaddafi regime, this is not the case in Syria. By contrast the Syrian opposition is deeply divided due to Syria's complex demographics and tensions between the sectarian divisions (74 per cent of the population is Sunni; significant minorities such as Christians, Alawites and non-Sunni Muslims each make up about 10 per cent) (Buckley, 2012).

5.4 Preliminary conclusion

The analysis of the Syrian crisis has shown that the RtoP did play a role in European responses but much less than it did in European responses to the Libyan crisis. France and the UK both reaffirmed their commitment to the emerging norm and declared their willingness to assume their responsibility as members of the international community. While Germany's crisis response was explicitly limited to non-coercive measures, the Franco-British approach did not exclude the possibility of using military force. They even agreed on the trigger to implement coercive measures – the use of chemical weapons of mass atrocities and justified their positions on the basis of the RtoP. In this context, there seemed to be a collective understanding – at least between France and Britain – on what the RtoP meant and entailed. The discourse, however, focused on the aim of punishing the Syrian government for the alleged use of chemical weapons rather than on protecting the civilian population. This justification for applying the RtoP seemed to be going beyond the original scope of RtoP referring to the four crimes – war crimes, crimes against humanity, genocide and ethnic cleansing.

As in the case of the Libyan crisis, the influence of the RtoP as an emerging international norm therefore remained moderate. Although it was used in the decision-making process on how to best respond to the crisis the proposed action did not match the prescriptions of the RtoP. Furthermore, the RtoP was seen as a legitimate basis to act upon only after the option of a military was openly considered. The Syrian case therefore confirms the assumption that the RtoP is increasingly linked to the use of force. This might explain why France and the UK, who were eager on participating in a military operation in Syria, openly supported and promoted the emerging norm. At the same time, the RtoP's increasingly coercive interpretation might be the reason why compliance with the RtoP was decreasing in Germany and the EU.

The EU in its role as security actor in the neighbourhood was able to deploy sanctions and deliver humanitarian aid. The 2012 Chicago summit aspiration of a greater role for the EU in defence, however, did not materialise in the case of the Syrian crisis. In the case of the Syrian crisis the EU did not act as norm entrepreneur for the RtoP either. Although acknowledging the commitment of RtoP crimes (i.e. crimes against humanity) and the failure of the Syrian regime to protect its civilian population, the EU discourse did not promote the RtoP any further. By contrast, it affirmed that the main responsibility had to be assumed by the Syrian government itself. Yet, in the aftermath and possibly as lessons learned from both the Libyan and Syrian crisis, the EU started to create new capabilities for the prevention of mass atrocities. The EU therefore supported the creation of a new Task Force on the EU Prevention of Mass Atrocities in January 2012.

With regard to the RtoP's development as an emerging international norm, four conclusions can be drawn from the Syrian crisis. First, the application of the RtoP in case of the Libyan crisis has increased reluctance among sceptics of the norm, such as Russia and China, but also Brazil and India, to agree to the application of non-coercive and coercive measure under emerging norm. Therefore, China and Russia referred constantly to the lessons learned from Libya when justifying their vetoes on UNSC draft resolutions on Syria (Brozus, 2012). Second, while European countries pointed towards the flexibility of international law, UNSC members Russia and China emphasised the dominance of the non-interference principle, national sovereignty and national interests. The Syrian crisis thus highlights the current limitations of the RtoP. Despite RtoP's emphasis on the protection of populations over the past decade, the UNSC veto system still creates situations in which states can commit mass atrocity crimes against their citizens without facing any consequences (Williams et al., 2012).

Third, as the US was pushing for military action in Syria after the alleged chemical weapon attacks by the Syrian government, President Obama managed to persuade some of its European partners to support his initiative. However, Obama did not make any reference to the RtoP but justified the need for military action on the basis of US national security interests. As in the case of Libya, the US did not act as norm entrepreneur for the RtoP either. Finally, and again as in the Libyan crisis, the Syrian conflict has shown that the RtoP is increasingly linked to the use of force and the question of whether to intervene militarily or not. Significantly, in the case of Syria, the RtoP became dominant in European discourses only after the option of a military response had been put back on the table.

Chapter 6: From Kosovo to Syria – what has changed?

The results of the case study analysis conducted in the two previous chapters shows that in both cases the RtoP's influence seems moderate and does not go beyond affecting the discourse. Still in the case of Libya, the RtoP was much more dominant in European discourses than it was in the case of the Syrian crisis. It has widely been argued that the application in case of Libya had a significant impact on the extent to which the international community in general would consider the use of the RtoP in the case of Syria (Brozus, 2012; Chesterman, 2011; Dunne and Gifkins, 2011; Jolyon, 2013). The link between Syria and Libya in terms of the application of the RtoP has also been present in the European discourses themselves. Yet, European discourses have frequently emphasised that the two crises are not comparable. Furthermore, references were made to the Kosovo crisis and intervention in 1999, against which this thesis assesses whether the RtoP actually makes a difference. This assessment chapter starts by looking at the references made in European discourses on the comparison of Syria, Libya and Kosovo, highlighting the link between the RtoP's practical application and its development as a norm. It also considers the existing academic debate on similarities and differences in the implementation of the military interventions in Kosovo and in Libya with the aim of assessing whether there is an actual difference in practice. The following section will then highlight the research results from the investigation of the Libyan and the Syrian crisis according to the chosen indicators for the case study analysis: the role of the UN and the EU as norm entrepreneurs, the crisis perceptions and the crisis responses. Potential lessons learned from the role of and the link between the RtoP and the EU in the Libyan and the Syrian crisis will be discussed in part three of this chapter before coming to a conclusion on the empirical analysis.

6.1 Relating Syria, Libya and Kosovo

In the French discourse it was stated on several occasions that the situation in Syria was not comparable to the crisis in Libya (Assemblée Nationale, 22 March 2011; Juppé, 24 March 2011; 23 May 2011; Araud, 8 June 2011). It was emphasised that the political, geographic and geostrategic situations in Libya and Syria were different. Alain Juppé highlighted that "even if there are several hundreds of thousands of deaths in Syria, the context is not the one we experienced in the attack on Benghazi" (Juppé, 23 May 2011). Juppé explained further that in the case of Libya, other Arab countries supported the military action and it was authorised by a UNSC resolution. By contrast, in the case of Syria the Security Council was unable to reach an agreement. The Foreign Minister stressed that the absence of a decisive response to the Syrian crisis was not due to the lack of willingness of France and other partners, the British in particular, but because the international context was not the same. France referred to the Libyan crisis response as an example in which the international community was successful in preventing further mass atrocities and assuming its responsibility as contained in the RtoP.

On the comparison between the situations in Libya and Syria, German Foreign Minister Guido Westerwelle affirmed that "in each country the situations are very different and that is why there can only be a tailored political response" (Euractiv, 2011). The UK, similarly to France, stressed in June 2011 that there was "no prospect of a UN Resolution similar to 1973 on Libya" and that the international community therefore needs "to work . . in other ways" (Hague, 12 June 2011). Cameron affirmed in September in 2011 that in the case of Libya there was an "ought" as well as a "could". While the international community had a "moral obligation" to intervene, it was also able, due to support of the Arab nations, the UNSC and NATO. The "could" was, on the other hand, not present in the case of the Syrian crisis (Cameron, 22 September 2011).

Similarly to the European official discourses, scholars have pointed out that the conflict in Syria is distinct from the conflict in Libya and does thus not precipitate for the same response (Buckley, 2012). Initially, the rebel operations in Syria for example have arguably not been near the scale of the rebel operations in Libya, while the latter did not have sectarian divisions comparable to those in

Syria[142]. Furthermore, aside the fact that the Syrian government's tanks and artillery have outmatched the rebels' rifles and homemade bombs, the Syrian regime controls an army that is unified and committed to forcefully suppressing the protests and thus cannot be compared to Libya where the military helped topple the unpopular leader (idem). Another significant difference is that the Syrian regime was continuously backed by its strong and long-standing alliances with Iran and Russia. However, from a people-centred perspective, the situation in Syria is very similar to the crisis in Libya, as the citizens have been protesting against poverty, lack of democracy and corruption, and their protests have been suppressed violently by their *de facto* leader.

Although in Syria 2013, an international military intervention could be averted, it is worthwhile taking a look at the similarities and differences between the military intervention in Libya in 2011 and the one in Kosovo in 1999. By contrast with Kosovo, the military intervention in Libya ended with initial combat operations. Furthermore, the Libya air campaign was significantly less intense, but lasted much longer (Chivvis, 2012). Regarding civilian losses during the military operation in Libya the numbers of victims vary. The UN International Commission of Inquiry on Libya reported that during 20 NATO air strikes, 60 civilians were killed in 5 of them (UN, 2 March 2012). The New York Times stated that during 25 air strikes at least 40, possibly more than 70 civilians, lost their lives (Chivers and Schmidt, 2011). Human Rights Watch claimed that the military intervention caused at least 72 civilians deaths (Bolopion, 2011). In comparison to that, an estimated number of 5000 civilians died during the air campaign over Kosovo. This might be related to the pace of NATO's operational tempo, which was significantly slower in Libya than in Kosovo (Vira and Cordesman, 2011).

142 Syria's complex demographics make it a difficult country to rule. It is believed that three-fourths of the country's roughly 22 million are Sunnis, including most of the Kurdish minority in the northeast (Bhalla, 2011). Most estimates put the number of Alawites in Syria at around 1.5 million, or close to 7 percent of the population. When combined with Shia and Ismailis, non-Sunni Muslims average around 13 percent. Christians of several variations, including Greek Orthodox and Maronite, make up around 10 percent of the population. Rather than exhibiting a clear Sunni-Shiite religious-ideological divide, Syria's history can be more accurately described as a struggle between the Sunnis on one hand and a group of minorities on the other (idem.). It is the divisions between the Syrian opposition that have prevented them from forming a unified force that the international community could support. President Assad belongs to the Alawite sect, a small, obscure branch of Shiism. Assad has concentrated power in the hands of his family and other members of the Alawite sect, which makes up the majority of the Syrian security forces (Buckley, 2012).

The Kosovo intervention was not authorised by the UN Security Council but was in the aftermath described as legitimate though illegal. While the Libya intervention was mandated by a UNSC resolution, it was still claimed that the military intervention was illegal as the mandate was extended *ex post* to target Muammar Gaddafi. The spectre of Kosovo thus remains in terms of the mismatch between the protection of civilians mandate and the declared aim of the intervening states to remove Gaddafi from power and to protect their national security (Dunne and Gifkins, 2011).

As to the role of the EU as a security actor, French President Nicolas Sarkozy claimed on 31 August 2011 that in Libya, Europe was able "to do the job" without "begging" the US for support as it had been the case in Kosovo in 1999. However, the question remains open whether without American operational support particularly during the first few days of the intervention, Europe would still be able to call the Libyan intervention a success. According to Nigel White (2012: 220), the change within the UNSC from the situation in Kosovo in 1999, where the UNSC could not agree on military action to protect the Kosovars, to Libya in 2011 is marginal, but sufficient to give the initial action a sound legal basis. That marginal push may have helped by the emergence in the early twenty-first century of the idea that there is a responsibility to protect on the part of the international community.

In comparison to the previous norm of humanitarian intervention which was contingent upon national interests, the RtoP would only make a difference if the crisis response was conducted from the point of view of those civilians in need, rather than those considering the intervention. The main difference of the RtoP is thus the focus on the protection of civilians based on the human security concept. The analysis of the Libyan crisis has shown that Europe talks about protection but lacks the according implementation. Significantly, the way the 2011 military intervention in Libya was implemented and conducted differed only slightly from the 1999 Kosovo intervention. In the case of Syria, Europe talks about punishment rather than protection and fails to act altogether. From this perspective, the RtoP does seem to make a slight difference on a rhetorical level but certainly not in practice.

6.2 Norm entrepreneurs, crisis perception and response

The roles of the UN and the EU

UNSC Resolution 1973 was the first time that the UN had taken such quick and decisive action, explicitly based on the RtoP and without government consent. From the outset of the crisis, UN officials warned of the imminent threat of mass atrocities and framed their response in the RtoP language. The analysis of the UN discourse has shown that the RtoP was taken into consideration and guided political decision-making in response to the Libyan crisis. Resolution 1973 stated explicitly that the primary goal of the intervention was the protection of Libyan civilians. Significantly, Resolutions 1970 and 1973 referred merely to Libya's responsibility to protect and did not explicitly mention the responsibility of the international community to protect the Libyan population.

In Syria, the UNSC remained blocked due to the repeated vetoes by Russia and China. In comparison to the Libyan crisis, the UN response to the Syrian crisis was not framed in the RtoP language until May 2013, two years after the outbreak of violence, when it called on the Syrian government to meet its responsibility to protect its population. While the UN identified the Syrian crisis as a threat to international peace and security and linked the unfolding events to terrorism, it did not actively promote the RtoP as a legitimate basis for the international community to respond to the conflict in Syria.

The EU clearly supported the RtoP but remained unable and incapable of reacting with means other than civilian. From the beginning, the EU emphasised that it was merely its responsibility to help. Instead of speaking of mass atrocities, the EU described the crisis in Libya as humanitarian emergency or disaster. The offer to deploy a military CSDP mission to support the delivery of humanitarian aid seemed more like an alibi than a serious proposal. The EU could have acted as norm entrepreneur for the RtoP in case of the Libyan crisis but failed to reach a consensus among its core member states.

HR Catherin Ashton's view of the EU as a civilian power was confirmed in the case of the Libyan crisis. From the member state's perspective, the EU's role as primarily a civilian actor was also affirmed. For both France and the UK, the military operation would naturally be conducted by NATO and not the EU. Although Germany emphasised the importance of the CSDP for the EU's global role, it was at the forefront of those calling for a peaceful response to the Libyan crisis on the basis of diplomacy and sanctions. While Europe was able to play a more decisive role in the case of Libya than it was in the case of the Kosovo in 1999, the military crisis response took place outside the EU institutional framework and with help of the US.

In Syria, the EU referred to the responsibility of the Syrian government as well as the responsibility of the UN Security Council, although acknowledging the failure of the Syrian state's responsibility to protect its citizens Europe's responsibility to protect was merely pointed out by the European Parliament. Holding on to the claim that the main responsibility in the Syrian crisis laid with the Syrian government itself, the EU did not act as norm entrepreneur for the RtoP. In comparison to the Libyan crisis, the EU advised against any form of military intervention due to the lack of local and regional support and the danger of regional instability. The EU managed to activate its Civil Protection Mechanism but remained inactive in the area of military crisis management. Furthermore, it applied a range of sanctions and other non-coercive measures. Among the 'Big 3', none seemed to have envisaged a particular role for the EU in the response to the Syrian crisis. Although European defence ministers emphasised the need for a stronger European defence policy in 2012, as a security actor the EU remained, along with the rest of the world, indecisive on how to best respond to the Syrian crisis.

The crisis perceptions and policy responses

The UK labelled the crisis in Libya as an RtoP case and in contrast to France and Germany, acknowledged that the Libyan government was failing in its responsibility to protect. However, initially it did not indicate who was supposed to assume the responsibility, if not the Libyan government. Moreover, the UK was the first to point out the potential consequences of the Libyan crisis to the wider region. France Germany and the UK seemed to agree that the RtoP applied to the Libyan crisis. The emphasis ranged from the RtoP of the international community (France), to the RtoP of the UNSC (Germany), to the failure of the Libyan government to assume its RtoP. The ambivalences within Europe on the exact meaning of the RtoP in practice were exposed even more in the decision-making processes on the actual policy response.

In Syria, France referred from the beginning to the commitment of mass atrocities and therefore emphasised its own responsibility as well as the responsibility of the UNSC. At the same time, France affirmed explicitly its commitment to the RtoP. It acknowledged that the Syrian regime had failed in its responsibility to protect the Syrian population and suggested an alteration of the voting rule in the UNSC. By contrast, the Syrian crisis was not very prominent in the German official discourse in general and German officials remained silent on questions of responsibility and the RtoP. The UK government described in detail the atrocities committed in Syria. Although initially not explicitly referring to the RtoP, it stressed the need of the international community to step in. Furthermore, the UK stipulated that the lack of action would undermine the UN's credibility, while Russia and China were already failing in their responsibilities as permanent members of the UNSC.

In line with its perception of the Libyan crisis, as massacres possibly constituting crimes against humanity, France was among the first countries calling for a military intervention. Although also highlighting the principle of non-interference, France took the view that a military intervention would still be legitimate, if based on (1) a clear legal basis, (2) a demonstrable need and (3) regional support. France actively persuaded the other members of the UNSC to assume their responsibility to protect the Libyan civilians.

In contrast to its French partners, Germany has described the crisis in Libya as a civil war from the beginning. Accordingly, its main argument against a response to the crisis with military means was to not to become a warring party in a protracted conflict. Germany's position on the Libya intervention reflected its general aversion against the use of force. Therefore, its crisis response focused on non-coercive measures. Germany agreed that the Libyan people needed to be protected but saw the responsibility to protect primarily with the countries in the region.

Britain's participation in the military intervention was justified with the argument that a failed Libyan state would be against the UK's national interest. Alongside a demonstrable need, regional support and a clear legal basis, the presence of national security interests seems to constitute a fourth condition for British involvement in the Libyan intervention. The UK therefore seemed to pursue a double-track. On the one hand the British government emphasised its commitment to the RtoP. On the other hand the UK seems to still adhere to the old norm of humanitarian intervention when it comes to the question of military intervention. David Cameron's discourse in the House of Commons on the debate about British military participation in Syria therefore very much resembles Tony Blair's discourse on the need to intervene in Kosovo in 1999.

From the outset, France expressed its willingness to participate in a military intervention in response to the Syrian crisis. However, only after the chemical weapons attacks, France justified the use of force on the basis of the RtoP. Despite focussing on the protection of civilians, France's response seemed to be motivated by the necessity to punish the use of chemical weapons of mass destruction as well as by the need to prevent further mass atrocities. Yet, a military operation was dependent on the decision of the US. Germany, on the other hand, did not depart from its focus on peaceful means in response to the Syrian crisis and did not make any references to the RtoP. But Germany also advocated the sanctioning of the use of chemical weapons. The UK initially focused on increasing the pressure on the Syrian regime with sanctions and diplomacy but, similarly to France, did not rule out any further action. Furthermore, for the UK government British national interests were vital. During the debate on the British participation in a military operation in Libya, the RtoP was used as basis for arguments in favour as well as against.

Europe and the rest of the world seemed to agree that Gaddafi had lost all his legitimacy as leader of Libya and that he had to step down. Although France and Britain strongly emphasised in their discourses that the sole objective of the military intervention was the protection of the Libyan civilians, achieving this aim seemed to be possible, only if linked to Gaddafi's removal. The lines between the goal of protection and regime change, which was not authorised by Resolution 1973, became blurred. In the case of the Syrian crisis, the RtoP was used as a justification for the proposed action, only after the chemical weapons attacks. There was a general consensus on the need to sanction the Assad regime for the use of weapons of mass destructions. Particularly those in favour of a military operation – namely France and the UK – referred to the RtoP as a legitimate basis for a military intervention. However, the call for punishment seemed to undermine the core aim of protection of the emerging norm. Similarly, in the Libyan crisis, the aim of protection was blurred by calls for regime change and *ex post* extension of the mandate given in Resolution 1973.

Assessing the presumptions

For the in chapter 4 developed presumptions, it can first of all be concluded that the RtoP does have influence. Although the RtoP's influence on actual practice remains limited, it seems to have an influence on European decision-making. The analysis has shown further that in specific cases the RtoP can be assumed to have an influence despite its absence. For the case of Germany, it can be assumed that the RtoP was either not very dominant, or not used at all because Germany disagreed with the coercive interpretation of the RtoP taken by France and the UK. This again confirms the argument that the influence of the RtoP is increasingly linked to the use of force. Significantly, France and the UK have referred to the emerging norm when justifying the proposal or actual use of military force.

Against the empirical findings elaborated on above, presumption III can partly be validated and partly be rejected. Presumption III stated: 'The perception of a crisis in RtoP terms (i.e. the four RtoP crimes) increases its influence but does not entail the implementation of the RtoP'. Yet, the commitment of mass atrocities or a specific number of civilian victims alone does not seem to be a trigger for the application of the RtoP, unless the proposed crisis response contains the use of military force. In other words, what seems to be a condition for the use of the RtoP in the foreign-policy decision-making process is not (only) the way the crisis is perceived and described but rather the question of whether a military intervention will be deployed or not. Moreover, the rhetoric use of the RtoP in the case of Libya and Syria has not led to an according implementation of the actual policies.

The empirical analysis has confirmed what has been suggested in presumption II: 'The EU's role as norm entrepreneur can reinforce its role as security actor'. Yet, the supposition has to be qualified further according to the findings of this study. The Libyan crisis showed that even though the EU supported the RtoP in its discourse, the actual crisis response took place mainly outside the EU framework. The EU's role as norm entrepreneur can potentially increase its role as security actor but only if the EU actively contributes to the implementation of the European crisis response. In the case of Syria, the EU did not act as norm entrepreneur nor did it take a decisive part in the crisis response.

At the same time, the analysis has shown that the role of the EU depends essentially on how the member states perceive the EU's part in the crisis response. Although France, Germany and the UK expressed the general desire for a greater role of the EU in the area of defence, in the specific cases of the Libyan and the Syrian crises member states saw the EU mainly as civilian or normative power. While general expectations on the EU to become a military actor match neither practice nor the EU's capabilities, the EU's understanding of its responsibility in the analysed crises in terms of primarily assisting and helping on the other hand seems to match practice and existing capabilities much better.

Finally, from the above conducted analysis it can further be concluded that presumption I has proven to be right. Presumption I stipulated that 'The existence of a norm entrepreneur can increase the collective understanding of the RtoP in a specific case but not in general'. The analysis has shown that collective understanding in one case can lead to less agreement or even contestation in another case. In the case of Libya, the UN, the EU and France acted as norm entrepreneurs for the RtoP. The UN promoted the RtoP in its general discourse on the Libyan crisis and in Resolution 1970 and 1973.

However, in Resolution 1973, the UNSC referred merely to the responsibility of the Libyan authorities and not to the responsibility of the international community. The EU supported the UN's approach to the RtoP but failed to reach a common position among its member states. Most actively, France persuaded its colleagues in the UNSC to agree on Resolution 1973 and promoted the RtoP in its official statements on the Libyan crisis. The three norm entrepreneurs – the UN, the EU and France – forged consensus on pillar 1 of the RtoP and to a limited extent on pillar 2. However, due to the *ex post* extension of the military operation to fight Libyan leader

Gaddafi the RtoP was not implemented accordingly. The shared understanding of the RtoP did thus not only remain limited to the case of the Libyan crisis but also made some members of the international community even more sceptical towards the emerging norm. The extent to which RtoP has an influence is therefore not only determined by the presence of norm entrepreneurs but also by previous applications of the RtoP.

Due to the recency of the case studies analysed in this thesis and with the Syrian crisis still ongoing at the time of writing, it is difficult to draw more general conclusions on the arguments discussed here or even make predictions for future cases. As events develop, a different set of questions may arise and the assumptions made here may change. Yet, when reviewing the Libyan and the Syrian crisis against the background of the development of the RtoP and the Kosovo crisis, the trend of linking the RtoP to the use of force and the option of a military intervention in response to mass atrocities seems to be persistent.

6.3 RtoP and the EU in Libya and Syria – lessons learned?

Jonathan Eyal (2012) has argued that the Libyan intervention constituted a missed opportunity for Europe to advance the RtoP as a new international norm. Through the way the military operation was conceived and implemented by France, Britain and the other powers and the subsequent expansion of the mandate, the Libyan intervention does not seem to differ much from the one in Kosovo in 1999. Significantly, another factor despite the RtoP that could have made a difference in Libya and Syria was the EU's CSDP and its role as a security actor. Yet, similar to the RtoP criticism it has been argued that due to the lack of a decisive response to the Libyan crisis, the EU has missed the "perfect" opportunity to make use of its common security and defence capabilities and to prove itself as a crisis manager in its neighbourhood. It seemed as if Libya was exactly the type of crisis for which the EU had been preparing since the experience in the Balkans in the 1990s. After having analysed the EU's mostly civilian crisis responses to the mass atrocities in Libya and in Syria the question arises to what extent the EU considers the lessons learned from these two events in the further development of its CSDP or whether the CSDP will remain 'dead' as claimed by Alain Juppé in the context of the Libyan crisis.

One reason for the disappointment with the CSDP in general and after Libya in particular were too high expectations. The Libyan civil war was the first security-related crisis after the entry into force of the Lisbon Treaty in 2009, which had stirred the expectations of a more effective, more coherent and more visible EU foreign policy. One year after the outbreak of the Libyan crisis, some diplomats and academics argue that it was actually a wake-up call for the CSDP (Koenig, 2012). It triggered a renewed debate on lessons learned within the EU's broader crisis management structures. This new impetus for learning lessons is reflected in the Foreign Affairs Council Conclusions on CSDP of 1 December 2011, which strongly emphasised the need for progress in CSDP.

Although the outbreak of violence in February 2011 called for a decisive and swift response, the planning process leading up to EUFOR Libya was lengthy and cumbersome. Recognising the lack of a permanent planning structure, the Council advocated in December 2011 the need for a significant improvement in planning and conducting civilian and military CSDP operations. It was agreed to enable the EU Military Staff and the Crisis Management and Planning Directorate to do more effective advanced planning with the aim to speed up decision-making at the political level. However, the Council did not specify how this would be done in practice.

In the course of the development of the CSDP since the lessons learned from Kosovo in 1999, the EU has developed civilian and military rapid reaction mechanisms, such as the Civilian Response Teams and the battlegroups. Yet, the Libyan crisis proved to be another example where the EU did not make use of these structures. The fact that the battlegroups remain unused, led to frustration among some member states (Koenig, 2012). Although the EU emphasised the further enhancement of the EU's rapid reaction mechanisms and particularly of the battlegroups in its Conclusions from 1 December 2011, no battlegroup was set on stand-by for the first semester of 2012. Finally, the Libyan crisis was yet another example for the lack of capabilities and the need of transatlantic support. EU member states, mainly France and Great Britain, were at the forefront of NATO's Libya intervention. However, approximately 90 per cent of the military actions against the Libyan regime would not have been possible without the support of the US (idem). The EU Council therefore suggested to work more efficiently with European resources and to avoid duplication by 'pooling and sharing' military capabilities.

Two years later and in the aftermath of an averted military intervention in Syria, the EU Council came together again to discuss the state of play and further development of the CSDP. During the 'European Defence Summit' from 19 to 20 December 2013, the European Council held for the first time since the entry into force of the Lisbon Treaty a thematic debate on the CSDP in the light of current and future security challenges. However, the Council recommendations on the further development of the CSDP seemed therein rather influenced by the economic circumstances as well as the shifting security priorities towards energy and cyber security. With regard to Syria, the EU merely emphasised the importance of its role as humanitarian aid donor.

While the CSDP did not play a major role in the EU's response to the Libyan crisis, it equally does not seem to reflect on the further development of the EU's security and defence policy. Although some have argued that the EU was following Catherine's Ashton's conceptualization of the EU as primarily civilian power (Brattberg, 2011) and others have claimed that the CSDP was "designed to make a contribution to global security rather to protect its borders with military force" (Kaldor, 2012), the EU Council did not depart from its aspiration to enhance the development of capabilities and to strengthen the European defence industry. At the same time, the 'Big 3' – France, Germany and the UK – seemed to disagree on how to "deepen European defence cooperation" (EU Observer, 2013).

During the December 2013 defence summit, French President François Holland called for a new EU fund to help member states fund unilateral military operations (such as the one conducted by France in Mali). In response Angela Merkel stressed that Germany would not fund any military operations in which Germany was not involved, while David Cameron made clear that he would block EU institutions from developing and operating their own military assets (idem). Head of NATO, Anders Fogh Rasmussen, agreed with Cameron and added: "Let me stress: It is not NATO or the EU that possess [military] assets. They are owned by the individual nations" (idem). Even after the experiences in Libya and Syria, the EU has not given up on its common security and defence policy but the gap between expectations, responsibility and capabilities seems to remain.

6.4 Conclusion

For Ramesh Thakur, RtoP was a "'game changer'" which acted as a powerful new galvanising norm" over Libya (Thakur, 2011). For Alex Bellamy, the concept "played an important role in shaping the world's response to actual and threatened atrocities there" (Bellamy, 2011: 263). It can be argued that the application of the RtoP in the case of Libya showed the biggest commitment of international community to assume its responsibility to protect civilians from mass atrocities since the inception of the emerging norm during the 2005 World Summit. At the same time, it seems as if the influence of the RtoP was mitigated in the aftermath of the Libyan intervention, leading to even greater reluctance in its subsequent test case, the Syrian crisis. While the RtoP became increasingly linked to the use of force during the Libyan intervention, the prospects for its future application have diminished significantly.

In this context, it has also been argued that parts of the debate of the Libyan crisis exaggerated the role played by the RtoP and that NATO's chosen means of implementing UNSC Resolution 1973 have been used by opponents of the RtoP to delegitimise the emerging norm (Morris, 2013: 1256-1266). Criticisms made in debates over Libya, of the manner in which NATO had implemented the UNSC mandate, came to contaminate discussions over Syria (idem: 1275). In Syria, arguments on the danger of doing more harm than good, in terms of both the internal humanitarian situation and the potential for triggering a wider regional conflagration, were much more strongly sided against intervention. RtoP in action in Libya has consequently been employed to justify inaction in the case of Syria.

What proved crucial to the passing of Resolution 1973 was the level of regional support for a more robust UNSC response: the African Union, the League of Arab States, the Gulf Cooperation Council and the Organisation of the Islamic Council all condemned the actions of Gaddafi's regime, with the latter three explicitly calling on the UNSC to impose a no-fly zone over Libya. Such support was cited by all three, France, Germany and Great Britain as essential to the legitimacy of the military intervention. Furthermore, US President Barack Obama, who was initially very reluctant to allow the US to get involved, was eventually persuaded of the compelling case for intervention by a trio of top advisers: Secretary of State Hillary Clinton, US Ambassador to the UN Susan Rice and especially Samantha Power, US Representative to the UNSC (Chesterman, 2011).

However, the US change of position and then support of the military operation did not seem motivated by the RtoP but was as Saira Mohamed notes "driven more by singular national interests than by any sense of responsibility" (Mohamed, 2012: 320). In addition to that, the French President Nicolas Sarkozy together with UK Prime Minister David Cameron seemed determined in the use of military force against Gaddafi. The main trigger cited was the seemingly murderous intentions of Gaddafi to exact indiscriminate revenge on large swathes of the Libyan people who had dared to rise up in protest (Howorth, 2013: 20). Finally, the last reason for the military intervention was that it was judged relatively simple in military terms (idem: 21).

As Julian Howorth notes "the case of Syria seems in many ways to be diametrically opposed to that of Libya" (2013: 23). To begin with, while decisions about military action in Libya were taken promptly within the time span of a month after the outbreak of violence, the Syrian crisis continued to unfold over a period of two and a half years (March 2011 to September 2013) with no decisive action taken by the international community until the end of August 2013. Second, as many as 30.000 people had died in Syria up to the beginning of 2013, making the relevance of the RtoP even more acute in Syria than in Libya. Furthermore, UNSC Resolution 2042 from April 2012 described the "widespread violations of human rights abuses [and] the death of many thousands of people", yet there was no mention of the prospect of military intervention until summer 2013, after the alleged chemical weapons attacks. Third, the preferred European course of action, even in France, was, alongside the US, the imposition of sanctions. Fourth, there was no regional support of any form of military intervention raised by Arab League or other organisations.

On the other hand, there were also fundamental reasons for the inaction of the international community in the Syrian case. First, the Syrian military is, unlike in Libya, a highly efficient, well-armed and well-trained force with bases all over the country. Furthermore, the opposition in Syria was extremely diverse, disunited and fractious. Finally, the possibly most important reason was that Syria had solid international backing not only from Russia and China but also from Iran. From the comparison between Libya and Syria it can be concluded that there are few clear prescriptions as to when in military intervention is and is not appropriate or justified.

Furthermore, Jennifer Welsh argued that

> *... RtoP was born in an era when assertive liberalism was at its height and sovereign equality looked and smelled reactionary. But as the liberal moment recedes, and the distribution of power shifts globally, the principle of sovereign equality may enjoy a comeback.* (Welsh, 2010: 428)

Thus a shift on global power may be as significant for normative structures as well as for material changes (Morris, 2013: 1279). The boldness of Russia's and Chinas rejection of the RtoP in general but specifically in the Syrian crisis might ultimately influence the development of the RtoP, as well as the dynamics of the global power distribution. If power continues to shift from its traditional Western grounds towards Russia, China and the other BRICS (Brazil, India and South Africa), who are sharing a "long-held mistrust of western-led military action" (Wagner and Jackman, 2013: 57), opposition to the RtoP may become more mainstream. In this context, Brazil's initiative on a 'Responsibility while Protecting', concerning the authorisation, implementation and review of uses of force for humanitarian purposes offers an interesting insight into how such shifts may manifest themselves and impact on the development of the RtoP.

How this exactly impacts on the RtoP in the future depends on how the emerging norm is conceived in the first place. According to Alex Bellamy (2011: 166) the question is whether the RtoP is primarily "a policy agenda in need of implementation" [or a] 'red flag' to galvanize the world into action". For Bellamy the answer is the former, with the RtoP "best employed as a diplomatic tool, or prism, to guide efforts to stem the tide of mass atrocities" but with "... little utility in terms of generating additional international political will in response to such episodes" (idem). On the other hand, Thomas Weiss has argued that it is "hard to fathom" why RtoP should be diverted from the key role it has to play as a potential antidote to international politics which "over the last decade" have resulted in the use of "not too much but rather too little armed force to protect human lives" (Weiss, 2011: 288-9). However, only time will tell how the recent developments will play out and what their implications for the RtoP will be. The constant danger of reading too much into current events and the temptation to exaggerate the inductive potential of individual (and potentially infrequent) cases must be guarded against.

In conclusion, the RtoP arguably influenced the European crisis responses in both cases – the Libyan and the Syrian crisis. At the same time the case study analysis has shown that interpretations of the RtoP vary from case to case. While the criteria of a flexible interpretation of the RtoP forms a part of the RtoP norm, as accepted in the 2005 World Summit Outcome Document, different interpretations of the norm do not *per se* undermine the further institutionalization of the international norm. More specifically if the focus and the aim of any application of the RtoP was consistently the protection of civilians from mass atrocities but merely the instruments to implement this aim changed, we would be likely to be able to speak about a consistent state practice of the RtoP. However, the analysis of the Libyan and the Syrian crisis has shown points in the opposite direction. The instrument of a military intervention in the form of a no-fly zone and its implementation has not changed from Kosovo to Syria despite technological innovations such as drones for example. Moreover, the crisis response has not exclusively aimed at the protection of civilians but also at regime change and at sanctioning an incumbent regime.

The increasing link of the RtoP to the use of military force against the will of a *de facto* government, envisaging different political aims than protection, prevents the emerging norm from further institutionalisation. It also implies that since its development in 2001, in response to the lessons learned from the Kosovo crisis, nothing much has changed than the discourse. While European actors make use of the RtoP language and speak of a responsibility to protect populations from mass atrocities, the actual policy response in form of (a proposed or actual) military intervention remains the same as in 1999. The concrete policy impact of the RtoP remains therefore limited.

Finally, Europe's – particularly France and the UK – association of the RtoP with the use of force turns the emerging norm against its founding principle human security. While the centre of attention remains with those considering the crisis response or more specifically the intervention, the change of perspective towards a people-centred conception of security remains unimplemented. For the link between the RtoP and human security this means that the RtoP did not only fail to implement its human security basis in Libya and Syria, but that its recent applications have actually started to contradict the very core of the concept of human security.

Chapter 7: Conclusion

This study has focused on the influence of the RtoP as an emerging international norm on European responses to mass atrocities in its neighbourhood. It has shown that the RtoP serves as legitimisation for the use of force in the crisis response. But it has also argued that it provides for little change when it comes to the actual implementation of proposed policies. The underlying research puzzle that sparked interest in conducting this study was to assess the impact of the concept of human security in post-Cold War Europe. Since its inception in the 1994 Human Development Report, the problem of operationalising the concept and thus turning it into a theoretically coherent and applicable concept, has not been solved. In order to circumvent the difficulty of operationalising the concept of human security and according to Keith Krause (2007), it has therefore been argued that human security can only be applied to practice when it is defined narrowly and it is linked to a specific policy initiative. Accordingly, in light of the narrowly-defined freedom of fear component of human security, it seemed sensible to choose the RtoP as an area of practical application of the human security concept.

In light of the failures of the international community to prevent mass atrocities in Rwanda (1994) and Bosnia (1995) and the lessons learned of the Kosovo intervention in 1999, the development of the RtoP was explicitly based on a people-centred conception of security. To recall Ramesh Thakur's (2006: 28) argument, the RtoP derived from the human security concept in the sense that it aimed at "an evaluation of the issues from the point of view of those seeking or needing support, rather than those considering the intervention." By contrast, humanitarian intervention, particularly the British interpretation, was contingent upon national interests and therefore linked to the notion of sovereign states having a 'right' to intervene. As an emerging international norm the RtoP was based on the concept of human security. Building on the redefinition of sovereignty as responsibility and shifting the centre of attention from the state to the people, it diverges from the 'old' norm of humanitarian intervention.

In this context, the underlying aim of this thesis was to assess the policy impact of human security in the form of the newly emerging international norm of the RtoP.

It was stipulated that if the RtoP had an impact on actual policy, as opposed to mere rhetoric, a change in the design and the direction of policies taking into account the human security concept would be visible. If, however, the RtoP and the people-centred focus were merely reflected in the discourse, the actual policy impact of human security and the RtoP would remain limited.

Having applied a social constructivist theoretical and analytical framework to the empirical analysis of two case studies – the Libyan and the Syrian crisis in the period from 2011 – 2013, it has been shown that the influence of the RtoP on European responses to these crises is mostly superficial. While the RtoP is present in the official discourses on the crises, the design and direction of the proposed policies seem to divert from the people-centred perspective and the aim of protection. Therefore it can be concluded that the RtoP makes little difference in practice.

Before we deny any potential policy impact of the human security concept, the presumed connection between the RtoP and human security has to be further qualified. The RtoP toolkit includes a range of measures, such as political pressure and economic sanctions that should be exhausted before the option of a military intervention is even considered. Yet, the RtoP has been used predominantly in connection with proposals to make use of military force in a crisis response, as this study has revealed. While a military intervention is not *per se* anti-human security, it is the implementation of such a policy in the form of a military no-fly zone, as in the case of Libya, that does not differ from the intervention in Kosovo in 1999 and is not designed effectively to protect civilians on the ground. Furthermore, the stated aim of protection was only superficially reflected in the implementation and conduction of the military operation on the ground in Libya. It became further blurred by the demands for regime change. The same is true for the case of Syria where the application of the RtoP was invoked with the aim to sanction the Assad regime rather than to protect the Syrian civilian population.

In practice, the RtoP seems thus to disregard its human security basis and the aim of protection, which could potentially make a real difference in response to cases of mass atrocities. Significantly, the applications of the RtoP in the case of Libya and Syria openly contradict the core principle of the human security concept – the people-centred perspective. The focus of intervention seems to remain with those conducting the intervention and not those in need of protection. In chapter 2 of this thesis, it had been assumed that there would be a shift after the Kosovo intervention in 1999 in the focus of interventions from national interests to human security, as well as from military action to the prevention of mass atrocities. For the two case studies analysed in this study, this shift can only be recognized on the rhetorical level but not in practice.

In the conclusion of chapter 2, it was argued that the normative development of the RtoP should not be seen as a precursor to its implementation but that it continues throughout the process of its application in practice. From the revision of the four RtoP cases prior to the outbreak of the Libyan and the Syrian crisis in 2011, four conclusions on the normative status of the RtoP were drawn. First, the RtoP is used by proponents and opponents of the norm. This assumption also applies to European responses to the Syrian crises, where in the French and British debate on a possible military intervention, the RtoP has been used as the basis for arguing in favour as well as against.

Second, it was concluded that the scope of the RtoP is limited to the four crimes as stated in the 2005 World Summit Outcome Document. In both the Libyan and the Syrian crises, the commitment of crimes against humanity and war crimes was constituted. Yet, this conclusion can only partly be confirmed for the two analysed case studies. While claims for (military) action were linked to the calls for regime change (in Libya) and to demands for punishment (in Syria), it seems as if the scope of the RtoP was significantly broadened in both cases. The third conclusion was that the toolbox of the RtoP remains unclear. Although the RtoP was not designed to be tantamount to military intervention, practice in the cases of Libya and Syria has shown that the recent normative development of the RtoP seems to be going in that direction.

Finally, the analysis in chapter 3 suggested that the implementation of the RtoP (and the CSDP) is challenged by the lack of political will from powerful states. This final conclusion can somewhat be rejected in the case of Libya and Syria (eventually), as at least France and the UK were willing also to react with military means. However, in the case of Libya EU member states were unwilling to apply the RtoP under the EU framework. Moreover, member states seemed deeply divided on the use of force in response to the Libyan crisis. With regard to Syria, on the international level powerful states such as Russia and China have long rejected any kind of coercive response to the Syrian crisis. The US, the UK and France were willing to consider a military intervention only after the chemical weapons attack by the Syrian government in summer 2013. The application of the RtoP (and the CSDP) therefore remains dependent on the political will of the actors involved.

As for the link between the RtoP and military intervention, Alex Bellamy has argued that the RtoP has the potential of making three important contributions to questions of military intervention (see chapter 3):

1. The RtoP can replace the older norm of humanitarian intervention with a broad range of measures directed mostly at preventing mass atrocities.
2. The RtoP thus advocates for a comprehensive crisis response.
3. The RtoP can provide a new framework for the implementation of policies by focusing on the protection of civilians.

From the analysis of the Libyan and the Syrian crisis, the RtoP seems, however, not to make a difference in the (proposed) military intervention but resembles the old norm of humanitarian intervention instead of replacing it. In its practical application, the RtoP seems to have turned against its human security foundation and therefore offers little added value to the actual protection of civilians.

It has further been contended that the RtoP had, amongst other drivers, an important impact on the EU's understanding of its responsibility and the development of the CSDP. The EU's foreign policy has been criticised for falling into the 'capability-expectations gap' (Hill, 1993) since the CSDP's creation during the St Malo summit in 1998 when some member states called for a greater role of the EU in the area of security and defence. Moreover, the US has, in the case of the Kosovo crisis as well as in the case of Libya, claimed that it is time for Europe to provide for its own security (see chapter 5, Obama quoted in Brown, 2011; Biscop, 2011b).

However, the EU fell short in developing sufficient military capabilities and the member states remain reluctant to act militarily under the EU umbrella. The famous 'capability-expectations gap' continues to characterize EU foreign policy. It will not cease to exist until an exclusively civilian role of the EU in the area of crisis management is accepted by its member states and transatlantic partners or member states enable the EU as a fully-fledged military actor to provide the respective defence capabilities and the political will to use them under the EU framework.

The EU's understanding of its responsibility as well as the perception of the 'Big 3' on its role in case of Libyan crisis and, to a limited extent, in the Syrian crisis seems to match its available capabilities much better. The EU's interpretation of the RtoP was from the beginning focused more on the prevention of mass atrocities with non-coercive means. During the Libyan and the Syrian crisis, the 'Big 3' and the EU itself promoted the image of a normative and civilian crisis manager and not of a hard security actor responding with military force. While the EU's sense of responsibility matches its crisis management capabilities, this also implies that, in comparison to the Kosovo crisis in 1999, the CSDP makes as much of a difference as the RtoP – only a rhetorical one. And although France claimed that Europe was able to respond decisively to the Libyan crisis, the military intervention took place outside the EU framework and would not have been possible without US support. While both the Kosovo crisis and the Libyan crisis have been designated as 'wake-up calls' for the CSDP (see Shepherd, 2009 on Kosovo and Koenig, 2012 on Libya), the results from this study suggest that the EU recognises the 'capability-expectations gap' in its discourse but fails to make the according changes to close it in practice.

The theoretical and analytical framework of the thesis was built on the argument that, due to the RtoP's indeterminacy, it is likely to be interpreted differently by diverse European actors. Although the analysis revealed different interpretations of what the RtoP means, entails and when it applies, there still seems to be an agreement among France, Germany, the UK and the EU institutions that the RtoP is strongly linked to the use of force and the question of military intervention. Amongst the 'Big 3', France, which was willing in both cases to participate in a military operation, seemed the strongest supporter of the emerging RtoP norm. The UK also supported the RtoP in both cases but appeared still to be leaning more openly towards the norm of humanitarian intervention, as any deployment of the British military has to be based on national (security) interests. In consequence of its history, Germany remained averse to the use of force and therefore presumably also abstained from supporting the RtoP in either of the crises analysed.

While European understandings of what the RtoP means and entails seem fairly convergent, the interpretation of when it applies and whose responsibility it is, are much more divergent. For France, the RtoP seems to apply in any crises involving the commitment of mass atrocities. It also understands it as its responsibility as part of the international community to act. The UK supports the application of the RtoP in crises where its national interests are at stake and emphasises the importance of assuming the responsibility collectively within the UN framework. Germany instead has increasingly underlined the responsibility of regional actors as well as of the state, in which the crisis is taking place itself. As we have seen, Germany does not subscribe to an RtoP that entails the use of military force.

RtoP as emerging norm: a (new) research agenda

Given the empirical analysis conducted in this thesis, further studies on the influence of the RtoP should take into account three arguments. The arguments presented below depart from the assessment of the four presumptions in chapter 7. By taking into account the empirical findings of this study, the presumptions tested in this analysis can be developed further in order to provide incentives for future research on the influence of the RtoP.

Building on the findings of chapter 2 and 3, it was stipulated that norm entrepreneurs can increase the collective understanding of the RtoP in a specific case, but not in general (presumption I). While this presumption has not been rejected after the analysis of the Libyan and the Syrian crisis, it should be revisited. The analysis has shown that the influence of norm entrepreneurs remains generally limited. The case of the Libyan crisis, however, is very likely to influence future applications of the RtoP. The focus should shift from the role of norm entrepreneurs to the effects that a collective understanding of the RtoP in one case, can have impact on its application in another. Against this background, the first argument future research should consider is:

1. The Libyan intervention will serve as a point of reference for future RtoP applications, most likely in a negative way.

Second, since the EU did not act as a norm entrepreneur for the RtoP in either of the two analysed case studies, the relation between the EU's role as a norm entrepreneur and as a security actor remains hypothetical (presumption II). The analysis has highlighted the importance of how member states, themselves, perceive the role of the EU in the area of security and defence. On this note, a question worth exploring further would be why member states remain unwilling to make use of military means for crisis management within the EU framework. This question could lead to an analysis of the conditions under which European states decide on the use of force in- or outside the EU framework. In this context, it would be equally interesting to explore further the conditions under which the application of the RtoP is considered. On this note, a second argument that could inspire future research is:

2. The conditions under which the application of the RtoP and the use of force in- and outside the EU framework are considered matter.

Finally, presumption III argued that there is no direct link between the perception of a crisis in RtoP terms (referring to one or four of the RtoP crimes in the discourse) and its according implementation. While the presumption has proven to be partly correct, the analysis has shown that the RtoP has become increasingly linked to the issue of military intervention. Therefore, future analyses should focus on whether the issue of military intervention serves as the main trigger for applying the RtoP rather than the crimes committed throughout the crisis in question. If this is the case, the actual implementation of the RtoP in terms of its people-centred approach appears even less likely. A third argument, from which future research could depart, is:

3. RtoP is likely going to be applied if a military intervention is considered no matter how severe the (humanitarian) crisis.

This thesis has focused on the influence of the RtoP as an emerging international norm on European responses to mass atrocities in its neighbourhood. As stated above, the focus has been on the impact of the RtoP as a norm and the question of to what extent it is used to legitimize a certain crisis response. Therefore this study did not aim to answer the question of why European actors responded to the crises analysed above in a specific way. This thesis can thus not draw any conclusions on the causes of European crisis responses or more specifically of military interventions and the use of force (see also chapter 1). Rather it intended to analyse how European responses to crisis in its neighbourhood involving mass atrocities are constructed and whether the RtoP and the CSDP make a difference therein.

In addition, this thesis has focused on the analysis of the official discourses of the 'Big 3', the EU and the UN. Therefore no interviews were conducted to investigate the motivations of member states' reactions 'behind the scenes'. The focus on the official discourse was in line with the chosen research question, which concentrated on the influence of the RtoP as legitimizing factor for action. Legitimacy, as assumed in this thesis, was mainly defined in the sense of justifying actions in front of broader domestic but also European and international audiences. The chosen research design and the selected methodology were able to provide an answer to the main research question of this study.

The results of the empirical analysis conducted in this study confirm the chosen constructivist agenda. The analysis has thus affirmed, firstly, that foreign policy actors do not see their interests through a narrow perspective of material gain but a broader one, allowing them to act on the basis of moral considerations. Secondly, the study has shown that these interests are socially constructed by the environment in which the actors involved find themselves. However, such findings have to be qualified by an important thread of realism, which has been detected at the beginning of this study, suggesting that altruism and compromise only go so far. National interest never disappears completely, though it may be reconceptualised, and because of this, turning rhetorical commitment into action on the ground will continue to be challenging for the foreseeable future.

Taking a slightly different angle and involving more time and resources, the analysis of the main research question of this study could focus more intensely on the internal foreign policy decision-making processes in Brussels, Paris, Berlin, London and even New York. Therefore, a large number of semi-structured interviews could be conducted with officials in the national capitals as well as in Brussels in order to scrutinise the impact of human security and the RtoP on the formation of the actual crisis response behind the scenes. A round of semi-structured interviews could be complemented further by a survey inquiring as to the reasons behind the choice for a specific crisis response in more than the three selected member states, which would provide the possibility to compare European crisis responses on a larger scale. Furthermore, attending a session of the General Assembly on the RtoP and conducting interviews at the UN headquarters in New York could provide important new insights on the further development of the RtoP as an emerging norm as well as on its role in the decision-making process on the international level.

Analysing the influence of the RtoP with a focus on the internal dimension, the theoretical framework of the study would have to be amended accordingly. While it would still be argued that a social constructivist approach is the most appropriate to analyse the impact of (emerging) international norms on European foreign policy, the focus on the internal political decision-making process would require the inclusion of a foreign policy analysis approach. Furthermore, the interactions between the different analysed levels – nation states, the EU and the UN – could be conceptualised in terms of a three-level game (see for example Bouchard, 2008).

The focus on the 'Big 3' in this thesis has been chosen on the basis of three reasons. First, due to their political impact within the EU and as a consequence, based on their potential as norm entrepreneurs. France, Germany and the UK are among the founding EU member states. They are also the biggest member states in terms of the size of their populations and their economies. Furthermore, the three, France and the UK in particular, have supported and promoted the creation of a common European security and defence policy since the St. Malo summit in 1998. Against this background, the focus of the analysis has been put on those member states that are powerful enough to decide on whether to invoke or contest the RtoP as an emerging international norm. For France, Germany and the UK this assumption has proven right. While France and the UK actively supported the RtoP in both crisis responses, Germany voted against the Franco-British approach in case of the Libyan crisis as mandated in Resolution 1973. Furthermore, it was concluded that the absence of the RtoP in the German official discourse, particularly in the Syrian case, could be seen as a form of silent contestation of the RtoP. Again, whether Germany contested the RtoP in the case of the Libyan and the Syrian crisis, or whether its choice of crisis response was motivated by other factors (such as state or federal elections), would have to be investigated in interviews.

Apart from the relevance of the core member states for the assessment of the RtoP's impact, doing this study differently, the analysis of the position of smaller member states on the influence of the RtoP and on the question of military intervention would also be valuable. In the case of Libya, the analysis of Italy's position, which was also in favour of a military intervention from the beginning and actively participated in Operation Unified Protector, would be particularly relevant. Furthermore, the analysis of the position of Poland could be considered. Significantly, Poland abstained in the voting on Resolution 1973 alongside Germany, Russia, China and Brazil.

In this context, and moving towards a more international perspective on the influence of the RtoP, a closer analysis of the Russian abstention on Resolution 1973 and its vetoes on several draft resolution on Syria in the UN Security Council could provide a further angle for the analysis that would well be worth investigating. It has been argued that Russia's blocking of any UNSC action on Syria has been motivated by the fact that Russia felt 'outplayed' or even cheated after the implementation of Resolution 1973 (von Eggert, 2012). Redoing the study could thus focus on the impact of the RtoP caught in the tensions between Russian *Realpolitik* and a European value-based foreign policy.

The point of view of other emerging powers as included in the BRICS (Brazil, Russia, India, China and South Africa) and particularly Brazil's position would be another approach to address the topic of this thesis. Significantly, in response to the application of the RtoP in the Libyan crisis, Brazil launched the initiative of a 'Responsibility while Protecting' (RWP) in 2012. The RWP emphasises that the use of force should be seen as a last resort and recommends the establishment of a mechanism that enhances the procedures inside the UN Security Council to monitor and access the implementation of resolutions mandating the use of force. In this context, Brazil might serve as important norm entrepreneur contributing to the further normative development of the RtoP.

Finally, for Europe the support of the US in terms of military capabilities and structures has proven to be crucial for the implementation of an intervention as in the case of Libya for example. Without the strikes conducted by the US military during the first days of the intervention in Libya, the operation would not have 'succeeded' the way it did. What changed in comparison to the Kosovo intervention in 1999, in which the US took the lead much more explicitly than in Libya, is the discourse and Obama's changing foreign policy doctrine towards the approach of 'leading from behind'. While this term is somehow misleading, as the US contribution in terms of military equipment and personnel was still significant, the Libyan crisis might nevertheless account for a change in transatlantic relations in the area of security and defence. Significantly, in the case of Syria, President Obama was the one seeking support for a military intervention from Europe, arguably less because of European defence capabilities than because of the need for partners to legitimise such an action internationally.

However, for the further development of the RtoP and the question of military intervention, the US position will be crucial. The US justified the Libyan intervention on the basis of national security interests, and proposed military action in Syria as punishment of the Assad government. It did not apply the RtoP.

There arise, inevitably, various ideas on how to re-do this study from different perspectives. In this context, there might also develop new research projects on the EU's CSDP, the RtoP and human security more broadly. Before, however, indulging in furthering this thesis's research agenda in alternative ways, the relevance of the topics analysed throughout this thesis should be reconsidered against the ever-changing research agendas in EU Studies and International Relations.

With the entry into force of the Lisbon Treaty in 2009 and its institutional innovations, such as the newly designed post of the High Representative of the Union for Foreign Affairs and Security Policy, as well as the establishment of the European External Action Service, EU External Action seemed an increasingly significant area of study. Furthermore, with the outbreak of the Arab Spring in December 2010 until present, the different policy areas included in EU External Action and particularly the EU's CFSP and CSDP would seem to have become more relevant in practice. At the same time, the Euro crisis that has been affecting European countries since 2009 has diverted political attention from foreign affairs towards internal EU policies specifically related to the Eurozone. While EU External Action in general will, due to the EU's economic weight, never be irrelevant, the EU is still far from representing a fully-fledged and capable security actor, as this study has shown. Therefore it is assumed that the centre of attention in EU studies will continue to focus on economic and financial policies. More specifically, research is likely to look at the power of single member states such as Germany in these policies areas, the question of further political integration, but also on migration and asylum issues as one consequence of the increased number of refugees arriving at Europe's borders and less on European defence and external security issues.

However, in light of the worsening of the situation in the Central African Republic (CAR) in January 2014, the EU provisionally agreed to send a military CSDP mission to secure the main roads leading to the CAR (EU Observer, 2014). Furthermore, the first European defence summit 2013 since the Euro crisis was convened in December 2013. Therefore, the EU's CFSP and CSDP should not be disregarded in future research. Whether the RtoP will play a role in future EU interventions or whether it may 'rest in peace' after the Libyan and the Syrian crisis, remains to be seen.

Against this background, studies in the area of the CSDP, human security and the RtoP have great potential to make further valuable contributions to knowledge and to practice. Since the focus so far has been on the European side, it would be worthwhile to aim in future studies at assessing the actual impact of the European security and defence policies on the ground. The investigation of CSDP missions in terms of their implementation of the human security concept would provide a further opportunity to assess the impact of the concept, since the presumed link between the RtoP and human security has proven to be spurious. In this context, research methods such as observing one or several CSDP missions on the ground or even actively participating as a member of the civilian staff could lead to highly relevant insights on the effects of the RtoP and CSDP on the ground.

Conducting fieldwork in Libya, for example, could provide for a further understanding of the effects of a military intervention, including technological innovations such as drones on the ground and in terms of its impact on the human security of the civilian population. While potentially producing interesting research results, fieldwork in Libya could only be conducted if the security situation was stable enough and with the support of an interpreter. Such a study would be practically informed rather than theory based and could help European governments in gaining a better understanding of how best to respond to crises involving mass atrocities. The assessment of situations post-intervention on the ground could also contribute to the further development of 'Responsibility while Protecting' initiated by the Brazilian government in 2012.

On the theoretical level, another study could focus on elaborating on the social constructivist framework to analyse the influence of (emerging) international norms. In chapter 4, it has been argued that the norm-life cycle (emergence, evolution and internationalisation) developed by Martha Finnemore and Kathryn Sikkink (1998) should not be regarded as a one-directional but rather as a two-directional process. This study has shown that, independent of its normative status, a norm can influence behaviour in the sense that it is used as legitimate basis for action. From the analysis of a norm's influence, however, conclusions can be drawn on the development of the norm. The three stages of norm development therefore influence each other rather than follow one after the other.

Amending the norm-life cycle, the newly developed framework should also contain a component conceptualising the superficial or hypocritical use of international norms. The constructivist perspective could thus be paired with a more rationalist perspective. As outlined previously, combining the social constructivist theoretical framework with a foreign policy analysis approach could account for the investigation of the influence of international norms on actors' internal foreign policy decision-making processes.

The EU, RtoP and the 'real world'

Before chancing a last look at the situations in Libya post-intervention and in Syria after the agreement on the dismissal of Syria's chemical weapons, some final conclusions on the role of the EU as a security actor in its neighbourhood should be drawn. In the two cases analysed in this thesis the EU has acted neither as a significant security actor nor as norm entrepreneur for the RtoP. The EU's low profile as security actor was explained by the lack of political will and capabilities in the case of Libya and by the EU simply getting in line with the rest of world's paralysis on how to respond to Syria. The EU has however claimed in both cases that its main responsibility is to help and to assist, particularly with reconstruction once the violent conflicts have been put to an end. Therefore it might be worthwhile having a brief look at the EU's engagement in post-intervention Libya. Notably, in the case of Syria, where the civil war continues at the time of writing, the focus of the crisis response is still on finding a political solution and on providing humanitarian relief.

In its conclusions from 1 December 2011, the Foreign Affairs Council affirmed its "readiness to provide further assistance to Libya across a range of possible sectors, including inter alia security sector reform and border management." Following the end of the fighting in Libya the EU shifted its humanitarian support to issues related to the field of development cooperation. The EU has provided two packages of short-term and medium-term support. Within the first package, ten million (Euros) have been allocated to support the Libyan government to build general public administrative capacities and to provide technical assistance. More specifically, the EU has funded civil society in Libya and a programme supporting the establishment of basic education for all children, but also including training of teachers and assisting the Ministry of Education in the formulation of an effective education policy.

Regarding the medium-term support, 50 million (Euros) had been made available for the cooperation with Libya for the period of 2012 until 2013. These funds were allocated according to the needs of the Libyan authorities, following the results of a coordinated needs assessment by the international community at the Paris Conference in September 2011[143]. In early March 2012, the EU sent an expert mission to Libya that aimed at assisting the Libyan authorities to assess their specific needs on border management. Consisting of ten experts, the mission is deployed for a period of three months in order to make recommendations to the EU for concrete action and support to an efficient border management regarding Libyan land, sea and air borders.

In comparison to previous cases, the EU's engagement in reconstructing Libya emphasised at all stages that the process was based on the process of local ownership. Accordingly, the EU would only support and assist in areas and with means that are required by local actors and based on their needs. In this context, the EU seems to keep its promises by playing a greater role in the post-conflict reconstruction process in Libya while also emphasizing the people-centred approach of its response. With a worsening security situation and the resurgence of the fighting in 2013 it seems, however, as if the EU's efforts in reconstructing Libya and guiding a process of political transition have come too early.

In the aftermath of Muammar Gaddafi's fall in August 2011, Stewart Patrick, former US State Department Official, concluded in *Foreign Affairs* that the Libyan intervention was "the first unambiguous military enforcement of the Responsibility to Protect norm, Gaddafi's utter defeat seemingly putting new wind in the sails of humanitarian intervention" (Patrick, 2011). However, a year after the intervention the state of Libyan affairs appears rather bleak, making the initial success of the RtoP look less compelling. Reports by human rights organisations and journalists have revealed that the country's transition has stopped due to rival groups and competing militias. Human rights abuses and corruption are widespread and, instead of developing stable institutions, Libya is becoming more and more fractured (Beaumont, 2012)

143 The Paris Conference on Libya brought together EU member states, the UN, the World Bank and the IMF as well as the Libyan authorities. The participants agreed to divide their assessments across 12 different sectors. The EU has initially been assigned the assessment in the areas of border management, civil society and media.

Ian Martin, the UN's envoy to Libya, explained at the beginning of January 2012:

> *The former regime may have been toppled, but the harsh reality is that the Libyan people continue to have to live with its deep-rooted legacy; weak, at times absent, state institutions, coupled with the long absence of political parties and civil society organisations, which render the country's transition more difficult.* (UN News, 2012)

The post-intervention assessment of the situation in Libya confirms the view that the intervention was not directed at the protection of civilians, but aimed and achieved the removal of the Gaddafi regime. As it was, to a certain extent, the case in Kosovo too, Libya is turning after the intervention into a fragile and corrupt state, in which the violence has by no means come to an end and the way to democracy is still long. By contrast, some have argued further that the NATO intervention in Libya has prolonged the conflict in Libya, spiking its death toll alongside increasing human rights abuses and weapons proliferation in the country (Kuperman, 2013).

Significantly, *The Independent* title in September 2013 was "We all thought Libya had moved on – it has, but into lawlessness and ruin" (Cockburn, 2013). While international attention focused on the chemical attacks in Syria in summer 2013, the fact that Libya slipped into a severe economic crisis remained almost unnoticed. Although the military intervention was justified on the grounds of the RtoP, the international community seemed to have ignored the continuously escalating violence since October 2011.

The destruction of Syria's chemical weapons arsenal began after the agreement reached between the US, the Russian and the Syrian government in September 2013. A political solution to the ongoing conflict in the country has, however, not been found by the time of writing and the violence continues to spread. David Cameron reminded in October 2013 that the chemical weapons agreement should not allow the international community to assume the Syrian crisis is over (The Independent, 2013). According to media reports, the UN has stopped updating the Syria death toll, as it could no longer verify the source of information, on which the last count of 100.000 deaths caused by civil war had been established in July 2013 (The Washington Post, 2014). The *Irish Times* (2013) reported in December that, according to the Syrian Observatory for Human Rights, the number of victims has risen to 130.000 assuming that the actual figures are much higher. The *Washington Post* further quoted an eyewitness in Syria doubting the effect of destroying the chemical weapons for the Syrian population.

> *"We have been killed for the last three years with all different kinds of weapons — tanks, mortar shells, snipers. Destroy the chemical weapons, or don't. That won't matter, because with chemical weapons or without them, the killing continues, the rivers of blood continue."* (Aya Mahaini, Syrian activist, quoted in Morris and Birnbaum, 2013)

Since the beginning of the Syrian crisis in March 2011, about 2 million people have fled the country while around 4.5 million people have been displaced internally (UNHCR, 2014). Refugees from the Syrian civil war have mostly fled to neighbouring countries Jordan, Lebanon, Turkey, and Iraq. Europe has been criticised for taking in only a small percentage of the 2 million Syrian refugees (Amnesty International, 2013). In January 2014, the UN called on the EU to open its doors:

> *Syria has become an unflinching contest for regional supremacy, anchored largely by the ancient regional power struggle between Tehran and Riyadh, but fuelled by more contemporary grievances. The volatile sectarian power tussle leaves little concern for the health and safety of millions of refugees, the majority of whom are women and children.* (Chulov and Grant, 2014)

Consideration of the situations in Libya and Syria in late 2013 reveals that although European responses to both crises were at least partly influenced by the RtoP, a military intervention or the destruction of weapons of mass destruction should only be the beginning of the international community's responsibility. At the time of writing neither of these conflicts had been resolved. The worsening security situations in both countries called for a greater European engagement, which went beyond the aim of regime change and the sanctioning of war crimes. Therefore, in Libya and Syria the only chance for the RtoP really to make a difference rested with the implementation of the responsibility to prevent and to rebuild.

When looking at the enduring crisis in Eastern Ukraine and the rise of violence linked to the Islamic State in Iraq and Syria throughout 2014, the questions for Europe and the RtoP seem to be the same as back in 1999: Where do we see Europe's responsibility and why does the RtoP seem to apply in some cases of mass atrocities and not in others? Although left with the difficulty of making generalizations and predictions, the RtoP will certainly have future influence on both political behaviour and scholarly debate in Europe. Assessing its significance empirically therefore remains imperative.

Annex I: Research notes

Part I of this thesis used mainly secondary sources on the development of the RtoP and the CSDP as well as on the four cases of RtoP implementation. A number of publicly available documents have crucially shaped the RtoP debate, beginning with the ICISS report, *The Responsibility to Protect*, through the report of the High Level Panel, *A More Secure World: Our Shared Responsibility*, Secretary-General Annan's report, *In Larger Freedom: Towards Development, Security and Human Rights For All*, culminating with the World Summit Outcome Document and ending with the most recent report of Secretary-General Ban, *Implementing the Responsibility to Protect*. These documents show the development from embryonic ideas to fleshed-out policy proposals and reveal differences from one stage to the next and what they mean for the roles and burdens of the actors involved.

The analysis of the European discourse on the four reviewed RtoP cases in chapter 3 built on official documents by the UN, EU as well as France, Germany and the UK where available. Furthermore, the analysis relied on existing scholarly publications and on newspaper articles quoting the French, German and British official positions on the four cases. The newspapers accessed for the national discourses analysed in chapters 2 and 3 were: *Le Monde, Frankfurter Allgemeine Zeitung* and *The Guardian.*

The second part of this thesis built first of all on the analysis of official documents of the UN, the EU and France, Germany and the UK. In addition to that, scholarly articles and think tank analysis on the background of the Libyan and the Syrian crisis have been included to back up the empirical analysis. The time frame for the case study on the Syrian crisis has been extended until September 2013, throughout the process of data collection (see chapter 5). Due to the recency of the Syrian crisis, the number of available secondary sources and scholarly analyses on the case remained limited at the time of writing. There is thus a slight imbalance in the availability of data in comparison to the case study on the Libyan crisis. Furthermore, the categories chosen for the discourse analysis (see chapter 5) were not equally represented in both case studies. Data on the national perceptions of the role of the EU in particular was much harder to find in the case of the Syrian crisis than in the case of the Libyan crisis.

At the time of writing the conclusion, the Libyan crisis – although ongoing – had disappeared vastly from the mainstream media. Yet, it was considered important to include a final section on the impact of the RtoP on the 'real' world. For the short press review conducted in the final section of the conclusion, a random selection of newspaper articles reporting on the most recent developments (at the time of writing) in the Libyan and the Syrian crises has been consulted.

The author herself translated all quotes from official French and German documents and speeches referred to in this thesis. The original quotations have been provided in footnotes. In order to facilitate the tracing of the data, the primary sources have been listed according to the chapters they have been used in (see references).

References

Primary sources

Introduction

Annan, Kofi (2000): *The Millennium Report: We the Peoples – the Role of the United Nations in the 21st Century*, United Nations, New York, available at: https://www.un.org/en/events/pastevents/pdfs/We_The_Peoples.pdf.

Blair, Tony (14 September 2005): "Statement of the European Union accompanying the speech of Tony Blair, Prime Minister of the United Kingdom of Great Britain and Northern Ireland, to the United Nations World Summit, available at: http://www.europa-eu-un.org/articles/en/article_5026_en.htm."

European Security Strategy (2003): "A secure Europe in a better world", Brussels, 12 December.

Fischer, Joschka (13 May 1999): "Rede beim außerordentlichen Parteitag in Bielefeld", http://staff-www.uni-marburg.de/~näser/kos-fisc.htm.

Report on the Implementation of the European Security Strategy (2008): "Providing Security in a Changing World", S 407/08, Brussels, 11 December.

Straw, Jack (17 September 2005): "EU Presidency Statement at the General Debate of the 60th Session of the General Assembly", available at: http://www.eu-un.europa.eu/articles/en/article_5032_en.htm.

United Nations General Assembly (2005): "2005 World Summit Outcome", UN Doc. A/RES/60/1 (24 October), available at: http://daccess-dds- ny.un.org/doc/UNDOC/GEN/N05/487/60/PDF/N0548760.pdf?OpenElement.

United Nations Secretary-General Ban Ki-moon (2009): "Implementing the Responsibility to Protect", UN Doc. A/63/877 (12 January), available at: http://globalr2p.org/pdf/SGR2PEng.pdf.

Chapter 2

France

Chirac, Jacques (3 May 1999): "Intervention radiotélévisée du président de la république, M. Jacques Chirac, sur l'évolution de la situation au Kosovo", in: *Politique étrangère de la France, Textes et Documents*, May, Paris, pp. 10–11.

Chirac, Jacques (6 April 1999): "Intervention radiotélévisée du président de la république, M. Jacques Chirac, sur l'évolution de la situation au Kosovo", in: *Politique étrangère de la France, Textes et Documents*, April, Paris, pp. 323–324.

Chirac, Jacques (24 March 1999): Déclaration du président de la république, M. Jacques Chirac, in: *Politique étrangère de la France, Textes et Documents*, March, Paris, pp. 195–196.

De Charette, Hervé (27 April 1999): "Séance du 27 avril 1999: Situation au Kosovo. Déclaration du gouvernement et débat sur cette déclaration, compte rendu intégral", available at: http://recherche.assemblee-nationale.fr

Hue, Robert (26 March 1999): "Séance du 26 Mars 1999: Situation au Kosovo. Déclaration du Gouvernement et débat sur cette déclaration, Compte rendu intégral", available at: http://recherche.assemblee-nationale.fr/search97cgi/s97cgi.exe?action=ViewandVdkVgw.

Jospin, Lionel (27 April 1999): "Intervention du Premier ministre, M. Lionel Jospin, à l'assemblée nationale, lors des questions d'actualité à l'assemblée nationale et réponse du Premier ministre aux questions des parlementaires lors du débat", in: *Politique étrangère de la France, Textes et Documents*, April, Paris, 448–457.

Jospin, Lionel (26 March 1999): "Intervention du Premier ministre, M. Lionel Jospin, à l'assemblée nationale, séance du 26 Mars 1999: Situation au Kosovo. Déclaration du gouvernement et débat sur cette déclaration", in: *Politique étrangère de la France, Textes et Documents*, March, Paris.

Germany

Fischer, Joschka (13 May 1999): "Rede beim außerordentlichen Parteitag in Bielefeld", http://staff-www.uni-marburg.de/~näser/kos-fisc.htm.

Fischer, Joschka (25 February 1999): "Rede vor dem Deutschen Bundestag", BT-Plenarprotokoll 14/22.

Gysi, Gregor (16 March 1999): "Rede vor dem Deutschen Bundestag", BT-Plenarprotokoll 14/31.

Kinkel, Klaus (16 October 1998): "Rede vor dem Deutschen Bundestag", BT-Plenarprotokoll 13/248.

Schröder, Gerhard (14 February 1999): "Rede vor dem Deutschen Bundestag", BT-Plenarprotokoll 14/21.

Ströbele, Christian (15 March 1999): "Rede vor dem Deutschen Bundestag", Plenarprotokoll 14/30.

The United Kingdom

Benn, Tony (23 March 1999): "Oral Answers and Questions", Column 168, House of Commons, http://www.publications.parliament.uk/pa/cm199899/cmhansrd/vo990323/debindx/90323-x.htm.

Cook, Robin (14 April 1999): "1999 Speech on Kosovo" at the Mansion in London, to in: *UKPOl*, http://www.ukpolitics.org.uk/node/2955.

Hague, William (23 March 1999): "Oral Answers and Questions", Column 164, House of Commons, http://www.publications.parliament.uk/pa/cm199899/cmhansrd/vo990323/debindx/90323-x.htm.

Mahon, Alice (23 March 1999): "Oral Answers and Questions", Column 172, House of Commons, http://www.publications.parliament.uk/pa/cm199899/cmhansrd/vo990323/debindx/90323-x.htm.

Tony Blair (22 April 1999): 'Doctrine of the international community', speech delivered to the Economic Club of Chicago, http://www.number-10.gov.uk/output/Page1297.asp.

The European Union

Council of the European Union (17 December 2004): "Civilian Headline Goal 2008", 15863/04, Brussels.

EU Council Secretariat (2006): "Factsheet: EU battlegroups", 2 November.

European Council (11 December 1999): "Presidency Progress Report to the Helsinki European Council on strengthening the Common European Policy on Security and Defence", 11 December.

European Council (4 June 1999): "Declaration of the European Council on strengthening the common European policy on security and defence", Cologne.

European Council (24-25 March 1999): "Presidency Conclusion", Berlin, http://www.consilium.europa.eu/uedocs/cms_data/docs/pressdata/en/ec/ACFB2.html.

European Council (21-22 February 1999): "2161st Council meeting General Affairs", C/99/44, Luxembourg.

Franco-British summit (1998): "Joint declaration", 4 December, St Malo.

Franco-British summit (2003): "Declaration on strengthening European cooperation in security and defence", 4 February, Le Touquet.

Laeken Declaration on the Future of the European Union (2001): http://european-convention.eu.int/pdf/lknen.pdf.

Official Journal of the European Union (2003): *Treaty on European Union (Maastricht Treaty)*, C191, 29 July, Luxembourg.

International/ UN

Geneva Conventions (1949): "1949 Conventions and Additional Protocols, and their Commentaries", available at: http://www.icrc.org/applic/ihl/ihl.nsf/vw-Treaties1949.xsp?redirect=0.

International Court of Justice (ICJ) (2007): "The Application of the Convention on the Prevention and Punishment of the Crime of Genocide (Bosnia and Herzegovina vs. Serbia and Montenegro)", Judgment, 26 February.

International Law Commission (ILC) (2001): "Draft Articles on the Responsibility of States for Internationally Wrongful Acts, 2001", A/CN.4/553, para. 10, available at: http://legal.un.org/ilc/texts/instruments/english/draft%20 articles/9_6_2001.pdf.

UNSC (26 March 1999): "Security Council rejects demand for cessation of use of force against Federal Republic of Yugoslavia", Press Release SC/6659.

Chapter 3

France

Jouyet, Jean-Pierre (7 February 2008): "Entretien de M. Jean-Pierre Jouyet sur la Slovénie, la Présidence de l'UE, la zone euro et la diplomatie de l'euro", French Embassy in London, available at: http://www.ambafrance-uk.org/Entretien-de-M-Jean-Pierre-Jouyet=10171.

Kouchner, Bernard (10 August 2008): "La Situation en Georgie, Entretien du Ministre des Affaires Etrangeres et Europeennes, M. Bernard Kouchner avec 'Europe 1'", French Embassy in London, available at: http://www.ambafrance-uk.org/spip.php?page=mobile_artandart=15976.

Kouchner, Bernard (15 January 2008): "Déclaration de M. Bernard Kouchner, ministre des affaires étrangères et européennes, lors de l'entretien conjoint avec M. Miguel Angel Moratinos, ministre espagnol des affaires extérieures et de la coopération à 'TV5 Monde'", available at: http://discours.vie-publique.fr/notices/083000163.html.

Point de presse (8 August 2008): "Georgie", Embassy of France in Washington, available at: http://ambafrance-us.org/spip.php?article1068.

The French White Paper on Defence and National Security (2008): New York: Odile Jacob Publishing Corporation.

Germany

Federal Ministry of Defence (2006): *White Paper 2006 on German Security Policy and the Future of the Bundeswehr*, Berlin.

Steinmeier, Frank-Walter (27 August 2008): "Erklärung zu Georgien der Außenminister Kanadas, Frankreichs, Deutschlands, Italiens, Japans, der Vereinigten Staaten und des Vereinigten Königreichs", Pressemitteilung, Auswärtiges Amt, available at: http://www.auswaertiges-amt.de/DE/Infoservice/Presse/Meldungen/2008/080827-G7-Erklaerung-Georgien.html.

Steinmeier, Frank-Walter (11 August 2008): "Auswärtiges Amt stellt eine Million Euro für humanitäre Hilfe in Georgien zur Verfügung", Pressemitteilung, Auswärtiges Amt, available at: http://www.auswaertiges-amt.de/DE/Infoservice/Presse/Meldungen/2008/080811-HH-Georgien.html.

Steinmeier, Frank Walter (2 February 2008): "Bundesregierung begrüßt Verständigung auf Friedensfahrplan und drängt auf Ende der Gewalt in Kenia", Pressemitteilung, Auswärtiges Amt, available at: http://www.auswaertiges-amt.de/DE/Infoservice/Presse/Meldungen/2008/080202-Friedensfahrplan-Kenia.html.

Steinmeier, Frank-Walter (27 January 2008): "Bundesregierung unterstützt Vermittlungsbemühungen in Kenia", Pressemitteilung, Auswärtiges Amt, available at: http://www.auswaertiges-amt.de/DE/Infoservice/Presse/Meldungen/2008/080127-BR-Vermittlung-Kenia.html.

Steinmeier, Frank-Walter (1 January 2008): "Bundesminister Steinmeier zu den Wahlen in Kenia", Pressemitteilung, Auswärtiges Amt, available at: http://www.auswaertiges-amt.de/DE/Infoservice/Presse/Meldungen/2008/080101-BM-Wahl-Kenia.html.

The UK

Her Majesty Government (2010): *A strong Britain in an age of uncertainty: The National Security Strategy*, presented to Parliament by the Prime Minister by Command of Her Majesty, October, London. Miliband, David (1 February 2008): "Statement by Foreign Secretary", Foreign and Commonwealth Office, available at: http://appablog.wordpress.com/2008/01/04/kenya-statement-by-foreign-secretary/.

Tatham, Michael (5 September 2012): "The UK is fully committed to implementing the Responsibility to Protect", Statement by Ambassador Michael Tatham at UN General Assembly Interactive Dialogue on the "Report of the Secretary-General on the responsibility to protect: Timely and decisive response", available at: http://responsibilitytoprotect.org/United%20Kingdom.pdf.

White Paper (2006): "The Future of the UK's Nuclear Deterrent", presented to Parliament by the Secretary of State for Defence of State for Foreign and Commonwealth Affairs, London: The Stationary Office, available at: https://www.gov.uk/government/uploads/system/uploads/attachment_data/file/27378/DefenceWhitePaper2006_Cm6994.pdf.

EU

Council of the EU (11 January 2008): "Declaration by the Presidency on behalf of the European Union concerning the AU mediation efforts in Kenya", European Union at the United Nations, available at: http://www.eu-un.europa.eu/articles/en/article_7654_en.htm.

Council of the EU (4 January 2008): "Declaration by the Presidency on behalf of the European Union concerning Presidential elections in Kenya", 5043/08, Brussels.

European Council (1 September 2008): "Presidency Conclusions", Extraordinary European Council, 12594/2/08/, 6 October 2008, Brussels.

UN

UNSC (2008): "Statement by the President of the Security Council", S/PRST/2008/4, New York.

UNSC (2007a): *Resolution* 1769, 31 July, New York.

UNSC (2007b): "'5519th' meeting of the Security Council", S/PV.5519, New York.

UNSC (2006a): *Resolution* 1706, 31 August, New York.

UNSC (2006b): *Resolution* 1674, 28 April, New York.

UNSC (2004): "5015th meeting of the Security Council", Press Release SC/8160, New York.

Chapter 4

France

Alliot-Marie, Michèle (25 February 2011): "Situation en Libye conseil des droits de l'homme déclaration du ministre d'état, ministre des affaires étrangères et européennes, Michèle Alliot-Marie", Paris.

Alliot-Marie, Michèle (24 February 2011): "Situation en Libye, Déclaration du Ministre d'Etat, Ministre des Affaires Européennes".

Araud, Gerard (10 May 2011): "Protection des civils dans les conflits armés intervention du président du conseil de sécurité, représentant permanent de la France auprès des nations unies", New York.

Araud, Gerard (23 March 2011): "Libye entretien du représentant permanent de la France auprès des nations unies avec le journal français des Etats-Unis d'Amérique 'France-Amérique'", New York.

Araud, Gerard (4 March 2011): "Libye - cote d'ivoire entretien du représentant permanent de la France auprès des nations unies, avec 'bfm tv'", New York.

Araud, Gerard (26 February 2011): "Libye intervention du représentant permanent de la France auprès des nations unies", New York.

Araud, Gerard (25 February 2011): "Conseil des droits de l'homme 15eme session spéciale: 'la situation des droits de l'homme en république de Libye' Intervention du représentant permanent de la France aux nations unies", Genève.

Assemblée Nationale (30 March 2011): "Assemblée nationale XIIIe législature Session ordinaire de 2010-2011", Compte rendu intégral, Séance du mercredi 30 mars 2011.

Assemblée Nationale (15 March 2011): "Assemblée nationale, XIIIe législature Session ordinaire de 2010-2011", Compte rendu intégral, Première séance du mardi 15 mars 2011.

Assemblée Nationale (22 March 2011): "Assemblée nationale XIIIe législature Session ordinaire de 2010-2011", Compte rendu intégral, Première séance du mardi 22 mars 2011.

Assemblée Nationale (8 March 2011): "Assemblée nationale XIIIe législature Session ordinaire de 2010-2011", Compte rendu intégral, Deuxième séance du mardi 8 mars 2011.

Assemblée Nationale (2 March 2011): "Assemblée nationale, XIIIe législature Session ordinaire de 2010-2011", Compte rendu intégral, Première séance du mercredi 2 mars 2011.

Communiqué de la Présidence (21 February 2011): "Situation en Libye", Paris.

Fillon, François (28 February 2011): "Entretien du premier ministre, François Fillon, avec 'rtl' - extraits", Paris.

Juppé, Alain (29 August 2011): "Conférence des ambassadeurs allemands entretien du ministre d'état, ministre des affaires étrangères et européennes, Alain Juppé, avec le quotidien allemand 'Frankfurter Allgemeine Zeitung' - extraits", Berlin.

Juppé, Alain (16 April 2011): "Colloque 'printemps arabe' discours de clôture du ministre d'état, ministre des affaires étrangères et européennes, Alain Juppé, à l'institut du monde arabe", Paris.

Juppé, Alain (6 April 2011): "Côte d'ivoire Libye entretien du ministre Juppé, avec 'France info' - extraits", Paris.

Juppé, Alain (24 March 2011): "Entretien du ministre d'état, ministre des affaires étrangères et européennes, Alain Juppé, avec l'"American Press Club'", Paris.

Juppé, Alain (17 March 2011): "Libye entretien avec la presse du ministre d'état, ministre des affaires étrangères et européennes, Alain Juppé", Paris.

Juppé, Alain (3 March 2011): "Conférence de presse conjointe du ministre d'état, ministre des affaires étrangères et européennes,Alain Juppé, avec le ministre d'état, ministre des affaires étrangeres du Royaume-Uni de Grande-Bretagne et d'Irlande du nord, William Hague - propos de M. Juppé", Paris.

Point de presse (21 October 2011): "Libye", Ministère des Affaires étrangères et européennes.

Point de presse (18 March 2011): "Adoption par le Conseil de sécurité des Nations unies de la résolution 1973 sur la situation en Libye", Ministère des Affaires étrangères et européennes.

Point de presse (24 February 2011): "Sanctions européennes contre la Libye", Ministère des Affaires étrangères et européennes.

Point de presse (22 February 2011): "Libye: rapatriement des Français: déclaration du ministre d'Etat, ministre des Affaires étrangères et européennes", Michèle Alliot-Marie, Ministère des Affaires étrangères et européennes.

Point de presse (21 February 2011): "Libye", Ministère des Affaires étrangères et européennes, http://www.diplomatie.gouv.fr/fr/ (24.06.2013).

Sarkozy, Nicolas (31 August 2011) "XIXème conférence des ambassadeurs discours du président de la républicue", Nicolas Sarkozy, Paris.

Sarkozy, Nicolas (24 June 2011): "Conseil européen conférence de presse du président de la république, Nicolas Sarkozy", Brussels.

Sarkozy, Nicolas (24 March 2011): "Conseil européen conférence de presse du président de la république, Nicolas Sarkozy", Brussels.

Sarkozy, Nicolas (11 March 2011): "Situation en Libye et en méditerranée conseil européen extraordinaire conférence de presse du président de la république, Nicolas Sarkozy", Paris.

Sarkozy, Nicolas (2 March 2011): "Visite d'état en France du président de la république d'Afrique du sud conférence de presse conjointe du président de la république, Nicolas Sarkozy, et du président de la république d'Afrique du sud, Jacob Zuma - propos de M. Sarkozy", Paris.

Sarkozy, Nicolas, and Cameron, David (28 March 2011): "Libye déclaration conjoint e du président de la république, Nicolas Sarkozy, et du premier ministre du Royaume-Uni de Grande-Bretagne et d'Irlande du nord", Paris.

S**arkozy, Nicolas and Cameron, David (10 March 2011):** "Libye lettre conjointe adressée par le président de la république, Nicolas Sarkozy et le premier ministre du Royaume-Uni de Grande-Bretagne et d'Irlande du nord, David Cameron au président du conseil européen, Herman Van Rompuy", Paris.

Wauquiez, Laurent (12 May 2011): "Union européenne réponse du ministre chargé des affaires européennes, Laurent Wauquiez, à une question d'actualité au sénat", Paris.

Wauquiez, Laurent (21 February 2011): "Entretien du ministre charge des affaires européennes, Laurent Wauquiez, avec 'Europe 1' - extraits", Paris.

Germany

Hoyer, Werner (24 February 2011): "Staatsminister Hoyer vor dem Deutschen Bundestag zur Lage in Libyen", Auswärtiges Amt.

Westerwelle, Guido (24 August 2011): "Libyen: 'Wirtschaftlicher Aufbau wird entscheidend sein' (Interview)", Auswärtiges Amt.

Westerwelle, Guido (30 April 2011): 'Außenminister Westerwelle im Interview mit dem 'Tagesspiegel' zur Situation in Libyen und in Syrien", Auswärtiges Amt.

Westerwelle, Guido (24 March 2011): "Außenminister Westerwelle in der Süddeutschen Zeitung zur Libyen-Politik", Auswärtiges Amt.

Westerwelle, Guido (23 March 2011): "Interview von Außenminister Westerwelle für die 'Passauer Neue Presse' ", Auswärtiges Amt.

Westerwelle, Guido (18 March 2011): "Regierungserklärung durch Bundesminister Westerwelle vor dem Deutschen Bundestag zur aktuellen Entwicklung in Libyen (UN- Resolution)", Auswärtiges Amt.

Westerwelle, Guido (17 March 2011): "Außenminister Westerwelle im Interview mit dem Deutschlandfunk zu Libyen", Auswärtiges Amt.

Westerwelle, Guido (16 March 2011): "Regierungserklärung durch Bundesaußenminister Westerwelle vor dem Deutschen Bundestag zum Umbruch in der arabischen Welt", Auswärtiges Amt.

Westerwelle, Guido (12 March 2011): "'Engste Partnerschaft beim demokratischen Aufbruch' (Interview)", Auswärtiges Amt.

Westerwelle, Guido (9 March 2011): "Libyen: 'Sanktionen und Humanitäre Hilfe' (Interview)", Auswärtiges Amt.

Westerwelle, Guido (28 February 2011): "Rede von Außenminister Guido Westerwelle vor dem Menschenrechtsrat der VN in Genf", Auswärtiges Amt.

Westerwelle, Guido (25 February 2011): "Interview: Bundesminister Westerwelle zur Situation in Libyen (Deutschlandfunk)", Auswärtiges Amt.

Westerwelle, Guido (22 February 2011): "Zur aktuellen Lage in Libyen", available at: http://www.auswaertiges-amt.de/sid_32B166C93223392B49E4D8DC37952BD0/DE/Mediathek/mediathek_video_node.html?id=583806 (12.06.2013).

Westerwelle, Guido (4 February 2011): "Außenminister Westerwelle: 'Europas Weg in die Welt'", Auswärtiges Amt.

Wittig, Peter (17 March 2011): "Explanation of vote by Ambassador Wittig on the Security Council Resolution 1973 on Libya", New York, available at: http://www.new-york-un.diplo.de/Vertretung/newyorkvn/en/__pr/Speeches/PM__2011/20110317_20Explanation_20of_20vote_20-_20Libya.html?archive=2984642 (12.07.2013).

The UK

Cameron, David (21 October 2011): "Prime Minister and Foreign Secretary on the death of Qadhafi", Foreign and Commonwealth Office.

Cameron, David (22 September 2011): "Libya and the Arab Spring shows the UN needs a new way of working not just united in condemnation, but united in action", UK Mission to the UN.

Cameron, David (14 March 2011): "'Britain will remain at the forefront of Europe in leading the response to this crisis'", Foreign and Commonwealth Office.

Cameron, David (28 February 2011): "Prime Minister's statement on Libya", Foreign and Commonwealth Office.

Foreign Office press release on NATO's Foreign Minister meeting (19 April 2011): "NATO Foreign Ministers meet in Berlin", Foreign and Commonwealth Office.

Foreign Office press statement (20 March 2011): "Libya: 'We will work with our Arab partners to enforce the resolution'", Foreign and Commonwealth Office.

Grant, Mark Lyall (17 March 2011): "United Nations Security Council resolution on Libya No-Fly Zone has been approved", Foreign and Commonwealth Office.

Hague, William (30 March 2011): "Libya conference outcomes: 'Clear international support for the people of Libya'", Foreign and Commonwealth Office.

Hague, William (15 March 2011): "UK is at the forefront of the international effort to isolate Qadhafi regime", Foreign and Commonwealth Office.

Hague, William (10 March 2011): "Foreign Secretary attends EU Foreign Ministers meeting on Libya", Foreign and Commonwealth Office.

Hague, William (23 February 2011): "UK calls for UN action on Libya", Foreign and Commonwealth Office.

Hague, William (22 February 2011): "Foreign Secretary on Libya", Foreign and Commonwealth Office.

Hague, William (20 February 2011): "Foreign Secretary speaks to Saif Qadhafi", Foreign and Commonwealth Office.

House of Commons (5 September 2011): "Debate, Oral Answers and Questions", columns 23-41.

House of Commons (30 March 2011): "Debate, Oral Answers and Questions", columns 345-364.

House of Commons (24 March 2011): "Debate, Oral Answers and Questions", columns 1109-1151.

House of Commons (18 March 2011): "Debate, Oral Answers and Questions", columns 611-651.

House of Commons (7 March 2011): "Debate, Oral Answers and Questions", columns 643-662.

EU

Ashton, Catherine (18 March 2011): "Remarks by High Representative Catherine Ashton at the VIP corner on the latest developments regarding Libya", Brussels.

Ashton, Catherine (20 February 2011): "Declaration by the High Representative, Catherine Ashton, on behalf of the European Union on events in Libya, Brussels".

European Commission, Humanitarian Aid and Civil Protection (ECHO) (2011): *Libyan Crisis Factsheet*, 21 June.

Foreign Affairs Council (2011): *Council conclusions on Libya, 3076th Foreign Affairs Council meeting*, 21 March, Brussels.

Official Journal of the European Union (2011): *Council Decision 2011/210/ CFSP*, 1 April 2011, L89/17.

Van Rompuy (23 February 2011): "Statement by Herman Van Rompuy, President of the European Council, on the developments in the EU's Southern neighbourhood".

Van Rompuy, Herman, and Ashton, Catherine (17 March 2011): "Joint statement by President of the European Council Herman Van Rompuy, and EU High Representative Catherine Ashton on UN Security Council resolution on Libya", Brussels.

International/ UN

League of Arab States (LAS) (2011): "The outcome of the Council of the League of Arab States meeting at the Ministerial level in its extraordinary session on the implications of the current events in Libya and the Arab position", 12 March, Cairo, available at: http://www.securitycouncilreport.org/atf/cf/%7B65BFCF9B-6D27-4E9C-8CD3-CF6E4FF96FF9%7D/Libya%20 7360.pdf.

UNSC (2011a): "Press Statement on Libya", 22 February, available at: http://www.un.org/News/Press/docs/2011/sc10180.doc.htm.

UNSC (2011b): *Resolution 1973*, 17 March, New York.

UNSC (2011c): *Resolution 1970*, 26 February, New York.

Chapter 5

France

Araud, Gérard (11 September 2013): "Responsabilité de protéger - Intervention du représentant permanent de la France auprès des Nations unies à l'occasion du dialogue interactif informel", New York.

Araud, Gérard (29 July 2013): "Syrie - droits de l'Homme - Intervention du chargé d'Affaires a.i. de la France auprès des Nations unies", New York.

Araud, Gérard (27 February 2013): "Syrie - Remarques du représentant permanent de la France auprès des Nations unies", New York.

Araud, Gérard (1 August 2012): "Syrie - Communiqué du ministre des Affaires étrangères, M. Laurent Fabius - Paris, 1er août 2012", Paris.

Araud, Gérard (29 July 2012): "Syrie - Entretien du représentant permanent de la France auprès des Nations unies avec 'ITELE'", New York.

Araud, Gérard (31 January 2012): "Syrie - Remarques à la presse de M. Alain Juppé, ministre d'État, ministre d'État, ministre des Affaires étrangères et européennes", Paris.

Assemblée Nationale (4 September 2013): "Assemblée nationale, XIVe législature Deuxième session extraordinaire de 2012-2013", Compte rendu intégral, Première séance du mercredi 04 septembre 2013.

Fabius, Lauren (8 September 2013) "Syrie - Entretien du ministre des affaires étrangères, M. Laurent Fabius, avec 'France 3' - extraits", Paris.

Fabius, Laurent (4 September 2013): "Syrie - Entretien du ministre des affaires étrangères, M. Laurent Fabius, avec 'France Info'", Paris.

Fabius, Laurent (27 August 2013): 'XXIe conférence des ambassadeurs - Syrie - Mali - Afrique - UE - Maghreb - Proche-Orient - G20 - Diplomatie économique - Français de l'étranger - Francophonie - Climat - Développement - Discours du président de la République, M. François Hollande", Paris.

Fabius, Laurent (24 September 2012): "Syrie/Mali - Remarques à la presse du ministre des Affaires étrangères, M. Laurent Fabius - New York, 24 septembre 2012", New York.

Fabius, Laurent (14 June 2012): "Syrie - Aggravation de la situation - Conférence de presse du ministre des Affaires étrangères, M. Laurent Fabius", Paris.

Fabius, Laurent (1 June 2012): "Syrie conseil des droits de l'homme des nations unies déclaration du ministre des affaires étrangères, M. Laurent Fabius", Paris.

Hollande, François (31 August 2013): "Syrie - Entretien du président de la République, M. François Hollande, avec le quotidien 'Le Monde' - extraits", Paris.

Hollande, François (14 March 2013): "Conseil européen - Syrie - UE - Point de presse du président de la République, M. François Hollande, lors de son arrivée au Conseil européen", Brussels.

Joint declaration of France, Australia, the UK, South Korea and Luxembourg (18 January 2012): "Syrie/Cour pénale internationale - Déclaration conjointe de la France, de l'Australie, du Royaume-Uni, de la République de Corée et du Luxembourg", New York.

Le Drian, Jean-Yves (7 June 2012): "Entretien du ministre de la défense, E. Jean-Yves le Drian, avec le quotidien 'Le Monde'", Paris.

Spokesperson of the French Foreign Ministry (14 June 2012): "Syrie - Aggravation de la situation - entretien du porte-parole du ministère des Affaires étrangères avec 'France 24'", Paris.

Germany

Hoyer, Werner (2 August 2011): "Staatsminister Hoyer zur Lage in Syrien (Interview)", Auswärtiges Amt.

Westerwelle, Guido (14 September 2013): "Außenminister Westerwelle begrüßt russisch-amerikanische Einigung zu Syrien", Auswärtiges Amt.

Westerwelle, Guido (1 September 2013): "Syrien: ‚Ich mache mir allergrößte Sorgen", Interview, Die Welt am Sonntag, Auswärtiges Amt.

Westerwelle, Guido (28 August 2013): "Syrien: ‚Ich warne vor einem Flächenbrand'", Interview, Die Neue Zürcher Zeitung, Auswärtiges Amt.

Westerwelle, Guido (14 January 2013): "Assad ist zu weit gegangen", Auswärtiges Amt.

Westerwelle, Guido (17 July 2012): "Erklärung von Bundesaußenminister Westerwelle zu Syrien", Auswärtiges Amt.

The UK

Brown, Jeremy (27 February 2012): "Foreign Office Minister discusses Syria at UN Human Rights Council", Foreign and Commonwealth Office.

Burt, Alistair (28 November 2011): "Foreign Office Minister comments on report detailing horrific human rights violations in Syria", Foreign and Commonwealth Office.

Hague, William (28 August 2013): "Foreign Secretary calls for strong international response to chemical attack in Syria", Foreign and Commonwealth Office.

Hague, William (20 May 2013): "Foreign Secretary statement to Parliament on Syria", Foreign and Commonwealth Office.

Hague, William (29 August 2012): "UK Intervention at the United Nations Security Council meeting on Syria", Foreign and Commonwealth Office.

Hague, William (20 July 2012): "Foreign Secretary sets out UK's approach to Syrian crisis", Foreign and Commonwealth Office.

Hague, William (30 June 2012): "Foreign Secretary's remarks at Syria Action Group meeting", Foreign and Commonwealth Office.

Hague, William (14 June 2011): "Foreign Secretary discusses Syria and Iran with Russian Foreign Minister", Foreign and Commonwealth Office.

Hague, William (11 June 2012): "Foreign Secretary: 'International unity' needed on Syria", Foreign and Commonwealth Office.

Hague, William (31 March 2012): "Foreign Secretary statement on political prisoners in Syria", Foreign and Commonwealth Office.

Hague, William (6 March 2013): "Foreign Secretary Statement to Parliament on Syria", Foreign and Commonwealth Office.

Hague, William (12 February 2012): "Foreign Secretary comments on 12 February Arab League meeting on Syria", Foreign and Commonwealth Office.

Hague, William (30 January 2012): "Foreign Secretary on Syria: 'We should unite behind the Arab League plan'", Foreign and Commonwealth Office.

Hague, William (28 January 2012): "Foreign Secretary condemns killings in Syria and says world must speak up for its people", Foreign and Commonwealth Office.

House of Commons (29 August 2013): "Syria and the Use of Chemical Weapons", columns 1424-1547.

House of Commons (5 September 2011): "Debate, Oral Answers and Questions", columns 1-49.

EU

Ashton, Catherine (13 March 2013): "Remarks by EU High Representative Catherine Ashton on the situation in Syria", Strasbourg, available at: http://eeas.europa.eu/top_stories/2013/140313_post_ep_plenary_en.htm.

Ashton, Catherine (18 June 2012): "EU HR Ashton gravely concerned by escalating violence in Syria", EU at the United Nations, available at: http://www.eu-un.europa.eu/articles/en/article_12310_en.htm.

Ashton, Catherine (7 June 2012): "Statement by the EU HR Ashton on violence in Syria", EU at the United Nations, available at: http://www.eu-un.europa.eu/articles/en/article_12261_en.htm.

Ashton, Catherine (19 August 2011): "Statement by High Representative Catherine Ashton on the broadening of restrictive measures against the government of Syria", Brussels.

Ashton, Catherine (8 July 2011): "Statement by the High Representative Catherine Ashton on the situation in Syria", Brussels.

Ashton, Catherine (18 March 2011): "Statement by the High Representative, Catherine Ashton, on the crackdown of demonstrations in Syria", Brussels.

EU Factsheet (1 March 2012): "The European Union and Syria", Brussels.

EU Joint Communication (24 June 2013): "Towards a comprehensive EU approach to the Syrian crisis", Brussels.

European External Action Service (13 September 2011): "Frequently Asked Questions on EU restrictive measures against the Syrian regime", Brussels.

European Parliament (15 December 2012): "'President Assad of Syria must step down immediately, says Parliament'", Plenary sessions, Strasbourg.

European Parliament (16 February 2012): "MEPs discuss Syria, EU foreign policy and the Arab Spring with Alain Juppé", Committee on Foreign Affairs / Subcommittee on Security and Defence, EP Press Release.

European Parliament (15 September 2011): "'Syria's Assad must go, and Libya's resources must benefit all Libyans say MEPs'", Plenary sessions, Strasbourg.

European Parliament (30 May 2011): "Syrian uprising: a spring not in bloom", Press Release.

Foreign Affairs Council (23 July 2012): "Council conclusions on Syria", 3183rd Foreign Affairs Council meeting, Brussels.

Foreign Affairs Council (14 May, 2012): "Council conclusions on Syria", 3166th Foreign Affairs Council meeting, Brussels.

Foreign Affairs Council (FAC) (22-23 March 2012): "Council conclusions on Syria", 3157th Foreign Affairs Council meeting, Brussels.

Németh, Zsolt (6 April 2011): "The EU urges national dialogue in three Arab countries", Hungarian Presidency of the Council of the European Union", Budapest.

Van Rompuy, Herman (30 January 2012): "Press statement on foreign policy issues", European Council, The President, Brussels.

International/ UN

Annan, Kofi (2012): "Six point-peace plan for Syria", as annexed to Security Council resolution 2042 (2012) of 14 April.

António, Guterres (2013): "Remarks to the United Nations Security Council António Guterres, United Nations High Commissioner for Refugees" 16 July, UNHCR, Geneva.

General Assembly (2013): *Resolution on Syria*, A/RES/67/262.

Obama, Barack (2013): "Statement by the President on Syria", 31 August, The White House, Office of the Press Secretary, available at: http://www.whitehouse.gov/the-press-office/2013/08/31/statement-president-syria.

Šimonovi, Ivan (2013): "Briefing for United Nations Security Council by Navi Pillay, High Commissioner for Human Rights, delivered by Ivan Šimonovi, Assistant Secretary-General for Human Rights: The Situation in the Middle East [Syria]" 16 July, UNHR, available at: http://www.ohchr.org/EN/NewsEvents/Pages/DisplayNews.aspx?NewsID=13545andLangID=E.

UNSC (2013a): *7000th meeting of the Security Council*, 16 July, S/PV.7000, New York.

UNSC (2013b): *Resolution 2113 (2013)*, S/RES/2118.

UNSC (2012a): *Resolution 2042 (2012)*, S/RES/2042.

UNSC (2012b): *Resolution 2043 (2012)*, S/RES/2042.

UNSC (2012c): *Resolution 2059 (2012)*, S/ERES/2059.

UNSC (4 February 2012): *6711th meeting*, S/PV.6711.

UNSC (4 October 2011): "France, Germany, Portugal and United Kingdom of Great Britain and Northern Ireland: draft resolution", S/2011/412.

UNSC (3 August 2011): "Security Council, in statement, condemns Syrian authorities for 'widespread violations of human rights, use of force against civilians'", 6598th Meeting, SC/10352.

Chapter 6

France

Araud, Gérard (8 June 2011): "Syrie entretien du représentant permanent de la France auprès des nations unies, avec 'i-tele'", New York.

Assemblée Nationale (22 March 2011): "Assemblée nationale XIIIe législature Session ordinaire de 2010-2011", Compte rendu intégral, Première séance du mardi 22 mars 2011.

Juppé, Alain (23 May 2011): "Conseil affaires générales conseil affaires étrangères conférence de presse du ministre d'état, ministre des affaires étrangères et européennes, Alain Juppé", Brussels.

Juppé, Alain (24 March 2011): "Entretien du ministre d'état, ministre des affaires étrangères et européennes, Alain Juppé, avec l'American Press Club", Paris.

UK

Cameron, David (22 September 2011): "Libya and the Arab Spring shows the UN needs a new way of working not just united in condemnation, but united in action", UK Mission to the UN.

Hague, William (12 June 2011): "Foreign Secretary discusses Syria with US Secretary of State John Kerry", Foreign and Commonwealth Office.

UN

Churkin, Vitali, UNSC (14 April 2012): "6751st meeting of the Security Council", S/PV.6751, New York.

United Nations (2 March 2012): "Report of the International Commission of Inquiry on Libya", Human Rights Council, Nineteenth session, Agenda item 4, A/HRC/19/68.

Secondary sources

Akande, Dapo (2011): "Does SC Resolution 1973 Permit Coalition Military Support for the Libyan Rebels?", *EJILTalk*, 31 March, available at: http://www.ejiltalk.org/does-sc-resolution-1973-permit-coalition-military-support-for-the-libyan-rebels.

Al Arabyia (2012): "Iran reaffirms full support for Annan's Syria peace plan", 10 July, available at: http://english.alarabiya.net/articles/2012/07/10/225485.html.

Alcalde, Javier, and Bouchard, Caroline (2008): "Human Security and Coherence within the EU: The Case of the 2006 UN Small Arms Conference", in: *Hamburg Review of Social Sciences*, 3(1), pp. 142–171.

Alkire, Sabine (2003): "A Conceptual Framework for Human Security", *Working Paper 2, Centre for Research on Inequality*, Human Security and Ethnicity, CRISE Queen Elizabeth House, University of Oxford.

Almond, Mark (1994): *Europe's Backyard War*, London: William Heinemann.

Amnesty International (2012): "Europe's race to the bottom on protecting refugees from Syria", *Op-Ed*, Elsayed-Ali, Sherif.

Amnesty International (2012): "Syria: Repression continues despite Annan plan hopes", 4 April, available at: http://www.amnesty.org/en/news/syria-repression-continues-despite-annan-plan-hopes-2012-04-03.

Badescu, Cristina G. (2011): *Humanitarian Intervention and the Responsibility to Protect*, London and New York: Routledge.

Badescu, Cristina G., and Bergholm, Linnea (2009): "The Responsibility to Protect and the Conflict in Darfur: The Big Let-down", in: *Security Dialogue, 40(3)*, pp. 287-309.

Ball, Patrick et al (2002): *Killings and Refugee Flow in Kosovo, March-June 1999: A Report to the International Criminal Tribunal for the Former Yugoslavia*, Washington: American Association for the Advancement of Science.

Barbier, Christophe (1999): "La politique à l'heure du Kosovo", in: *L'Express,* 15 April, pp. 28-30.

Barnutz, Sebastian (2010): "The EU's logic of security: politics through institutionalized discourses", in: *European Security, 19(3),* pp. 377-394.

Baun, Michael (2005): "How Necessary is a Common Strategic Culture?", in: *Oxford Journal on Good Governance,* 2(1), pp. 33-37.

BBC News (2013): "Syria death toll at least 93,000, says UN", 13 July, available at: http://www.bbc.co.uk/news/world-middle-east-22886730.

BBC News (2008a): "Fears Burma Strom Toll Could Soar", 7 May.

BBC News (2008b): "UK warns of Russia 'catastrophe'", 12 August.

Bederman, David J. (2001): *International Law Frameworks,* New York: Foundation Press.

Bellamy, Alex J. (2011a): *Global Politics and the Responsibility to Protect: From Words to Deeds,* London: Routledge.

Bellamy, Alex J. (2011b): "Mass Atrocities and Armed Conflict: Links, Distinctions, and Implications for the Responsibility to Prevent", *The Stanley Foundation Policy Analysis Brief,* February.

Bellamy, Alex J. (2010): "The Responsibility to Protect-Five Years On", in: *Ethics and International Affairs, 24(2),* pp. 143–169.

Bellamy, Alex J. (2008): "The Responsibility to Protect and the Problem of Military Intervention", in: *International Affairs, 84(4),* pp. 615-639.

Bellamy, Alex J. (2006): "Responsibility to Protect or Trojan Horse? The Crisis in Darfur and Humanitarian Intervention after Iraq", in: *Ethics and International Affairs, 19(2),* pp. 31–54.

Bellamy, Alex J., and McDonald, Matt (2002): "'The Utility of Human Security': Which Humans? What Security? A Reply to Thomas and Tow", in: *Security Dialogue, 33(3),* pp. 373–377.

Beaumont, Peter (2012): "One year on: chaotic Libya reveals the perils of humanitarian intervention", in: *The Guardian*, 19 February.

Biscop, Sven (2011a): "A Long-Term Strategy for Libya and the Mediterranean: Over to the European Union", *Egmont Security Policy Brief*, No. 17.

Biscop, Sven (2011b): "The future of EU-US security and defence cooperation: what lies ahead?", *Debate*, Institute for Security Studies, Paris, 28 September, available at: http://www.iss.europa.eu/fr/publications/detail-page_213/article/q-the-future-of-eu-us-security-and-defence-cooperation-what-lies-ahead-3/.

Björkdahl, Anna (2002): "Norms in International Relations: Some Conceptual and Methodological Reflections" in: *Cambridge Review of International Affairs*, 15(1), pp. 9–23.

Bloching, Sebastian (2011): "CSDP and EU Mission Update – April 2011", *European Security Review Briefing 3*, ISIS Europe, 3-15 April.

Blomfield, Adrian (2008): "Georgia: Russia enters into 'war' in South Ossetia", in *The Telegraph*, 8 August.

Bock, Christian W.D., and R. Miller, Leland (2004): "Darfur: Where is Europe?", in: *The Washington Post*, 9 December.

Bolopion, Philippe (2012): "After Libya, The Question: To Protect or Depose", in: *L.A. Times*, 25 August.

Bouchard, Caroline (2008): *Managing Expectations: The European Union and Human Security at the United Nations*, Doctoral Thesis, University of Edinburgh, available at: https://www.era.lib.ed.ac.uk/bitstream/1842/3261/1/C%20Bouchard%20PhD%20thesis%2008.pdf.

Boxx, Edward (2013): "Observations on the Air War in Syria", in: *Air and Space Power Journal*, March-April, pp. 147-168.

Brattberg, Erik (2011): "Opportunities lost, opportunities seized: the Libya crisis as Europe' s perfect storm", European Policy Centre *(EPC) Policy Brief*, June.

Bretherton, Charlotte, and Vogler, John (2006): *The European Union as a Global Actor*, 2nd ed. London: Routledge.

Brosig, Malte (2011): "The Emerging Peace and Security Regime in Africa: The Role of the EU", in: *European Foreign Affairs Review, 16*, pp. 107-122.

Brown, Chris (2011): "Recent actions in Libya show that 'liberal interventionism' to support the human rights of civilians is not exempt from politics", *LSE Blog*, 15 April.

Brozus, Lars (2012): "Improving Mass Atrocities Prevention, Guidelines for Effective and Legitimate Implementation of the Responsibility to Protect", *SWP Comments, 38*, December, Berlin.

Buckley, Caitlin A. (2012): "Learning from Libya, Acting in Syria", in: *Journal of Strategic Security, 5(2)*, pp. 81-104.

Carroll, Rory (1004): "Sudan massacres are not genocide," in: *The Guardian*, 10 August, available at: www.guardian.co.uk/world/2004/aug/10/eu.sudan.

Cassese, Antonio (1999): "*Ex iniuria ius oritur*: Are We Moving Towards International Legitimation of Forcible Humanitarian Countermeasures in the World Community?", in: *European Journal of International Law*, 10 (1), pp. 23-30.

Chandler, David (2008): "Review Essay: Human Security: The Dog That Didn't Bark", in: Security Dialogue, 39(4), pp. 427–438.

Chandler, David (2005): *From Kosovo to Kabul: Human Rights and International Intervention*, London: Pluto Press.

Chesterman, Simon (2002): "Legality Versus Legitimacy: Humanitarian Intervention, the Security Council, and the Rule of Law", in *Security Dialogue, 33(3)*, pp. 293–307.

Chesterman, Simon (2011): "Leading from behind': the responsibility to protect, the Obama doctrine, and humanitarian intervention after Libya", in: *Ethics and International Affairs, 25(3)*, pp. 279–85.

Chivers, C.J. and Schmitt, Eric (2011): "In Srikes on Libya by NATO, an Unspoken Civilian Toll", in: *The New York Times*, 17 December.

Chivvis, Cristopher S. (2012): "Libya and the Future of Liberal Intervention", *Survival, 54(6)*, pp. 1–23.

Chulov, Martin, and Grant, Harriet (2014): "EU must open doors to avoid refugee catastrophe, says UN", in: *The Guardian*, 13 January.

Coelmont, Joe (2011): "First Lessons from the Libya Operations", *Egmont Security Policy Brief*, No. 18.

Cohen, Roberta (2009): "The Burma Cyclone and the Responsibility to Protect", in: *Global Responsibility to Protect, 1(2)*, pp. 253-257.

Cockburn, Patrick (2013): "Special Report: We all thought Libya had moved on - it has, but into lawlessness and ruin", in: *The Independent*, 3 September.

Cortell, Andrew P., and Davis, James W. Jr. (2002): "Understanding the Domestic Impact of International Norms: A Research Agenda", in: *International Studies Review*, 2(1), pp. 65–87.

Cotler, Irwin, and Genser, Jerad (2011): "Libya and the Responsibility to Protect", *International Herald Tribune*, 1 March 2011.

Cross, Marie (2010): "Co-operation by Committee: The EU Military Committee and the Committee on the Civilian Crisis Management", *Occasional Paper 82*, EU Institute for Security Studies, Paris.

Daddow, Oliver (2009): "'Tony's war'? Blair, Kosovo and the interventionist impulse in British foreign policy", in *International Affairs, 85(3)*, pp. 547–560.

Dagher, Sam, and Fassihi, Farnez (2013): "Syria Presses Offensive, Shrugs Off Gas Attack Claims", *The Wall Street Journal*, 22 August.

Deighton, Anne (2011): "The European Union, Multilateralism and the Use of Force", in: *The Changing Character of War*, Strachan, Hew, and Scheipers, Sibylle (eds.), Oxford: Oxford University Press, pp. 315-333.

Dembinski, Matthias, and Reinold, Theresa (2011): "Libya and the Future of the Responsibility to Protect – African and European Perspectives.", *PRIF*-Report, No. 107, Frankfurt a. M.

Deng, Francis, Kimaro, Sadikel, Lyons, Terrence, Rothchild, Donald, and Zartman, William I. (1996): *Sovereignty as Responsibility: Conflict Management in Africa*, Washington: Brookings Institution Press.

Duncanson, Clair, and Eschle, Catherine (2008): "Gender and the Nuclear Weapons State: A Feminist Critique of the UK Government's White Paper on Trident", in: *New Political Science, 30(4)*, pp. 545-563.

Dunne, Tim, and Gifkins, Jess (2011): "Libya and the state of intervention", in: *Australian Journal of International Affairs, 65(5)*, pp. 515–530.

Eminue, Okon, and Dickson, Monday (2012): "The United Nations Resolutions on Syria: Exploration of Motivation from Russia and China", in: *International Affairs and Global Strategy*, 10, pp. 5-13.

Euractiv (2011): "Gewalt in Syrien: Deutschland für EU-Sanktionen", 27 April, http://www.euractiv.de/globales-europa/artikel/gewalt-in-syrien-deutschland-fuer-eu-sanktionen-004723.

EuBusniess (2011): "New EU Sanctions put the Squeeze on Libyan Oil Sector", 12 April, http://www.eu- business.com/news-eu/libya-conflict-oil.9ji.

EU Observer (2013): "France, Germany and UK show discord on EU defence", 20 December 2013.

EU Observer (2014): "EU countries provisionally agree African mission", 10 January.

Evans, Gareth (2011a): "R2P is breaking a new ground in the development of global governance", Interview, Yale Global online, 15 April, available at: http://yaleglobal.yale.edu/content/gareth-evans-responsibility-protect-transcript.

Evans, Gareth (2011b): "End of Argument", in: *Foreign Policy*, 28 November, http://www.foreignpolicy.com/articles/2011/11/28/gareth_evans_end_of_the_argument.

Evans, Gareth (2007): "The Responsibility to Protect: Creating and Implementing a New International Norm", Address made to Human Rights Centre, Melbourne, 13 August and to Community Legal Centres and Lawyers for Human Rights, Sydney, 28 August.

Evans, Gareth (2006): "From Humanitarian Intervention to the Responsibility to Protect", Keynote adddress to Symposium on Humanitarian Intervention, University of Wisconsin-Madison, 31 March, https://www.fh-muenster.de/humanitaere-hilfe/downloads/Evans_-_Responsibility_To_Protect.pdf.

EXACT Webpage: www.exact-training.net (14 January 2014).

Eyal, Jonathan (2012): "The Responsibility to Protect: A Chance Missed", in: *Short War, Long Shadow*, Johnson, Adrian, and Mueen, Saqeb (eds.), Royal United Services Institute for Defence (RUSI), pp. 53-62.

Fargues, Philippe, and Fandrich, Christine (2012): "The Syrian Response to the Syrian Refugee Crisis, What Next?", *Migration Policy Centre Report, 14*, Florence.

Fermor, Christopher (2012): "NATO's decision to intervene in Libya (2011): Realist principles or humanitarian norms?", in: *Journal of Politics and International Studies, 8(Winter)*, pp. 323-361.

Finnemore, Martha (1996): "Constructing Norms of Humanitarian Intervention", in: *The Culture of National Security, Norms and Identity in World Politics*, Katzenstein, Peter (ed), New York Columbia University Press, pp. 153-185.

Finnemore, Martha, and Sikkink, Kathryn (1998): "Norm Dynamics International and Political Change", in: *International Organization, 52(4)*, pp. 887–917.

Finnemore, Martha, and Sikkink, Kathryn (2001): "Taking Stock: The Constructivist Research Program in International Relations and Comparative Politics", in: *Annual Review of Political Science, 4*, pp. 391–416.

Florini, Ann (1996): "The evolution of international norms", in: *International Studies Quarterly, 40*, pp. 363–389.

Forsberg, Tuomas (2011): "Normative Power Europe, Once Again: A Conceptual Analysis of an Ideal Type", in: *Journal of Common Market Studies, 49(6)*, pp. 1183–1204.

Fortmann, Michel, and Viau, Hélène (2000): "A Model Ally? France and the US during the Koso-vo Crisis of 1998-99" in: *The France-US Leadership Race: Closely Watched Allies*, Haglund, Dave (ed.), Kingston, Ontario: Queens Quarterly 2000, pp. 87-109.

Francesco, Francioni (2005): "Balancing the Prohibition of Force with the Need to Protect Human Rights: A Methodological Approach", in: *Customary International Law on the Use of Force. A Methodological Approach*, Cannizzaro, Enzo, and Pacchetti, Paolo (eds.), Leiden and Boston: Nijhoff, pp. 269-292.

Francioni, Francesco (2000):"Of War, Humanity and Justice: International Law after Kosovo", in: *Max Planck Yearbook of United Nations Law, 4*, 107-126, available at http://www.mpil.de/shared/data/pdf/pdfmpunyb/francioni_4.pdf.

Frankfurter Allgemeine Zeitung (FAZ) (2008a): "Nach dem Zyklon, Bundesregierung: Internationale Hilfe für Burma erzwingen", 10 May, http://www.faz.net/aktuell/gesellschaft/zyklon/nach-dem-zyklon-bundesregierung-internationale-hilfe-fuer-burma-erzwingen-1541248.html.

FAZ (2008b): "Nach dem Zyklon, EU setzt auf politischen Druck gegen Burmas Junta", 13 May, http://www.faz.net/aktuell/gesellschaft/zyklon/nach-dem-zyklon-eu-setzt-auf-politischen-druck-gegen-burmas-junta-1540972.html.

FRIDE (2008): "The International Response to Darfur", *Activity Brief*, 9 April, Madrid.

FRONTEX News (2011): "Hermes 2011 Starts Tomorrow in Lampedusa", 19 February.

Gänzle, Stefan, and Grimm, Sven (2010): "The European Union (EU) and the Emerging African Peace and Security Architecture", in: *Crafting an African Security Architecture: Addressing Regional Peace and Conflict in the 21st Century*, Besada, Hany (ed.), Farnham: Ashgate, pp. 73-88.

Geiß, Robin, and Kashgar Maral (2011): "UN Maßnahmen gegen Libyen: Eine völkerrechtliche Betrachtung", in: *Vereinte Nationen*, 3, available at: http://www.dgvn.de/fileadmin/user_upload/PUBLIKATIONEN/Zeitschrift_VN/VN_2011/Gei%C3%9F_ Kashgar_Beitrag_3-11_7-6-2011.pdf.

George, Alexander L. (1979): "The causal nexus between cognitive beliefs and decision-making behavior: The 'operational code' belief system", in: *Psychological models in international politics*, Falkowski, Lawrence S. (ed.), Boulder, Colombia: Westview, pp. 95-124.

George, Alexander L., and Bennett, Andrew (2005): *Case Studies and Theory Development in the Social Sciences*, Cambridge (MA): Belfer Centre for Science and International Affairs.

Gibbs, Jack P. (1966): "The Sociology of Law and Normative Phenomena", *American Sociological Review, 31(June)*, pp. 315-325.

Glenny, Misha (1996): *The Fall of Yugoslavia*, London: Penguin.

Global Centre for the Responsibility to Protect (2009): "UN General Assembly Debate on Implementing the Responsibility to Protect, 2009", 18 October, available at: http://www.globalr2p.org/resources/343.

Gottwald, Marlene (2012a): "Humanizing Security? The EU's Responsibility to Protect in the Libyan Crisis", *Finnish Institute of International Affairs (FIIA) Working Paper*, 75, April.

Gottwald, Marlene (2012b): "Options for EU Engagement in post-conflict Libya", Trans European Policy Studies Association *(TEPSA) Brief*, 9 March.

Grevi, Giovanni (2009): "ESDP Institutions", in: *European Security and Defence Policy: The First Ten Years*, Grevi, Giovanni, Helly, Damien and Keohane, Daniel (eds.), Paris: European Institute for Security Studies (EU ISS).

Grevi, Giovanni (2007): *The Common Foreign, Security and Defence Policy of the European Union: Ever-Closer Cooperation, Dynamics of Regime Deepening*, Doctoral Thesis, Free University of Brussels, June 17, available at: http://theses.ulb.ac.be/ETD-db/collection/submitted/ULBetd-11182008-174845/restricted/fullversion_grevi.pdf.

Gya, Giji (2010): "The EU's role in the Darfur Crisis from 2003 until today", in: *The Gap between narratives and practices, Darfur: the responses from the Arab World*, FRIDE, March, Madrid.

Halbach, Uwe (2009): "The European Union Mission in Georgia: Peacekeeping on a Controversial Footing", in: *The EU as a Strategic Actor in the Realm of Security and Defence? A Systematic Assessment of ESDP Missions and Operations*, SWP Research Paper, 14, December, Berlin.

Hehir, Aidan (2009): "NATO's 'Humanitarian Intervention' in Kosovo: Legal Precedent or Aberration?" in: *Journal of Human Rights, 8*, pp. 245–264.

Hill, Christopher (1993): "The Capability-Expectations Gap or Conceptualizing Europe's International Role", in: *Journal of Common Market Studies*, 31(3), pp. 305-328.

Holzgrefe, J. L. (2003): "The humanitarian intervention debate", in: *Humanitarian Intervention, Ethical, Legal and Political Dilemmas*, idem, and Keohane, Robert O. (eds.), Cambridge: Cambridge University Press, pp. 15-52.

Howorth, Jolyon (2013): "Humanitarian Intervention in the post-Cold War era: a provisional balance-sheet in light of Libya, Syria and Mali", Paper given to *Fundacion Chile*, 21 March, Santiago.

Howorth, Jolyon (2007): *Security and Defence Policy in the European Union*, Basingstoke: Palgrave Macmillan.

Howorth, Jolyon (2000): "Britain, France and the European Defence Initiative", in: *Survival, 42(2)*, pp. 33-55.

Hyde-Price, Adrian (2004): "European Security, Strategic Culture, and the Use of Force", in: *European Security, 13(4)*, pp. 323-343.

Independent International Commission on Kosovo (IICK) (2000): *The Kosovo Report: Conflict, International Response, Lessons Learned*, Oxford Scholarship Online.

International Coalition for the Responsibility to Protect (ICRtoP) (2011): "Impact of Action in Libya on the Responsibility to Protect", *ICRtoP FAQs*, available at: http://www.responsibilitytoprotect.org/index.php/component/content/article/35-RtoPcs-topics/3436-icrtop-2-page-faq-on-the-impact-of-action-in-libya-on-rtop.

International Commission on Intervention and State Sovereignty (ICISS) (2001): *The Responsibility to Protect*, Ottawa, available at: http://www.iciss.ca/report-en.asp.

International Crisis Group (2013): "Syria's Metastasising Conflicts", *Middle East Report*, No. 143, 27 June, Brussels.

Ischinger, Wolfgang (2011): "Es gibt keine gerechten Kriege – aber notwendige", in: *Cicero*, May 2011, available at: http://www.cicero.de/839.php?ausgabe=05/2011.

Jørgensen, Knud Erik (1997): *European Approaches to Crisis Management*, The Hague: Kluwer Law International.

Kaldor, Mary (2012): "The EU as a New Form of Political Authority: The Example of the Common Security and Defence Policy", in: *Global Policy, 3* (December), pp. 79–86.

Kaldor, Mary, Martin, Mary, and Selchow, Sabine (2007): "Human security: a new strategic narrative for Europe", in: *International Affairs, 83(2)*, pp. 273–288.

Katzenstein, Peter J. (1996): "Introduction: Alternative Perspectives on National Security", in: *The Culture of National Security, Norms and Identity in World Politics*, idem (ed), New York: Columbia University Press, pp. 1-32.

Kelsen, Hans (1954): *The Law of the United Nations: A Critical Analysis of its Fundamental Problems*, New Jersey: The Lawbook Exchange, LTI Union.

Kendall, Bridget (2008): "Western words fall on deaf Russian ears", in: *BBC News*, 10 August, http://news.bbc.co.uk/1/hi/world/europe/7552016.stm.

Kerkkänen, Ari (2014): "The Failure of the Security Paradigm in Syria, The Human Security Perspective", *Finnish Institute of International Affairs (FIIA) Working Paper*, No. 79, January.

Koenig, Nicole (2012): "Libya: A Wake-up Call for CSDP", *Trans European Policy Studies Association (TEPSA) Brief*, 15 March.

Koenig, Nicole (2011): "The EU and the Libyan Crisis: In Quest of Coherence?", *IAI Working Papers*, 11, 19 July.

Koenig, Nicole (2010): "The EU and NATO: Towards a Joint Future in Crisis Management?", *EU Diplomacy Paper*, No. 11/2010, Bruges: College of Europe.

Koutrakos, Panos (2013): *The EU Common Security and Defence Policy*, Oxford University Press.

Kuperman, Alan (2013): "Lessons from Libya: How Not to Intervene", *Policy Brief*, Belfer Center for Science and International Affairs, Harvard Kennedy School, September.

Kratochwil, Friedrich V. (1989): *Rules, norms and decisions, On the conditions of practical and legal reasoning in international relations and domestic affairs*, Cambridge Univeristy Press.

Krause, Keith (2007): "Towards a Practical Human Security Agenda", *Geneva Centre for the Democratic Control of Armed Forces Policy Paper*, No. 26.

Krieg, Andreas (2013): *Motivations for Humanitarian Intervention, Theoretical and Empirical Considerations*, Dordrecht: Springer.

Lehne, Stephan (2012): "The Big Three in EU Foreign Policy", *The Carnegie Papers*, July, Washington DC.

Larsen, Henrik (1997): *Foreign Policy and Discourse Analysis: France, Britain and Europe*, London: Routledge.

Le Figaro (2008): "La junte birmane accusée de crime contre l'humanité", 17 May.

Lucarelli, Sonia (2006): "Introduction", in: *Values and Principles in European Union Foreign Policy*, Lucarelli, Sonia, and Manners, Ian (eds.), London and New York: Routledge, pp. 1-18

Lucarelli, Sonia, and Menotti, Roberto (2006): "The use of force as coercive intervention", in: *Values and Principles in European Union Foreign Policy*, Lucarelli, Sonia, and Manners, Ian (eds.), London and New York: Routledge, pp. 147-163.

MacFarlane, Neil S., and Khong, Yueng Foong (2006): *Human Security and the UN, A Critical History*, Bloomington: Indiana Univeristy Press.

MacFarquhar, Neil (2012): "Syrian Protesters Emerge Amid Clashes and Bombing During a Holiday Ceasefire". *The New York Times*, 27 October.

McKinnon, Ian and Tran, Mark (2008): "Brown condemns 'inhuman' Burma leaders over aid", in: *The Guardian*, 17 May.

Manners, Ian (2002): "Normative Power Europe: A Contradiction in Terms?", in: *Journal of Common Market Studies*, 40(2), pp. 235–58.

Manners, Ian (2006): "Normative power Europe reconsidered: beyond the crossroads", in: *Journal of European Public Policy, 13(2)*, pp. 182–199.

Manners, Ian (2006): "The constitutive nature of values, images and principles in the European Union", in: *Values and Principles in European Union Foreign Policy*, Lucarelli, Sonia, and Manners, Ian (eds.), London and New York: Routledge, pp. 19-41.

Matthews, Max W. (2008): "Tracking the emergence of a new international norm: The responsibility to protect and the crisis in Darfur", in: *Boston College International and Comparative Law Review, 31(1)*, pp. 137-152.

Mardsen, Chris (2011): "Divisions on European summit on Libyan intervention", *World Socialist Website* (wsws.org), 13 April.

Mohamed, Sara (2012): "Taking Stock of the Responsibility to Protect", in: *Stanley Journal of International Law, 48*, pp. 319-339.

Morris, Justin (2013): "Libya and Syria: R2P and the spectre of the swinging pendulum", in: *International Affairs*, 89(5), pp. 1265–1283.

Morris, Loveday, and Birnbaum, Michael (2013): "Syria has destroyed chemical weapons facilities, international inspectors say", in: *The Washington Post*, 31 October.

Murray, Robert W., and McKay, Alasdair (2014): "Introduction", in: idem (eds.), *Into the Eleventh Hour: R2P, Syria and Humanitarianism in Crisis*, Bristol: E-International Relations, p. 10-17.

Mydans, Seth (2008): "Myanmar Faces Presures to Allow Major Aid Effort", in: *The New York Times*, 8 May.

Nadelmann, Ethan A. (1990): "Global Prohibition Regimes: The Evolution of Norms in International Society", in: *International Organization, 44 (Autumn)*, pp. 479–526.

Natsios, Andrew S. and Scott, Zachary (2012): "Darfur, Sudan", in: T*he Responsibility to Protect, The Promise of Stopping Mass Atrocities in Our Time*, Genser, Jared and Cotler, Irwin (eds.), Oxford: Oxford University Press, pp. 235–259.

O'Neill, Andrew (2008): "Kosovo aid model", in: T*he Australian*, 14 May.

Onuf Nichols G. (1998): "Everyday Ethics in International Relations", in: *Millenium Journal of International Studies, 27,* pp. 669–93.

Onuf, Nicholas G. (1989): "Constructivism: A User's Manual", in: *International Relations in a Constructed World*, Onuf, Nicholas G. Kulbáková, Vendulka and Kowert, Paul (eds.), Armonk, NY and London: M.E. Sharpe, pp. 58–78.

Patrick, Stewart (2011): "Libya and the Future of Humanitarian Intervention, How Gaddafi's Fall Vindicated Obama and RtoP", in: *Foreign Affairs*, 26 August.

Pattison, James (2008): "Legitimacy and Humanitarian Intervention: Who Should Intervene?" in: *The International Journal of Human Rights, 12(3)*, pp. 395–413.

Parekh, Bhiku (1997): "Rethinking Humanitarian Intervention", in: *International Political Science Review, 18(1)*, 49-69.

Percy, Sarah (2007): "Norms, Their Influence, And How They Can be Studied", in: *Mercenaries: The History of a Norm in International Relations*, idem, Oxford Scholarship online, pp. 1–43.

Peters, Anne (2012): "The Responsibility to Protect and the Permanent Five", in: *Responsibility to Protect, From Principle to Practice*, Hoffmann, Julia, and Nollkaemper, André (eds.), Amsterdam: Amsterdam Univeristy Press, pp. 199–212.

Peterson, John (2003): "The US and Europe in the Balkans", in: *Europe, America, Bush, Transatlantic Relations in the Twenty-First Century*, Peterson, John and Pollack, Mark A. (eds.), London and New York: Routledge, pp. 85–98.

Pillay, Navi (2011): "Pillay calls for international inquiry into Libyan violence and justice for victims", 22 February, available at: http://www.ohchr.org/en/NewsEvents/Pages/DisplayNews.aspx?NewsID=10743andLangID=E.

Posen, Barry (2000): "The war for Kosovo: Serbia's political-military strategy", in: *International Security, 24(4)*, pp. 39–84.

Preston-McPhie, Meredith, and Sharma, Serena (2012): "Kenya", *The Responsibility to Protect, The Promise of Stopping Mass Atrocities in Our Time*, Genser, Jared and Cotler, Irwin (eds.), Oxford: Oxford University Press, pp. 279–297.

Prunier, Gerard (2007): *Darfur: The Ambiguous Genocide?*, revised ed., Ithaca: Cornell Univeristy Press.

Ramet, Sabrina, and Phil Lyon (2001): "Germany: The Federal Republic, Loyal to NATO", in: *The Kosovo Crisis – The last American war in Europe?*, Weymouth, Anthony, and Henig, Stanley (eds.), London et al: Pearson Education, pp. 83–105.

Raymond, Gregory A. (1997): "Problems and Prospects in the Study of International Norms", in: *Mershon International Studies Review, 41(2)*, pp. 205–245.

Reisigl, Martin (2008): "Analyzing Political Rhetoric", in: *Qualitative Discourse Analysis in the Social Sciences*, Wodak, Ruth, and Krzyanowski, Michał (eds), London: Palgrave Macmillan, pp. 96–120.

Risse, Thomas and Sikkink, Kathryn (1999): "The Socialization of international human rights norms into domestic practices", in: *The Power of Human Rights: International Norms and Domestic Change*, Risse, Thomas, Ropp, Stephen C. and Sikkink, Kathryn (eds.), Cambridge: Cambridge University Press, pp. 1–38.

RP Online (2013): "USA und Russland einig über Syrien-Abrüstung", 14 September, available at: http://www.rp-online.de/politik/ausland/usa-und-russland-einig-ueber-syrien-abruestung-aid-1.3676670.

Rubin, James P. (2013): "Syria is Not Kosovo", in: *The New York Times*, 4 September.

Rupnik, Jacques (2011): "The Balkans as a European Question", in: *The Western Balkans and the EU: 'The Hour of Europe'*, idem (ed), Chaillot Papers, No. 126, Paris: Institute for Security Studies, pp. 17–30.

Seppä, Tarja (2011): "Humanising Security: Reponsibility to Protect", in: *Muutosten Aikoja*, Lappalainen, Toimittajat P., Seppä, Tarja, and Soininen, Suvi, Jyväskylä: electronic book, available at https://jyx.jyu.fi/dspace/bitstream/handle/123456789/26673/Muutosten%20a ikoja.pdf?sequence=1.

Seibert, Bjoern H. (2008): "EUFOR Tchad/RCA – A Cautionary Note", *European Security Review*, No. 37, ISIS Europe, March.

Seybolt, Taylor B. (2008): *Humanitarian Military Intervention: The Conditions for Success Failure*, Oxford: Oxford University Press.

Shepherd, Alistair J. K. (2009): "'A milestone in the history of the EU': Kosovo and the EU's international role", in: *International Affairs, 3(March)*, pp. 513–530.

Simma, Bruno (1999): "NATO, the UN and the use of force: Legal aspects", in: *European Journal of International Law, 10*, pp. 1–22.

Smith, Hazel (2002): *European Union Foreign Policy: What It Is and What It Does*, London: Pluto Press.

Smith, Karen E. (2000): "The End of Civilian Power EU: A Welcome Demise or Cause for Concern?", in: *The International Spectator, XXXV(2)*, pp. 11–28.

Stahl, Bernhard (2008): "Nationale Geschichte(n) für den Krieg – der deutsche und französische Diskurs im Kosovo-Krieg und in der Irak-Krise", in: *Zeitschrift für Vergleichende Politikwissenschaft, 2(2)*, pp. 1–30.

Stahl, Berhard (2010): "National (hi)stories of war – German and French discourses in the Kosovo war and the Iraq crisis", in: *Zeitschrift für Vergleichende Politikwissenschaft, 6(S2)*, pp. 47–76.

Stahn, Carsten (2007): "Responsibility to Protect: Political Rhetoric of Emerging Legal Norm", in: *The American Journal of International Law, 101(1)*, pp. 99–120.

Strauss, Ekkehard (2009): *The Emperor's New Clothes? The United Nations and the Implementation of the Responsibility to Protect*, Baden-Baden: Nomos.

Stroobants, Jean Pierre (2011): "L'Alliance atlantique étale ses division à Bruxelles sur la gestion de la crise libyenne", in: *Le Monde*, 22 March.

Techau, Jan (2013): "Will Europe ever agree on the use of force?", *TGAE Policy Paper*, No. 65, Carnegie Europe and Notre Europe, 13 January.

Thakur, Ramesh (2009): "Ban a Champion of UN's Role to Protect", Daily Yomiuri, 10 March, available at: http://www.responsibilitytoprotect.org/index.php/component/content/article/35-r2pcs-topics/2187-ramesh-thakurban-a-champion-of-uns-role-to-protect.

Thakur, Ramesh (2006): *The United Nations, Peace and Security: From Collective Security to the Responsibiliyt to Protect*, Cambridge: Cambridge University Press.

The Economist (2011): "Lessons of Libya", 19 May 2011, available at: http://www.economist.com/node/18709571

The Economist (1999): "Sorting out Kosovo", 17 June, available at: http://www.economist.com/node/213471.

The Independent (2013): "Editorial: 'Hell beyond hell': The situation in Syria is actually getting worse", 20 October.

The Irish Times (2013): "Death toll from Syria's civil war climbs to 130,000", 31 December.

The Times of India (2012): "Kofi Annan resigns as UN Syria envoy", 2 August 2012.

The Washington Post (2014): "UN decides to stop udpating Syria death toll", 7 January.

Thomas, Nicholas, and Tow, William T. (2002): "The Utility of Human Security: Sovereignty and Humanitarian Intervention", in: *Security Dialogue, 33(2)*, pp. 177–192.

Tonra, Ben, and Christiansen, Thomas (2011): "The Study of EU Foreign Policy: Between International Relations and European Studies" in: *The Hague Journal of Diplomacy, 9(1)*, pp. 11–29.

Toope, Stephen J., and Brunnée, Jutta (2010): "The Responsibility to Protect and the Use of Force: Building Legality?" in: *Global Responsibility to Protect, 2(3)*, pp. 191–212.

Tutu, Desmond (2008): "Taking the responsibility to protect", in: *The New York Times*, 9 November, available at: http://www.nytimes.com/2008/02/19/opinion/19iht-edtutu.1.10186157.html?_r=0.

Ulfstein, Geir, and Christiansen, Hege Føsund (2013): "The legality of the NATO Bombing in Libya", in : I*nternational and Comparative Law Quarterly, 62(1)*, pp. 159–171.

United Nations (2008): "The United Nations and Kenya – Briefing note", 7 February 2008, available at: http //responsibilitytoprotect.org/Feb%20 2008%20Kenya%20UN%20brie fing%20note.pdf.

UN High Commissioner for Refugees (2014): "Syrian Regional Refugee Response", http://data.unhcr.org/syrianrefugees/regional.php (20.01.2014).

UN News (2008): "UN Genocide Advisor Urges End to Violence in Kenya, Sends Staffer There", 28 January, available at: http://www.un.org/apps/news/story.asp?NewsID=25425andCr=kenyaandCr1.

UN News (2012): "Libya facing challenging transition, but authorities striving to succeed", 25 January, available at: http://www.un.org/apps/news/story.asp/ www.wmo.int/story.asp?NewsID=41040andCr=libyaandCr1=#.UtvzL_04m2w.

UN News (2013): "Interview with Valerie Amos, Under-Secretary-General for Humanitarian Affairs and Emergency Relief Coordinator", 28 March, available at: http://www.un.org/apps/news/newsmakers.asp?NewsID=87.

Van Landingham, Rachel E. (2012): "The Stars Aligned: The Legality , Legitimacy, and Legacy of 2011' s Humanitar an Intervention in Libya" in: *Valparaiso University Law Review*, 46(3), pp. 859–890.

Vira, Varun, and Cordesman, Anthony (2011): "The Libyan Uprising: An Uncertain Trajectory", *Centre for Strategic and International Studies*, 20 June, Washington D.C.

Vlasic, Mark V. (2012): "Europe and North America" in: *The Responsibility to Protect, The Promise of Stopping Mass Atrocities in our Time*, Genser, Jerad, and Cotler, Irwin (eds.), Oxford: Oxford University Press, pp. 159–181.

Von Eggert, Konstantin (2012): "Why Russia is standing by Syria", BBC News, 15 June 2012, available at: http://www.bbc.co.uk/news/world-europe-18462813.

Waging Peace (2007): Press Release, 15 February, http://www.wagingpeace.info, www.sudantribune.com/spip.php?article20310.

Wagner, Daniel, and Jackman, Daniel (2011): "BRICS form unstable foundation for multilateral action", in: *Foreign Policy Journal*, 2 April, available at: http://www.foreignpolicyjournal.com/2011/04/02/brics-form-unstable-foundation-for-multilateral-action/?.

Weaver, Matthew (2012): "What next after failed ceasefire?", in: *The Guardian*, 30 October.

Weiss, Thomas G. (2011): *Humanitarian Intervention: Ideas in Action*, 2nd ed., Cambrigde: Polity Press.

Weller, Marc (1999): *The Crisis in Kosovo 1989–1999: From the Dissolution of Yugoslavia to Rambouillet and the Outbreak of Hostilities, International Documents and Analysis*, Vol. 1, Cambridge: Documents and Analysis Publishing.

Welsh, Jennifer M. (2012): "The Responsibility to Protect and Humanitarian Intervention", in: *Responsibility to Protect, From Principle to Practice*, Hoffmann, Julia, and Nollkaemper, André (eds.), Amsterdam: Amsterdam Univeristy Press, pp. 185–198.

Welsh, Jennifer M. (2010): "Implementing the 'responsibility to protect': where expectations meet reality", in: *Ethics and International Affairs, 24(4)*, 415–430.

Welsh, Jennifer M., and Banda, Maria (2010): "International Law and the Responsibility to Protect: Clarifying or Expanding States' Responsibilities?", in: *Global Responsibility to Protect, 2*, pp. 213–231.

Wendt, Alexader (1992): "Anarchy is what states make of it: the social construction of power politics", in: *International Organization, 46*, pp. 391–425.

Werthes, Sascha, and Debiel, Tobias (2006): "Human Security on Foreign Policy Agendas: Introduction to Changes, Concepts and Cases", in: idem (eds.), *Human Security on Foreign Policy Agendas. Changes, Concepts and Cases*, INEF Report 80/2006 idem (eds.), University of Duisburg-Essen: Institute for Development and Peace, p. 7-20.

Wheeler, Nicholas (2000): *Saving Strangers: Humanitarian Intervention in International Society*, Oxford: Oxford University Press.

White, Nigel (2012): "Libya and Lessons from Iraq: International Law and the Use of Force by the United Kingdom", in: *Netherlands Yearbook of International Law 2011, 42*, pp. 214–229.

Wiener, Antje (2007): "Contested meanings of norms: a research framework", in: *Comparative European Politics, 5*, pp. 1–17.

Williams, Paul D., and Bellamy, Alex J (2012): "Principles, Politics, and Prudence: Libya, the Responsibility to Protect, and the Use of Military Force", in: *Global Governance, 18*, pp. 273–297.

Williams, Paul R., Ulbrick, Trevor, J., and Worboys, Jonathnn (2012): "Preventing Mass Atrocities Crimes: The Responsibility to Protect and the Syria Crisis", in: *Case Western Reserve Journal of International Law, 45(1)*, pp. 474–503.

Wodak, Ruth (2008): "Introduction: Discourse Studies - Important Concepts and Terms", in: *Qualitative Discourse Analysis in the Social Sciences*, Wodak, Ruth, and Krzyanowski, Michał (eds), London: Palgrave Macmillan, pp. 1–29.

Yee, Albert S. (1996): "The causal effects of ideas on policies", in: *International Organization, 50(1)*, pp. 69–108.

Yin, Robert. K (2003): *Case Study Research, Design and Methods, 3rd* ed., Thousand Oaks and London: SAGE Publications.

Youngs, Richard (2004): "Normative Dynamics and Strategic Interests in the EU's External Identity", in: *Journal of Common Market Studies, 42(2)*, pp. 415–35.